PSYCHOVERTICAL

PSYCHOVERTICAL

Andy Kirkpatrick

HUTCHINSON
LONDON

Published by Hutchinson 2008

2 4 6 8 10 9 7 5 3 1

Copyright © Andy Kirkpatrick 2008

Andy Kirkpatrick has asserted his right under the Copyright, Designs
and Patents Act 1988 to be identified as the author of this work

First published in Great Britain in 2008 by
Hutchinson
Random House, 20 Vauxhall Bridge Road,
London SW1V 2SA

www.rbooks.co.uk

Addresses for companies within The Random House Group Limited can be found at:
www.randomhouse.co.uk/offices.htm

The Random House Group Limited Reg. No. 954009

A CIP catalogue record for this book
is available from the British Library

ISBN 9780091920968

The Random House Group Limited supports The Forest Stewardship
Council (FSC), the leading international forest certification organisation. All our
titles that are printed on Greenpeace approved FSC certified paper carry the FSC logo.
Our paper procurement policy can be found at
www.rbooks.co.uk/environment

Mixed Sources
Product group from well-managed
forests and other controlled sources
www.fsc.org Cert no. TT-COC-2139
© 1996 Forest Stewardship Council
FSC

Typeset by Palimpsest Book Production Limited, Grangemouth, Stirlingshire
Printed and bound in Great Britain by
Clays Ltd, St Ives PLC

To the patient people who helped
gather up the words that almost escaped me

El Capitan

Contents

Illustrations

All photographs, maps and line illustrations are by the author, unless otherwise attributed.

Acknowledgements

Thanks to Mandy, who unlocked many doors, and helped me discover who I could be – and for being my toughest critic. And for giving me Ella and Ewen, gifts that will take me a lifetime to unwrap.

To my Mum, the strongest person I've ever met. It's a shame people don't write books about people who climb real mountains every day. I finally get what you mean about the world being my oyster.

To my Dad Pete, who gave me my thirst for adventure to begin with – one of the greatest people I've ever known The older I get the more I understand.

To my brother Robin (you're a real hero, not the wimp I've made you out to be). I just want to say sorry for pushing you in the docks that time (and all the other stuff . . . like the fish tank). To my sister Joanne who has climbed her own mountain to become the type of teacher every child deserves, and to another teacher, Mr Peterson of Villa Junior School, who took the time to see between my spelling mistakes.

To Karen Darke for stopping me from writing, and reminding me that having adventures is more important than writing books about them.

To Tony Whittome, Marni Jackson, Jim Perrin, and Andrew and Sharisse Kyle at Mount Engadine Lodge and everyone at the Banff Centre for giving me the chance, and the push I needed, to write this book. And to Bill Gates for Word, without which I'd never have written a word in the first place. Thanks to Duane Raleigh and Alison Osius at Climbing magazine who made me believe I was a writer, plus they would actually pay me for my words, and not forgetting all those poor editors that came afterwards who pulled their hair out with my never-ending 'eny's' and 'becouse's' that slipped past the spell checker.

To Dick Turnbull for giving me a job, but never giving me an easy ride, and for inspiring me to suffer in the first place. I am also indebted to the support from Berghaus, Black Diamond, British Mountaineering Council, Buffalo, Lyon Equipment, Petzl, PHD, Mount Everest Foundation, Sportiva, and Patagonia, without which I'd never have been able to afford to go away, or replace the thousands of pounds of kit I lost or dropped over the years. I also want to single out Chris Watts and Siobhan Sheridan at First Ascent for always going out of their way to help and making me feel like a sponsored hero.

Lastly to all my climbing partners, who I expect, if you bump into them and ask about their role in this book, will tell you that every fall was half as far, and every near-death experience was nothing to write home about. Don't believe them, they're all in denial, it was always worse. But it was always more fun than it sounds . . . wasn't it?

Prologue

I sat alone in the small white room, my attention drifting from the snow that built up on the windowsill outside to the two test papers on the desk in front of me. I fidgeted with my pencil, chewing the end until my lips were speckled with red chips of paint. My mouth tasted of damp wood. The wind rattled across the corrugated roof of the building. The sound of air being sucked under draughty doors and past ill-fitted windowpanes grew loud, taking my concentration away with it.

Time was running out.

Although this was an exam I had sought out, it felt no better than all the others. I felt small, awkward and stupid. The first paper had been easy, but the second had turned my brain into a thick slow glue as the numbers fell from their places, lost upon the page. Even though the room was cold, I was feverish with that familiar panic which I had thought I'd never feel again. It was as if I were back at the school I had hated. An old self-loathing returned, but I pushed my brain to form some answers out of the murk.

None came.

Drifting out of the storm, we trench through deep snow until we come to the edge of the loch, its surface frozen beneath a winter blanket. My partner takes a bearing and shouts into my ear that it isn't far. The buttress above comes into view for a moment as the cloud spins away from its summit.

We have left the car in the dark, woken early by the wind buffeting it on that empty high mountain road. Groggy with the long journey north from England, we had dressed while still in our seats, fighting like Houdini to pull on boots and salopettes in our confined quarters – neither of us really wanting to venture outside until the last possible moment. The early start has proved useful in the long approach through the deep snowdrifts. With luck it will allow enough time to climb the route.

We recheck our bearings, wanting to avoid the avalanche-prone slab to the left of the loch, and gain another quick glimpse of the wall when the cloud thins. It is steep and covered in rime ice, which clings to the rock just like ice clings to the inside walls of a freezer. It offers an equivalent security.

The conditions are far from perfect, but this is Scottish-winter climbing. Here you just climb routes as you find them, not as you'd like to find them. It has been pointed out by a visiting Slovene climber that here in Scotland we 'ski on the grass and ice-climb on rock', but at least today the rock looks wintry enough. Stuffing the map away and pulling on goggles, we take the easy option and set off across the loch's creaking edge.

I turned the paper over and looked up at the snow, lying thick as a bed on the sill. I had a few minutes left until the examiner was due to return, but I knew from experience that it would take more than time to get these answers right.

Teachers always said I was lazy, that I lacked concentration or was a slow learner, then went on to label me as having some kind of learning disability. The schools I went to were filled with 'problem children' and I was just one more. I remember learning in biology that the brain has two sides. It came as a bit of a revelation at the time. It seemed to explain why sometimes I felt slow and stupid, one of the school's stigmatised, remedial kids, while at other times I felt bright and intelligent, capable of producing drawings or solving puzzles that were beyond the others. Most of the time I kept the dark side in the background, concentrating on what I was good at, but at school that wasn't easy when the narrowly focused world of school subjects gave you almost no way of shining.

The route looks hard. A tenuous mixed line up a steep wall and arête, it is a classic rock climb in the summer, but now, with a coating of ice, it is one of the hardest climbs on the crag. I visualise the moves, how I'll link up those rounded horizontal cracks and vertical seams, digging through the wall's thick winter coat of rime for secret places in which to twist and hook the picks of my axes.

I've wanted this route for a long time, storing in my head every scrap of information I can find. Although I can't spell the name of the routes, or the corrie we are in, I can list everyone who's tried them, what else they've done and why they failed.

As I step up to the base, I remember the discouraging words of a climber who has failed on this route twice: 'You'll never climb it, there's a really long reachy move on it – you're too short.'

Flicking my picks into the hard cold turf that sprouts in patches on the climb I close my eyes and visualise the route as a puzzle, the pieces jumbled in the snow. I see the first piece and start to climb.

The examiner opened the door and asked me to stop.

I looked out of the window feeling sick and empty.

At school my worst nightmare had been the times table. The teacher would start in one corner of the classroom and go around, making each child stand up at their desk and say the next figure. As the moment snaked nearer, the blood would drain from my face as my heart beat faster and faster. I would feel hollowed-out and sick. The dark half would scramble any thought as I struggled to calculate an answer. Finally, on shaky legs, I would stand and speak. I always got it wrong. The other kids would laugh as I sat back down, thankful the ordeal was over.

Totally immersed in the climbing, my brain is powered up and energised, working to its full potential, its limited memory freed from all those confusing hoops it has had to jump through in the real world. Up here everything is real. No numbers. No words. The only calculations are physical, the only questions how to progress and how not to fall off.

Winter climbing is 10 per cent physical, 90 per cent mental. If you're good at jigsaws you'll probably be good at this sort

3

of climbing. It's simply a frozen puzzle, your tools and crampons torquing and camming the pieces to fit – and like a jigsaw, the moves are easy. It's just finding them that's hard.

The examiner picked up the sheets and asked me to come to his office while he marked the papers. Seeing I was pensive he chatted about the storm as we walked through the old Victorian building.

It wasn't leaving school with few qualifications that mattered to me or to anyone else; it was leaving with the belief, created by society, that these things really mattered. At sixteen I thought I had been graded for life. The only skill that I knew I possessed was my ability to be creative. This initially manifested itself in painting and drawing, but, like anything that comes easy, I had no way of knowing that this was any kind of skill at all. I found it hard to get people to take me seriously when they found I couldn't remember my date of birth or the months of the year. I was always fearful that I would be found out, that people would dismiss me as thick or stupid. Yet slowly, as I grew older, I found ways around this by trying to avoid any contact with words or numbers.

I left home and moved into a squat near the city's university, and slowly I began to mix with people who could get things right, people I had never met in my remedial world. It was like meeting people from another culture, and yet I found we weren't that different – and that in some ways I had skills they lacked, or maybe even envied. I slowly learnt that I had to tag abstract words or numbers with images for reference words, and that way could bypass the sludgy part of my brain. My party piece back then was trying to remember all twelve months of the year, and get them in order, something for the life of me I just couldn't do. It was only at that point that my new acquaintances made me see that this and all the other things that once did matter meant nothing at all. One night at a party someone said my linear brain function was perhaps a sign of dyslexia and maybe I should be tested, just to find out what exactly was wrong with my brain – and that's how I found myself doing this one final test, wondering if, at nineteen, it no longer mattered.

*   *   *

I get to the place where the other climbers have failed. Two spaced, flared, horizontal cracks, the gap too wide to span with my axe. I hunker down on my tools and try to solve the problem.

Hammering my axe into the crack at chest level, I mantle up on it, palming down on its head, straightening my arm, one crampon point scratching near its spike, the other crampon latched around a corner. It feels as if I'm about to do a handstand. I blindly scrape away the thick stubborn hoar with my other axe, searching for a secure home for its pick. There is nothing.

I think about backing off, about failing, but I'm not sure I can. I imagine the good nuts set in poor icy cracks below and feel committed to the move, as I blindly scrape for something to hang. With my arms cramping, I'm forced to commit to laying away off the rounded arête, the teeth of my pick skittering and skating around until I pull down hard and trust it, wiggling my other axe out as I slowly stand up straight, my body hanging on tenterhooks.

I try not to shake too much.

I take a deep breath and look for the next piece.

The first test paper had comprised a hundred complicated cubes, with four options of how they would look opened out. The other paper had been covered in words and numbers. The boxes were easy and I had wondered if I'd been given this by mistake. Then I had come to the other sheet and the lights had gone out. Feeling like an idiot, well aware I hadn't done well on the second sheet, I sat and watched him mark the answers, ticking them off as he went.

Reaching easy ground, easy in comparison to what it took to reach it, I race up a hanging corner, sacrificing protection for speed. I pop up onto a narrow foot ledge, a grassy escape route into an easier climb on the left. I hesitate. Above, the wall looks compact and steep. It would be so easy to avoid what waits there. Plenty of possible excuses. The dark. The storm. I look down at my partner Dick and think of the hollowness of giving up now. I know he doesn't care as long as I get a move on.

With a nut placed at my feet I boulder out the moves above

the ledge until I'm committed. I can see where I'm headed: across the wall to a ledge on the arête. Sweeping away hoar as I go, I try not to think about getting pumped as I scratch until I find one good tool placement on round edges, crampon points poised on sloppy holds that look like flattened chicken-heads. Matching tools together I look down at my partner far below as he tries to stay balanced in the wind, his flapping red jacket barely visible through the blown snow. The two ropes arch, plucking out questionable protection, but the big one stays put. There should be great fear, there should be great doubt, but all I see is possibility.

The teacher looked up from his marking and removed his glasses. 'Remarkable. You've scored 99 per cent in the spatial test. I've only ever had one other person score so high. He was a headmaster. As for the other test . . . I'm afraid you only scored 16 per cent.'

My overwhelming joy was quickly crushed: the second test was much more important to real life. Being able to recognise what boxes look like opened out would get me a job in a card-board box factory.

'You're a classic dyslexic,' he said. 'One side of your brain doesn't work as it should, so the other half compensates.' He told me the symptoms of dyslexia and my pieces finally fitted.

Lateral thinking gets me below a small ledge. Holding my breath on nothing foot-holds I tickle at a frozen tuft of grass with my pick. The pick bites with a dull, shallow thwack. With time running out, I blindly swap feet, then hang off one tool as I bring the other across to join it. I feel the dice roll. Will they rip out when I pull?

My brain does some quick calculations and says no. I do. They don't. I'm there.

I mantle up onto the arête. I'm so aware of everything around me: the snowflakes blowing across my face, the line of sweat rolling down between my shoulder blades, a twist of frozen heather emerging from the snow, the wind, the darkness, the cold. My body is hot, my brain burning as I suck in the speeding snow. The next thirty feet is unprotected. If I fall I'll die, but there is no time for melodrama; this is where I have always wanted to be. I think how strange it is that brain power can get me here, yet it still fails to do so many other things. I know now that all things are balanced, but on the mountain such details no longer matter. There is no need for words here. With the pieces together I can see the picture. Who needs to know its name?

Hooking both axes onto a flake I pull off the ledge and head into the darkness.

The doctor showed me to the door and handed me a brown envelope containing my results. 'Andrew, with a score of 99 per cent you should find something you enjoy that involves three-dimensional problem-solving, something creative, where you can turn these things into an advantage.' I shook his hand and I said thank you, then walked home through the snow, wondering where such a strange gift would lead me.

All rising to great place is by a winding stair.

Francis Bacon

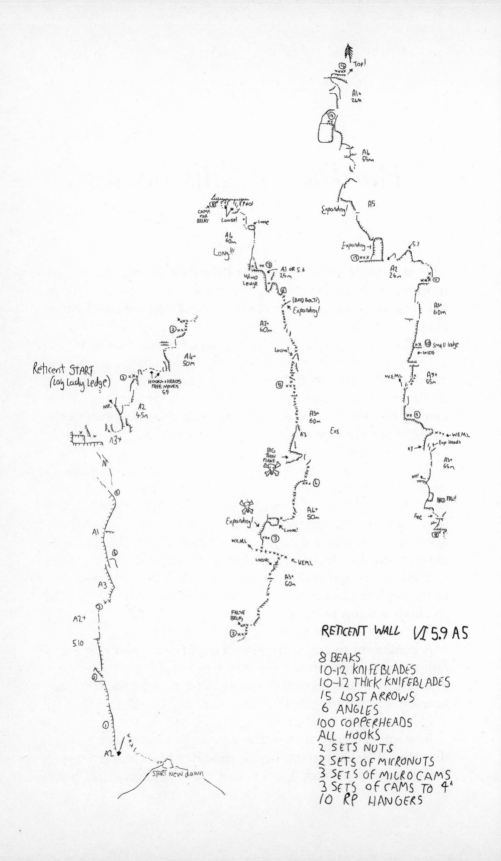

Top!

A1+
26m

A4
55m

A5

Expanding!

Expanding →

5.7

A2
26m

A3+
60m

small ledge
+ WIDE

W.E.M.L

A3+
55m

W.E.M.L

Exp Heads

A3

A3+
65m

No!

BAD FALL!

Free

CAMS FOR
BELAY

No!
Loose!

Loose

A4
60m

Long!!!

WIND
Ledge

A1 or 5.6
25m

(BAD BOLTS)
Expanding!

A2+
60m

Loose!

A3+
60m

A3

Exs

BIG
THIN
FLAKE

Expanding!

W.E.M.L

Loose!

LOOSE

← W.E.M.L

A3+
60m

FINE
BELAY

A4+
50m

Reticent START
(Lay Lady Ledge)

HOOKS + HEADS
FREE MOVES
5.9

A4+
50m

No!

A2
45m

13+

N

A1

A3

A2+

5.10

A2

START NEW DAWN

RETICENT WALL VI 5.9 A5

8 BEAKS
10-12 KNIFEBLADES
10-12 THICK KNIFEBLADES
15 LOST ARROWS
6 ANGLES
100 COPPERHEADS
ALL HOOKS
2 SETS NUTS
2 SETS OF MICRONUTS
3 SETS OF MICRO CAMS
3 SETS OF CAMS TO 4"
10 RP HANGERS

Hard work kills horses

The taxi came at 6 a.m., beeping twice. It was a Sunday morning early in June 2001, the beginning of my journey to solo one of the hardest climbs in the world, certainly the hardest climb of my life.

And my life was falling apart. I was running away.

I'd lain awake on the settee most of the night waiting, my mind a mess; in part this was the usual jumble of worry and doubt about the climb, and in part it was the presence of darker clouds, the worry of what it meant to be sleeping down in the living room alone while my wife slept upstairs.

Did she sleep?

All night I'd tried to order my thoughts, put things in perspective, get my life straight in my head before I left. It was impossible. I thought about writing her a letter, to try to explain why I was going, why I was so compelled to climb. But I just knew those words would be transparent and wouldn't come close to how I really felt. No words could explain why. Nothing I could say would make her understand. There was no sense to it, only the absurdity of travelling halfway round the world to climb a lump of rock.

You don't have to go.

A pendulum swung within my thoughts, its point rising and falling, one moment making me feel invulnerable, the next draining away all my self-belief, making me just want to stay here forever with my wife Mandy and my daughter Ella.

How can you leave them?

It would be easy to tell the taxi to go away, to creep up the stairs and slip into our bed. I could hug Mandy and whisper that I wanted to stay. For once she would know that I put her first. I could still be here when Ella woke up. See her smile.

But what about tomorrow?

You have to go.

I lay and imagined myself lying in a pool of my own blood, shattered bone sticking out of me at crazy angles, slowly dying on the climb, imagined the feeling of loss, knowing I would never see them again, their world shattered like my body.

What will you find there that will justify risking everything you have here?

The taxi beeped again.

I wished it was still dark. In the night I would often feel the most level-headed about climbing hard routes. Getting out of a warm bed to go to the toilet, I would stand naked in the dark, shivering with cold, knowing all I wanted to do was get back under the covers with the woman I loved. The thought of being anywhere else, sleeping in a snow hole, perched on the side of an icy north face, or forced to abseil through the night would seem ludicrous. Pointless.

You sound like her.

There is a point.

I could think of no rational reason for climbing anything. I just knew I had to do it.

The climb is the question.

I would be the answer.

I was about to leave, and travel halfway across the world to solo one of the longest routes on the planet, a climb only a handful of people had ever dared to attempt, one which had taken one of the greatest climbers in the world a staggering fourteen days to solo. I knew the route was out of my league. I knew I could die, or worse, yet I slept alone on the settee.

You might never come back.

The taxi beeped once more.

I stood up and, already dressed, began lifting the huge vinyl haul bags that held my climbing gear out of the house and to the taxi. Each one was the size of a dustbin, made from indestructible material designed to line landfill sites and adapted to withstand being scraped against rock for miles of climbing. For the next few weeks they would be my only company. Half carrying, half dragging them out of the back door, I went round the side

of the house to where the car waited. The taxi driver got out slowly and helped me lift the first bag into the boot, then pushed the second one sideways onto the passenger seats in the back.

Each bag was the size of a small person. It weighed around fifty kilos and contained the equipment I'd need for my coming climb: ropes, karabiners, slings, pegs, nuts, storm gear, sleeping bag, my portaledge (a folding bed used to sleep on vertical walls), and a hundred other vital items, a decade's worth of accumulated climbing equipment.

The bags were hard to lift and painful to carry. They had to be moved in relays unless I could find wheels, whether taxi, bus or trolley, but even when I felt my knees were about to buckle or my vertebrae compress down like an empty Coke can, I enjoyed carrying them. Pain like that is simple, honest, and feels invigorating as muscles and mind are pushed beyond their norms. Carrying stops you thinking.

The longer you go without thinking the better it feels when you experience it again.

Each bag made the car sag further, and the taxi driver's eyebrows rose as his wheel arches dipped towards the gutter.

'You might need another taxi, mate,' said the driver, kicking his tyres with concern.

'Only got one small one left,' I said, as I nipped back down the alley to my house.

13

I walked through the back gate, past Ella's frog-shaped sand-pit and small red scooter, and in through the back door of our tiny Sheffield terraced house.

My last bag lay on its side surrounded by Ella's toys.

There was one more thing I had to do. I crept up the steep narrow stairs and slipped into her bedroom. She lay on her side, her thumb in her mouth. Perfect. Nothing in my life seemed to fit together properly any more, my marriage, work, climbing. Nothing but her. She was the only thing in my life that I didn't doubt.

But even she wasn't enough.

You have to go.

I wanted to kiss her, but knew if she woke up I wouldn't be able to leave.

I spent a lot of time wondering what she would think when she grew up, if I were to die climbing, and I thought about it again now: the selfishness of what I was about to do, risking my life once more, and in turn, risking her life and future. Many climbers, or people who do dangerous things, give it up once they have kids, but for me her birth had come at the start of it all.

At that time, people made judgements about me as a climber and a father, often asking me how I could do it. I didn't know, all I had was excuses. I'd said that you shouldn't sacrifice who you are for your kids, but I wasn't so sure. Wouldn't it be me sacrificing them for what I wanted? But I knew that if I didn't, I wouldn't be a person worth having as a father, and in a way that was why I was here now, about to set off on another climb. The more I tried to quit, the more the pressure built inside me.

What if you never see her again?

I told people I didn't want to die before she was born, just as much as after she was born. But the truth is dying is never in any climber's plan.

She made sense, but she also made what I loved even more senseless. Mountains don't care about love.

I wanted to stand there forever. I could. But I wouldn't.

I crept out of her bedroom, closed the door, and turned to see the stairs leading up to our bedroom, where Mandy probably lay awake. She would be angry with me, leaving her again to go climbing. She wanted so little: a normal life, a normal husband. I couldn't give her that, but we were both stubborn and we'd been together for ever. We didn't quit, so here we were. Still fighting. We also loved each other.

I knew she would be lying in bed hating me now, yet wanting me to climb the stairs and say goodbye, or even to say I'd stay – not because she was weak, but because she loved me.

I was about to solo a climb so hard only the best had attempted it, a route I doubted I could do. Yet in that moment the thing I most feared was climbing those stairs, climbing up to face her and say goodbye.

What if you never see the baby growing inside her?

I went out to the garden and tried to compose myself, not wanting the taxi driver to see I was upset. I was everything I despised.

They will be better off without you.

As I'd done so many times before, I opened a box in my head and placed the feelings inside, closed the lid, and moved on.

'Where to?' the taxi driver asked as I sat next to him and clipped in my seat belt.

'The station, please.'

We drove down the hill, and through the empty streets.

'Where you off to?'

'America, to a place called Yosemite.'

'Oh aye, I've heard of that. Are you a climber, like?'

'Yeah . . . sort of.'

'Are you going by yourself?'

'Yes.'

'Isn't that dangerous?'

'No,' I lied, 'just more work.'

'You want to be careful with those bags of yours, they're bloody heavy.'

'Oh, they're OK, they keep me fit.'

'No mate,' the driver said, looking at me with concern, 'remember, hard work kills horses.'

Bird rock

I was hanging in space, my fingers clamped tight, holding on, above a new and startling world of light and sound. People often ask me how long I've been climbing and I suppose it all began here. It was 1971 and I had just squeezed my way out of my mother.

The doctor held me above my mum, my tiny untested fingers wrapped around his and hanging on in terror, something that is often mistaken as strength.

'My, Mrs Kirkpatrick,' said the doctor, dangling me before her like a zoo keeper dangles a baby chimpanzee in front of a TV crew. 'You have got a very strong baby here. He's as strong as an ox.'

My childhood was full of high places, of holding on, hanging, swinging, and falling, and so it's no surprise that as an adult I would be drawn towards the heights and a life off the horizontal.

My first high place was a hill named Bird Rock, a mountain carved in half by some geological fluke, exposing a limestone face set in a valley not far from our house, and visible from our tiny garden. It always seemed strange and exotic, always there on the horizon, mysterious, its summit seemingly in-accessible amongst the more pedestrian rolling green hills that surrounded the Welsh village where I grew up. I'd seen films like *King Kong, Tarzan* and Sir Arthur Conan Doyle's *The Lost World*, where strange rock faces yielded prehistoric lands and lost species. I wondered if Bird Rock was the same, its craggy face perhaps hiding dodos, pterodactyls and giant eagles that would have to be fought off.

I was five and it was my first mountain, and my dad always promised that when I was a little older we would climb it together.

My father was a mountaineering instructor in the RAF, based at a Joint Services camp in the Welsh seaside town of Tywyn, running courses for the army, navy and air force. That is the perfect job for a sadist: running poor recruits around the hills in the rain, making them shimmy across greasy ropes above ponds of vile green liquid, pushing them to near hypothermic death in foaming rivers, all in the name of training. My dad threw himself into the job with gusto, thinking up increasingly devious ways of scaring and stretching recruits in the outdoors, always setting an example by going first. I can still remember creeping into my parents' warm bed on dark winter mornings, as my dad got up to take a load of recruits down to the sea for an early morning swim, his face grinning with the craziness of it all. You could say he was very pre-health-and-safety.

He was pretty unconventional for someone in the RAF in the 1970s. Rather scruffy and prone to bend the rules, he never went too far in his long career, generally being placed out of harm's way in the outer reaches of the RAF: mountain rescue teams, officer development, and outdoor education. His only advice to me growing up, apart from how to tie knots, roll kayaks or light a stove, was 'Only work hard when people are looking.' No doubt this tongue-in-cheek approach didn't serve him well when it came to making air chief marshal, but fundamentally all he wanted to do was just go climbing.

He was charismatic, a fantastic story teller and a great 'people person', which is probably why they didn't just boot him out. These skills trumped a pair of well-ironed trousers or polished shoes any time. His enthusiasm for the mountains was also infectious, whether you liked it or not. He pursued climbing and adventure with a passion, and at that time the only way to do this was to work as an instructor in the forces, where you could use the system to go away on trips you would never have been able to afford otherwise. Throughout those early years there were big gaps when my dad was away on courses or expeditions, but I never stopped idolising him, and still remember my heart leaping when, sitting on our back fence, I saw him for the first time in weeks, coming out of the base and across the playing field to our house. Coming home.

He applied many of his military training techniques to my upbringing, such as exposing people to danger in a controlled environment, so as to better prepare them for real danger in the future: war in Europe, global Armageddon, primary school. My mother still tells the story of her coming home to our flat when we were posted to Sardinia, and finding him watching the TV, while I sat in my nappy in the kitchen playing with the largest carving knife in the cutlery drawer. I was two at the time. On being challenged by my mum, my dad's only response was, 'You have to cut the apron strings some time.'

Very often in my childhood, while I was standing on a tiny ledge, walking across a plank above a big drop, or about to jump into an icy lake, my dad would shout, 'A real man would do it,' to which I would always reply, 'But I'm not a man, Dad.'

The closest this exposure came to unravelling was one Christmas afternoon, when he took me down to the sea for a walk as a huge winter storm raged, and surf crashed over the sea defences. The most hazardous spot was the boat ramp that led into the sea, the waves rushing up it and fanning out behind the sea wall. Dressed in my black donkey jacket and red wellies, I ran backwards and forwards, trying to race the waves down and back again without getting too wet, when all of a sudden a huge wave overtook me, knocking me over and sucking me back into the sea.

Luckily my dad was close by, and was used to swimming in the cold Irish Sea. He dived in and managed to pull me back to shore. I was frozen, my eyes were full of sand, but I was alive. My strongest memory is of being run home in his arms and then plonked in a warm bath, the remaining contents of a bottle of Matey bubble bath being added to the water as a treat. I suppose it was an early lesson that when you survive a life-threatening trauma, people tend to treat you nicely.

My dad had joined the air force at seventeen. It's strange he found himself having a role in the mountains, since he was born in Hull, one of the flattest places in Britain. I often wonder if having an adventurous spirit is genetic, as my dad's father and grandfather had also been in the military, his dad fighting in Egypt and in Ireland during its civil war. It's hard to imagine now how limited people's lives and careers were back then, born and dying in the same town, taking up the trade of their fathers. For most, joining the navy or army was the only way to break free.

My dad's two brothers were also rather unconventional. Eddy Kirkpatrick had been a salvage diver whose hair-raising adventures deserved their own book: diving on sunken German U-boats in primitive gear for their brass torpedoes, and searching for Nazi gold lost in the North Sea. His life must have been lived by the seat of his pants. Doug Kirkpatrick had worked on Baffin Island in the Arctic as a radio operator, and later as a hunter in New Zealand, before he settled down to normal life as an insurance salesman.

Maybe this wanderlust comes from the place where you are born. The fictional adventure of Robinson Crusoe had begun in the port of Hull and I wonder if maybe this spirit for adventure was part of the genetic heritage of the city. It is a place from where boats sailed all over the world, where seamen once signed on for white-knuckle rides to hunt whales in Greenland, and to fish on the violent northern oceans, a city whose heart was laid waste by the cod wars. Whatever the reasons, the Kirkpatricks are a strange breed, a mixture of many roaming people, Russian, Scottish, Romany. Whoever they were, they all seemed to be afflicted with wanderlust, and were single minded and incredibly stubborn.

Since I had been born we had moved around the country several times, and a lot of my early memories involve playing in wooden RAF-issue packing cases. However, my dad's posting in Tywyn was long enough for it to become the place I see as my first home, and I can think of no better place to grow up. It was nestled between mountains and ocean, and we lived next to the camp. The military and mountaineering seem to produce larger than life characters, men who jumped straight from the war films on the telly, and many of them made an impression on me. Our next-door neighbour was a man called John Bull, who seemed to be able to communicate only by shouting. He was in the army and was a lifer like my dad. He was a fellow instructor and would always be thinking of new ways to torture the recruits. In his house he had a full-size Greenlandic kayak he'd brought back from an expedition.

On Sundays we would go to the sergeants' mess for lunch, where there were pictures of mountains, and walls full of plaques, polished ice axes and mountaineering mementos. On one wall was a giant picture of Mount Everest, with its camps marked, part of an upcoming military expedition. Standing there in my best clothes, I felt I was in a special place, a place of men. Even to a five-year-old, there was such a feeling of being wrapped up in the military, of being one institutional family. I can understand how soldiers can carry on fighting in wars that they feel are unjust, or illegal. It was a home.

I was a very physical child who was always running, climbing and generally getting into the type of trouble that such kids usually do. My clothes were always a collection of patches, ripped, scuffed, torn and then mended, with shoes lasting me no more than a few weeks, meaning cheap rubber wellies and shorts became the only answer for my despairing mum. My legs were always brown with bruises, and scabby. The arrival of my brother Robin had given me another person to play with, but, because I was a rough child, Robin would often come off worse: falling off, falling down, being hit, knocked out or generally injured in any playtime we had. One of my strongest memories is of my mum often slapping me, my brother standing crying behind her, while she shouted, 'Your brother must have rubber bones.' It was a phrase repeated so often I actually believed such a thing was possible, no doubt further adding to Robin's misery. I used to think that our family were borderline freaks, as not only did my brother have rubber bones but my mum also had 'eyes in the back of her head'.

Other children were not fortunate enough to have rubber bones, and for a while I was in big trouble after pushing a twelve-year-old girl off the top of the slide and breaking her arm. I wasn't a bad child or a bully in any way, only a child who 'always took things too far'.

I was a very happy-go-lucky boy, but Robin was less easy to please. My mum would often tell him to stop whining, sometimes slapping him on the legs and telling him 'Now you have something to whine about.' She often put the disparity in our characters down to the fact that the doctor had run him under the cold tap as soon as he'd been born, a shock he'd never quite recovered from.

My mum had met my dad at a dance, and they were married not long afterwards. She was also from Hull. She had wanted to go to art school, but instead had been forced to give up such fancy notions and work in a bakery. I suspect this had had a major effect on the rest of her life, as she would often tell us this story, wanting us never to compromise what we wanted to do. My mum was far from pushy, but she always told us that the world was our oyster – not that I ever really understood what that meant.

What she wanted most of all, though, was children, and I had been her firstborn, in 1971, Robin coming along a year later. Times were hard for her, with my dad's pay low, and she would often repeat the phrase, 'I don't know how we'll make ends meet', which I mistook as 'hen's meat', often wondering if hen's meat tasted just like chicken. Although we were poor, my mum hid it well, and did things that were free: going for walks, playing on the beach, drawing and painting, and giving the priceless gift of a parent's attention. My mother's side of the family had been craftsmen, her father a carpenter, his father a head gardener, her great-grandfather a stone mason. From her I learnt to draw, something that would prove invaluable later in life. I scribbled on anything at hand as soon as I could hold a crayon.

Like my dad, my mum wanted fun and adventure, and a life less ordinary than the one she had left behind in Hull, but not at the cost of security for her and her kids.

We lived on the military estate on the edge of the camp, not far from the beach. Even at the age of five I was a bit of a loner and a daydreamer, happy to be by myself, playing for hours in the garden, making up imaginary worlds. I was lucky enough to have the freedom to do my own thing and wander around the estate by myself, in the days before people even knew anything about paedophiles, where there were only 'funny men'. I was only reined in after I went missing one day and didn't come home for lunch, and the whole camp was mobilised to look for me. Several hundred soldiers and airmen combed the sea shore, fields and rivers looking for my body. In the end I turned up asleep in a collection of hay bales a few hundred metres from our house. My mum belted me with relief, shouting, 'I was worried sick,' a phrase that was now added to her everyday lexicon.

After that I had to stay with Robin, although this almost cost him his life on more than a few occasions.

My worst youthful scrape, and one of my earliest fully formed memories, was going to our next-door neighbour's house with Robin to look at their aquarium. It stood on a wooden stand near the front door, looking like an enormous TV filled with fish. We would stand with our noses pressed up against the glass, and watch the fish race around. On this day, my mum stood talking on the doorstep to the couple who owned the fish, my dad being away on an expedition. She had probably taken us around to see the fish as a distraction because I was missing him.

We were playing our usual fish-spotting game, eyes tracking the red, blue and purple flashes darting around the tank. The couple who owned the house would always tell us that we had to be careful as the tank held piranhas, and that they would bite us if we got too close. I always wondered if they really would. If I were to stick in my hand, would the flesh be ripped off it in seconds like I'd seen in an old film once on our black and white TV?

I wanted to find out if it was true.

The fish darted away from the glass as I moved round to the side of the tank, trying to grab the top so I could pull myself up and dip my hand in. I would probably have lifted Robin up so he could dip his hand in, but already he had learned not to get involved in any of my games and would probably have started crying.

Being small for my age I found the tank was too high, so, looking for another option, I saw that I could maybe climb up between the wall and the tank, using the skirting board as a foothold. I started by squeezing my leg in, my welly sticking well to the edge of the skirting as I tried to squirm up the gap, which widened as I pushed in.

I looked through the glass as I moved up, seeing through the drifting green murk my brother's tiny face, his eyes fixed on the dancing fish. I pushed up. I slipped back. I pushed harder.

The tank moved . . . then moved some more . . . then crashed over onto Robin. An explosion of glass and water shot through the porch, a tsunami raging out of the front door and knocking everyone off their feet.

There I stood, my back to the wall, looking down at the floor littered with glass, pebbles, soggy green plants, twitching fish and, right in the middle, the tips of two small red wellies – my little brother.

Incredibly Robin made a swift recovery, and after a night in hospital he left with only a few cuts, being declared by the doctor as having a very strong heart.

Personally, I put it down to his rubber bones.

Not long afterwards my sister was born. My mum had always wanted a daughter, and had become so desperate she'd taken to clothing Robin in dresses when he was a baby. Joanne was born in 1976 and from the beginning everything changed.

She never stopped crying, screaming non-stop for six months. The calm, fun house I'd known existed no longer. Mum and Dad became steadily worn down, tired and strung out. My dad could escape but not my mum.

Then one day my mum took us all to the hospital, and I can remember me and Robin waiting in the hallway while she talked to the doctor. Then I could hear her crying and screaming, appearing in the hallway distraught. They had asked her if either I or Robin had dropped Joanne. It appeared her hip was broken. Soon, though, it was discovered she had been born with an undiagnosed congenital hip defect, meaning she had no hip bone, and had been in terrible pain since her birth.

Soon after that, Dad was posted to another camp in Llanwrst on the edge of Snowdonia and a few weeks later we followed him, Joanne's tiny body encased in plaster. We were leaving the happiest period of my childhood behind.

Everything was different. New school, new house, new friends and, worse still, new parents. I hated school. I felt like an outsider. Starting from scratch. I was no longer at the centre of my parents' universe: Joanne took up much of my mum's time, while my dad seemed to be away more and more. When he was around he seemed bad tempered, or not really there at all. He was about to go on a trip to Yosemite, a name I only understood from Yosemite Sam on the TV, and this further added to the stress, leaving my mum with me and Robin, both unsettled, and Joanne. I suspect that the pressure was too much for my dad: his happy and conventional life, a life where he could have the freedom to climb and still have a family, began to collapse. Demands began to be made of him. He was forced to choose.

One night, Robin and I woke up and could hear noises downstairs. We crept down to the dining room where our mother was at the table with our dad. She was crying.

There had never been crying before we moved from Tywyn, but now it seemed to be happening all the time. We had always been happy; we had never had much but at least we had that; there had never been room for sadness. This was all to change. He was telling her something. Something she was shocked to hear. Her world and future falling apart. Her heart broken. Another woman.

The following morning we were bundled out of bed by Mum, quickly dressed, and walked down to the train station. It was early; a fog obscured the line. I wondered if this meant I didn't have to go to school. My mum wasn't talking. It took all her strength just to keep it together.

The train appeared out of the mist and slowed to a stop.

We stood, no longer the family we had once been, our bags all packed for a new life in Hull, a place far removed from my world of sand dunes and hills, from beaches and green fields full of sheep, and from my dad. I had no idea where we were going, or that we would never come back – that Dad and I would never climb Bird Rock together.

The valley

Tired after my long rambling journey, passed backwards and forwards from taxis to trains, trains to planes and back again, my mind began to come slowly back to life as the final leg drew to a close and the tiny shuttle bus wound its way up into the Yosemite Valley.

The valley had been carved in the Ice Age, a mighty glacier cutting deep into the perfect Sierra Nevada bedrock, its slow retreat leaving behind a 3,000-foot-deep, five-mile-wide valley of incredible walls and towers. The valley was a magical place of mighty faces, thundering waterfalls and giant sky-scraping sequoias. It had captivated the minds of all who had visited, made famous first by the words of John Muir in the 1800s and later in the definitive black-and-white big-wall shots of Ansel Adams. It was one of the wonders of the world and a Disneyland for climbers, with rides both big and small, fun and terrifying.

The little vehicle was full of the usual flotsam and jetsam

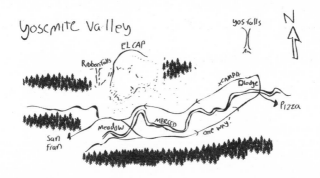

found on American buses: the poor, the desperate, the foreigners. It was packed with a mixture of seasonal employees heading back to their concession jobs, hotel clerks, swimming-pool attendants and bus boys, all returning to the safety of the valley. Then there were the climbers, drawn from around the world, all buzzing with excitement at finally reaching the crucible of climbing, the danger of the rock faces.

The landscape outside the window of the bus changed slowly as we went from sea level into the high Sierras, from the flat California grass lands, parched brown after a long hot summer, into thick forest as the floor of the valley rose, creating a space of rock, water, wood and shadow. It seemed timeless after the alarm-bell ringing of the modern world behind us.

It grew colder and darker in the bus, light and warmth flickering less and less across the windows as we moved higher, among growing trees whose trunks expanded in size until they looked mighty and prehistoric. You could tell who was who on the bus by the way they reacted to the change. The valley workers slumped over in their seats with headphones on their ears, eyes closed or heads buried in books. The climbers pressed against the windows, jabbing and pointing at the increasing majesty of the views beyond, jumping from one side of the bus to the other as it wound up the valley, like kids on a school trip.

An old hand at the trip, I played it cool. This was my fifth visit to the valley, but in reality I felt just as excited as the first time. This and every other trip was a pilgrimage, and like all pilgrims I had been nervous the first time that El Cap wouldn't live up to the hype. I'd read and been told so many things about the Captain – that it was a mecca of climbing, an expanse of rock so huge and overpowering it almost had its own gravitational pull, well at least on climbers, and that I wouldn't ever see anything as awe-inspiring – that I had been afraid it would not live up to its reputation. Now I was afraid that it might let me down, that El Cap would be diminished somehow by the nine ascents I'd already made.

It never had. It never would.

Out of the trees appeared the mightiest, most beautiful wall on the planet.

The first thought on seeing El Cap, springing up from a meadow and leaping into the sky, is one of disbelief. The scale of it is hard to set against anything else you've seen before. It is taller by hundreds of metres than the highest building on earth, three times taller than the Eiffel Tower. A ripple of excitement and gasps went through the climbers, those who had seen it before turning with smiles to their friends who had not, with a look of 'I told you so' splashed across their faces.

Its hugeness was as hard to comprehend as the first time, a vast expanse so large it was impossible to fit it within the viewfinder of a camera, or to hold its scale within memory. I loved this piece of rock.

When we reached the bus stop, we found the usual gaggle of tourists milling around. I stepped down from the bus and collected my bags, then began moving them in relays to Camp 4, the world-famous climbers' camp site situated a couple of hundred metres away.

Life on a wall is simple, there is no place for 'why', only for 'do'. A climb can take many days, even weeks, distilling your complicated life back to Stone-Age simplicity: eat, crap and stay alive. This most of all was what I had come to find.

I dragged my last bag across the dusty car park to the camp site, throwing my luggage into a heap in the closest space I could find that was free. I looked around at the picnic tables, and lines of washing strung up on old ropes criss-crossing from tree to tree, and listened to the faint chatter of resting climbers talking about 'what next', and the occasional power shout as a climber slapped the top of the world famous boulders that lay on the edge of the camp site.

For the first time in ages I felt almost relaxed.

I began opening my bags and laying out my gear. Experience had told me that there were many reasons for failure – bad weather, ill partners, a lack of will – but the biggest of all was fucking around, not getting down to the task at hand.

Most climbers would arrive and spend a few days getting used to the place, maybe doing some short climbs, and probably another wall before jumping on the 'big one'. It is often nice to build up your psyche before embarking on a tough climb, especially if it's going to be the hardest one of your life.

You don't have time.

I do.

You have to start tomorrow.

I have all the time in the world.

The longer you wait the greater the chance you're going to bottle it.

That would be worse than dying trying.

The longer you stay down here, the greater the chance you'll tell someone and they'll talk you out of it.

I don't want to be talked out of it.

I laid out my old tatty plastic tarp and began setting out all my gear, checking that nothing had been forgotten.

First I put my camming devices in a row: thirty alloy tools, designed to expand into cracks, ranging in dimension from the size of my fingertip to the size of my head. Each one would be invaluable on the climb. Even the smallest were good enough to hold a falling climber, although I hoped that wouldn't be put to the test. I also knew that this route had minimal placements for bomber gear like this: if I had the chance of finding such a placement I would have to have the correct size to fit. My life could depend on it.

Next I laid out my wired nuts: thirty loops of incredibly strong and robust steel cable, fitted with a small curved rectangle of aluminium or brass, designed to be slotted into the rock. These were split into sets, each set clipped to a large karabiner, and racked so that if one set was dropped I would have two in reserve. I checked over the nuts, some marked as mine with

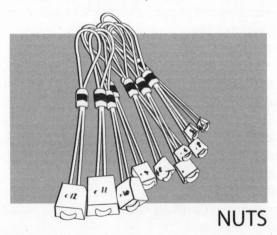

NUTS

green electrical tape, others with foreign markings and probably found on other climbs, or gone astray from the racks of past climbing partners. I picked up a number seven Chouinard nut and felt it in my fingers. It was the size of a small box of matches, and was oily and sticky with age, its size and manufacturer, stamped into the alloy, almost invisible under the scratches of a lifetime's worth of placements. It had been given to me by my dad ten years before as part of my first rack, second-hand, loved and cherished. Back then everything I owned for climbing would fit on a single karabiner; now it wouldn't fit in a single dustbin.

I set the nut down amongst the others and hoped I'd get to use it just once.

Would he ever have imagined I'd bring you here?

You think too much. It's just an old nut.

I pulled out my karabiners, over a hundred, clipped together in neat bunches ready to be racked onto my harness, and began sorting them. The route comprised twenty-one long pitches, many close to seventy metres in length, and these karabiners would be vital to clip every piece of protection to the rope. They were the glue that held everything together.

As I was pulling out the last of the karabiners, a small wooden train tumbled out with them and fell into the pine needles that covered the ground. I picked it up. It was Ella's, no doubt thrown in with the rest of my gear while packing. I thought of us setting up her wooden train track in the living room, her telling me what had to go where. I wished I'd taken more time to play with her. I stuck the toy in the pocket of my fleece.

I continued to lay out the karabiners, then noticed two climbers were watching me from a nearby picnic table, arms folded, checking out my gear, no doubt wondering what I had planned.

Everyone wants to climb El Cap, but, although many try, the majority fail. I used to joke that there are two types of climbers in Yosemite: those who want to climb El Cap and those who have failed. I wondered what group the climbers that watched me were in. Had they just failed and were now looking for some beta from a fellow big-wall climber, or had they just climbed it, and wanted to bask in the glory of telling someone else? Climbing El Cap by any route is an achievement, so any glory is well earned.

They walked over.

'What you planning?' asked the taller climber, his grubby shorts and dirty sandalled feet showing he'd been here a while.

Don't tell them!

'Not sure,' I said, lying.

Ignore them.

'We've just got down off the Shield,' said the other climber, a scab on the bridge of his nose a sign that he'd smashed a piece of gear into his face on the climb: probably a peg while he was testing it.

'Well done.'

The Shield was one of the harder classic routes on El Cap, a line that shot up one of the steepest parts of the wall. It had been my first big wall, but keeping this a secret and not bursting their bubble was more rewarding than telling them that.

'Yeah, it was cool,' the climber carried on, 'but I sure could have done with a rack like yours though. You must be planning on something hard . . . Aurora, Pacific Ocean Wall, maybe Lost in America?' He reeled off some of the harder routes.

Don't tell them.

'Not sure,' I said, not adding that I'd ticked those routes over the last five years.

'Wyoming Sheep Ranch?' asked the other, crouching down to sift through my rack of sky hooks, tiny hooks of steel designed to latch onto holds as small as a matchstick. The Ranch was one of the hardest and most sought after routes on El Cap, its crazy myth-busting name giving away nothing of the danger involved.

'No, sounds a bit too loose,' I said, as I started laying out my knife-blade pegs, sorting them in size from the smallest scalpel-thin pegs, up to those of butter-knife thickness, each invaluable for hairline cracks.

'Come on, tell us what you've got planned,' said the tall climber, now looking at my birdbeaks, tiny tomahawk-shaped hooked pegs, their blades as small as a fingernail, to be used when knifeblades were too fat to fit. 'You must be planning something hard with this lot. We won't tell.'

I set down a couple of Lost Arrow pegs, thick chunky steel pegs for cracks too large for knife-blades, and felt their weight

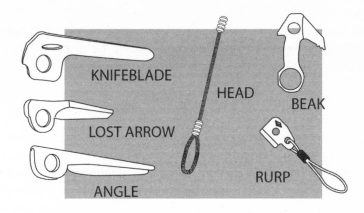

as they passed from my fingers to the tarp, imagining the sound of them driving home in the rock.

A ranger passed by on a mountain bike and smiled at us, no doubt making a mental note to come back later and check we'd all paid our camping fees.

'We know who you are,' said the climber with the scabbed nose. 'You're Andy. You're hardcore.'

If only he knew.

I laughed, but it felt nice for someone to think I was good at something for a change. For most of the last few years I'd just felt more and more useless – the harder the route, the greater my apparent inadequacies. I didn't see myself as a climber, yet climbing consumed me. Perhaps my problem was being married to someone who saw climbing only as a negative; there was no room for hero-worship or ego with Mandy. She saw through the bullshit. The greater the climb the greater the pain for her. She saw it as an end-game. Her mother had died when she was six. Her father had kept them apart so as to make it easier. She didn't remember her, only the loss. Now she thought I would die and leave her too. No climb, no matter how hard, would impress her, only my return.

'The Reticent Wall,' I said almost sheepishly.

Their jaws dropped, their mouths opened, but the words were almost too scary to say in the confines of this valley where they meant so much.

'Holy fuck, Andy,' the tall climber said as he dropped the bird-beaks and straightened up. 'You seem like a nice guy, be careful.'

'I will,' I said with a laugh that was designed to hide my embarrassment, turning my head back to the task at hand to signal I didn't want to talk about it.

'I mean it, man.' He paused. 'Be careful.'

I finished selecting gear and began placing each rack of hardware in haul bags ready for tomorrow, when I'd carry them up to the base of the climb and then begin fixing my ropes over the next two days.

When the gear was packed, I sat on a nearby picnic table and sketched out the food I would need, how much water to take, and anything I had to buy before I left – wet wipes, batteries for my Walkman, sun-cream.

I pulled out the book I'd brought for my trip – *The Periodic Table* by Primo Levi – and opened it to reveal two photos. They were poor-quality shots of Ella and Mandy, poor quality because I knew they would get trashed on the climb and probably lost. One was of Ella sitting in her high chair, red tights poking out beneath the table, a cowboy hat on her head. It was her second birthday. The second was the reflection of Mandy, Ella and me in a shop window, taken in Scarborough a few months before. Ella is on my shoulders, her hands resting on my head, Mandy is standing beside me, her arm through mine. We're all smiling. The smiles seemed so long ago.

Why weren't they enough?

They were then.

They are now.

I sat for a while and tried to feel the calmness of the place around me, the call of birds, the gentle creak of the trees, the low hum of the occasional car passing by. It would be nice to stay a while and be normal, to sit with other climbers and talk shop, maybe even get my ego stroked some more.

There would be no peace. The drums were beating inside me.

If you want to be happy again, you have to go.

Pebbledashed

The perfect life I had known changed when I was seven, my tiny seaside house swapped for a damp top-floor maisonette in a tower block in the city of Hull. I retreated inside myself and fed on memories. I wanted my old bedroom. My old house. My school. My friends. My toys. To turn back the clock and sit on our garden fence and see my dad coming home across the field. I wanted things to be as they had been. I wanted my dad. My old life became nothing more than a film in my head that I would watch for the rest of my life.

From my bedroom you could see the Humber estuary to the south, its waters brown like cheap chocolate and slow with silt, pollution, and history. The hills and ocean of my past, with its freedom and space and happiness, had changed overnight to mountains of concrete, tower blocks with families packed in tight; a world of spiralling stairs and piss-stinking lifts, a dark and dirty world beside a dirty river, a body of water that matched my surroundings perfectly, just as the sea had matched my previous life.

We had stepped down from the train into a dark city. We might as well have landed on an alien world.

We had had very little before, and had been poor, but now we had even less and were poorer still. My mum, however, was forever strong and positive. She never let her guard slip, even when I knew she was crumbling to nothing inside. She had lost more than we had. We were all she had left. Now she had to find a new map of our future. From her I learnt that often the only way to get through life is to hide how you feel when others depend on you appearing strong.

The only time my mum ever articulated how she felt was

33

when she told me she could physically feel that her heart was broken. I imagined her heart, red and solid, unbeating, like a piece of broken pottery, and knew I could do nothing to help except be as strong as she was.

Council housing had been in short supply, but she found us a new home on an estate of pebbledashed tower blocks nicknamed 'the misery maisonettes' by the local paper. They were set out like a prison, and it had been some city planner's sick joke to name them after villages in the Lake District. We moved into Buttermere House. It was only on the day she got the key and we moved in that she found out from the next door neighbours why the flat hadn't been snapped up. The previous tenant had hanged himself in the maisonette's stairwell. He'd tied the rope to the banister that would soon stand a foot from the head of my bed, and the mark was still there to see. At night when the building cooled, the banister would begin to creak. The flat had two small balconies, and sometimes I would dream I saw the dead man, who looked like the Yorkshire Ripper, standing there looking through the curtains.

It would be easy to look back and feel hard done by in such difficult times, but, like most poor children, on the surface at least we slowly adapted, started new schools and made do with a new world. Inside, I was bewildered and lost, but we had the gravity of our mum's love to pull us all in, and we knew that this would never change. The years passed and I adapted who I was to where I was. The space of my childhood in Tywyn expanded with my imagination, becoming just as boundless as any landscape. The Hull estate, in my mind fed by films like *Star Wars* and comics such as *2000 AD*, changed from a collection of pebbledashed flats into some post-apocalyptic city. My new friends and I began to play ever more complex games, and build up worlds of imagination. The dim and dark corners of our world turned into something exciting and startling. Sacred amongst all these places were the green open areas: the playing fields, the small park, the squares of dog-shit-covered green grass, and the trees. We gobbled these places up, our skin tingling for nature even though we didn't know it then. I imagined myself an alien who had come from a different world from the other kids, a world that made me different from them and to which I would have given anything to return.

School was amazing. The teachers were experienced and positive, able to deal with a lot of problem kids with a firm but supportive hand. Somehow they made every child feel unique, special and wanted. Nevertheless I struggled in many subjects, finding it hard to do what many of the other kids took for granted, both academically and, more embarrassingly, socially, unable to master reading the time or tying my shoe laces. I began special lessons, the teachers helping me to catch up, and learn new ways of learning. There was never a name given to my slowness of understanding, or stigma, only acceptance that I required help.

Luckily my saviour was the fact that I could draw, a fantastic outlet for my out-of-control imagination. Unable to read, I looked at comics, a braille of pictures becoming my language, the stories I wanted to tell produced in images. I was a real daydreamer, finding it hard to concentrate in class, and I was forever in trouble for scribing in book margins and on desks, rather than getting down to work. I always seemed to be somewhere else. I spent all my spare time drawing, lying on my stomach in front of the TV. My mother's brother, who owned a printing company, kept me supplied with off-cuts of paper and card.

My dad's visits were erratic. Often he went months without seeing us, something that's hard to understand when you're a child – or a father. I wonder if perhaps it would have been better to have never seen him again, because of the amount of upset it caused when he had to leave – two days or a week not being enough to fill the hole inside us. Even so I loved him unconditionally, and held on to his image, both because he was my dad, and because he was the only link back to my old life. We, however, were changing fast. Joanne was out of her plaster and a cheerful little girl, and both Robin and I were growing up. In the early days I would pray that Mum and Dad would get back together, but as the years moved on I knew they never would.

When I knew my dad was going to visit us, I'd count down the days as if to Christmas. Then I would stand on a chair and look out at the road, the height of the flats allowing me to see for a long way, waiting for his car to turn off the main road and drive into the flats' car park. I would pine for him. Nothing else mattered. I could feel the pain of longing, and wondered if my heart was broken like my mum's and if hers felt like this. But I always forgave him.

When he came to see us he would often take us to the park, and occasionally we'd go climbing and camping in the Peak District, a few hours away. The camp site was only a few miles from Sheffield, but for me it was a magical place of valleys, forest and streams, and a real escape from the city.

One morning I woke up early, crept out of the tent and walked up the hillside, through the wet ferns, and scrambled up a band of rocks called Stanage Edge. It was dawn, and mist hung in the valley below. I didn't want to go home to the city. I wanted to stay, but I knew I couldn't. I promised myself that one day I wouldn't have to leave.

Perhaps it was the memory of Tywyn, or the visits to the Peak District, but I yearned for adventure – wherever it could be found.

We had many trips to Switzerland as children: not the country, but a disused quarry named Little Switzerland set beside the mighty Humber Bridge. We would go there in a big gang and explore its overgrown depths and flooded pools, sometimes abseiling with the rope and home-made harness my dad had given me. I took on the role of twelve-year-old climbing instructor, the rope tied off to some railings, designed to stop people falling over the edge. Now it makes my blood run cold just thinking about it. After we'd done our exploring, imagining we were in the jungles of Vietnam, following in Rambo's footsteps, we'd make the long nine-mile march home. Often we'd return to the estate looking like a rag-tag army, covered in mud, with dads on bikes shouting at us because they'd been out looking for us for several hours. Generally my mum would send us to bed, having yet again been made sick with worry.

Between the river and our flat lay the docks, vast and sprawling over tens of miles. Once part of one of the greatest ports in the world, like most of the nation's industrial strongholds they had slowly fallen into a decline. The North Sea trawlers, Arctic whalers, the ships full of wood, wool and, at one time, slaves, had been replaced by rusting prams, oily bobbing polystyrene, and bloated dead dogs.

These docks, along with the bombed-out buildings at the edge of the estate, became my wilderness, a place as dangerous, remote and grand as any Arctic wasteland, an expanse of freedom and possibility.

In those days there was no reason to go to the docks, and the only people you would find there were prostitutes, tramps, anglers and the kids who lived in our estates along their northern edge.

Most of the prostitutes came from our estate, with their children going to our school, and it was not uncommon for one kid to taunt another in the playground with the line, 'Your mum's a prozzie,' to which they would reply 'Yes . . . what about it?'

I knew about prostitutes long before I knew about sex, and their trade was often a good source of fun as we sped around on our bikes at dusk like the BMX bandits, flushing out all the local working spots such as the old graveyard that bordered the docks, and watching the punters either run or stand their ground and shout and chase us.

The tramps who inhabited the docks came from the Salvation Army building on the estate, and were of the old variety; the hospitals had yet to be cleared of the mentally ill, so the down-and-outs were mainly elderly, smelly, bearded men – no doubt soldiers who never made it home. They drank meths – or at least that was what we believed – and huddled together on the stairs of the church, waiting for the off-licence to open. They would often fall into the docks, either to be plucked out by the fire brigade or to sink below the quick mud and drown. One story at school was of a tramp who survived a jump one night from the sixth floor of Grasmere House – but the bones of his legs went right through his feet. He was left sticking out of the ground, a foot shorter, screaming, until the fire brigade could dig him out.

Although I didn't actually see this event, the image that it conjured haunted me through my childhood, especially when we were older and would dare each other to climb onto the roof of the flats by squeezing up behind the rubbish chutes, with an unsurvivable drop waiting below.

We were always climbing things, running along walls, messing around on roofs, the heights being the domain of the brave or of policemen with ladders. The bigger the drop, the bigger the thrill.

The estate was full of stories of derring-do and disaster: kids falling from balconies when their washing-line ropes snapped, or people falling down lift shafts. One landmark was a cracked paving stone below one of the 'proper flats'. It was said to have been the impact point of a woman who committed suicide by jumping from the twentieth floor. This was perhaps the reason the 'proper flats' had more respect from us kids; they guaranteed death from the top. The word 'maisonettes' was also deemed to be a bit pretentious, not that we knew what that was. I thought a lot about death as a child – perhaps I was a bit disturbed, maybe it was thinking too much about the man who had hanged himself in our maisonette.

In the docks, the anglers fished for the eels which seemed to thrive on the decay. This was also a popular pastime among us kids, once we could afford a rod, although most fishing trips to the docks involved very little fishing. We'd cycle down there with our rods tied to our bikes, and after the initial excitement threading hooks and bait, our attention would soon wander. One popular activity was finding druggies' hypodermic syringes down within the oily Victorian gears of the rotating bridges that joined up the docks. We'd stick them in our bait maggots, and pump these up till they popped. There was always loads of junk that could be thrown in the water, glass windows to break on derelict buildings, or we'd use catapults and see who could hit far-off dead animals that floated like bloated pigs in the water.

When they drained the dock a few years later, to make way for a shopping centre, the workmen came across a dying giant fish over two metres long. Unidentified and looking darkly prehistoric, the fish was held up for a photo to go in the local newspaper. It must have lived in the sealed-up dock for decades, feeding off eels and rats.

The only thing I ever fished out of the docks was Robin, who would always end up falling in – usually because I pushed him. One summer he got a second-hand bike for his birthday, a yellow Raleigh Boxer, and we cycled down to the docks so he could show it off. When he wasn't looking, I tied a piece of old rope to it, attached the other end out of sight onto a rusty iron bollard by the edge of the drop, then, shouting, 'Hey Robin, watch this . . .', I chucked it in. Unfortunately, before I could haul it back up again, he burst into tears and ran off home. Twenty years later he still can't see the funny side of this.

One of our most popular, and hazardous, pastimes was swimming in the docks, something that generally ended up with somebody getting hurt or almost drowning. You would strip down to just your shorts, then line up along the rounded stone edges and try to find someone brave enough to jump in first. It was never me.

Taking a running jump, the first boy would launch himself out into the water, disappearing with a loud splash and a cheer from the onlookers, who would then remain silent for a few moments until he bobbed up from the blackness.

Eventually it would be my turn and, trembling a little with fear (fear of the cold water, fear of what lay beneath it, fear of not coming up), I would step forward. Those who had already done it would stand shivering as well, arms crossed, watching until everyone else had jumped. You knew you had no choice, you were going in one way or another.

Taking a few steps back I would do the running jump and launch off into space with a scream that was half bravado, half fear, shooting out high over the water, eyes closed. The drop was several metres and you seemed to be in the air an impossibly long time. As you fell down towards the water you would feel that thrill of the freedom of the choice being made, there was no way back, you were committed to fate. Then you would hit.

The impact was hard, the cold stunning, the water so black you expected to bounce, but down you would go, deep. There was always the anticipation of hitting something, until finally you stopped and, following the sounds of your friends, swam upwards towards the surface, where you would climb out via a ladder and stand, arms crossed, dripping dirty oily water, like the rest.

Of course, the trick to swimming in the docks was not to swallow any water, or get entangled on anything below the surface, or bump into a dead dog or worse. I would often imagine the zombied bodies of dead tramps or murdered prostitutes crawling along on the bottom, trying to catch my feet – perhaps more of an indication of my video choices than of a vivid imagination.

Every summer, kids would drown, and the headmaster would give a stern warning in assembly about not going near the docks. The worst thing that ever happened to me, and the last time I jumped in the docks, was when I landed on something very sharp and cut my feet so badly I couldn't walk, and had to be pushed home on someone's bike, blood dripping out of my Dunlop trainers all the way. Up until then, whatever the dangers, these things never stopped me. After all, it was an early lesson in life, that games without risk are just that – games. Anyway, the local swimming baths had been bulldozed to make way for a new bypass. For us it was the docks or nothing.

Someone once told me that a wilderness was an area of several thousand miles with no infrastructure or human impact. They were wrong. Looking back I think the docks, Little Switzerland, and the bombed-out buildings gave me something immeasurably valuable as a child, something that I would hang on to for the rest of my life. These industrial wastelands of cut stone and dank water were a wilderness as precious to us as any tundra. They were where we explored both without and within ourselves.

The early years of my life in Hull seemed to be one long hot summer: the roads were always quiet, and weekends and holidays never seemed to end. We were poor, but so was everyone else, so this never seemed much of a problem. Mine was probably the last urban generation to have an old-fashioned childhood, fairly free of consumerism save for the odd *Star Wars* figure. It was consumerism that later created real poverty and, worse still, the realisation of how poor people were. Back then, everyone on the estate was hard up, so we were all equals. Having a TV that was rented, and required you to feed it 50p coins to make it work, was normal, as were free school dinners and grants to buy clothes with. Nowadays I reflect on the fact that I still get free clothes – only now they are from outdoor companies and I get paid to wear them.

Unlike the mothers of most of my friends, my mum would always try and save enough money to take us to the seaside for the day at least once a month on the train, our family British Rail railcard making it possible. I used to wonder how we could be a family, without our dad, but obviously BR was pragmatic on such sticking points. We would arrive in Scarborough on the earliest train possible, and disembark carrying everything we needed for the day. 'Now,' my mum would say as we walked towards the beach, 'we have £5 to spend, and when it's spent that's it.' It was amazing how far that money could go.

She once said that *we* were never poor, but that *she* was poor, and it's true that she kept many of her hardships secret, well apart from the need to make 'hen's meat'. Nevertheless, growing up I was aware that life for her was a juggling act between paying bills and having money for trips to the seaside, toys or little luxuries that made the flat a home for us. Her life was full of small disasters, unexpected bills, lost or damaged clothes she had to replace, and I would often see her despair, only to rally later and fight back. One of her most common sayings was, 'If that isn't the story of my life!', used whenever something went wrong. She seemed to have so much bad luck, with life constantly making her tough life even tougher. It was only later that I understood that poor people tread such a fine line that even the slightest thing can push them over the edge, yet each time she climbed back and carried on. 'Never mind, it's the story of my life' became so common that it seemed like an automatic defence, an acceptance of what life threw at us. One such occasion was when, on our way to Scarborough, the train began sounding its horn, then slammed on its brakes, eventually coming to a sudden stop, depositing the passengers on the floor. 'I'm very sorry,' said the guard as he walked through the carriages. 'We seem to have hit a cow on the line.' Our nice day out ruined, Mum just looked at us. 'Well, if that's not the bloody story of my life.'

If my early memories of Hull seem to be captured in rays of summer sun, then the years that followed are cast in autumnal gloom, beginning when I moved up into senior school. This was an all-boys' school, the classes packed tight, the atmosphere tense. Its hallways and balconies were like a prison wing. It seemed as if I had been taken from a small, hard-working and positive school, where children felt special and valuable, and then poured into the grinder of a factory for the disillusioned and bewildered. A school system should attempt to bring to life that special gift each of us is given at birth, to blow on that ember of skill and help you to realise something you perhaps could be. This school, and many like it, simply tipped the lot of us into a bucket and stirred for five years.

Overnight I went from being a happy child who had a few problems with writing and reading, to a 'REM'. I was stuck in remedial classes where teaching was simply about containment. Kids ran wild. They pushed teachers out of their classrooms, they set fire to desks, they threw their books out of windows. The threat of physical violence hung in the air. All you could do was hide behind bluff and show, or slink to the furthest corners at breaktime. No one could show any interest in learning for fear of being labelled a swot and ostracised by the pack. We were all going to hell.

At the end of our time there, it was decided that our failing school would be amalgamated with another failing school, thus doubling the problem and halving the resources to deal with it. Many teachers were just seeing their time out, ineffectual, exhausted and plodding. You felt they hated teaching us just as much as we hated being taught by them. What was lacking was passion of any sort, but then, with three-and-half-million unemployed, they knew they were serving out a sentence just like us and thought they weren't paid enough for passion. They went on strike for more pay, and soon the kids joined them, the local radio station coming down to interview them standing at the gates, not realising the strike had in reality already been going on for years on both sides. With so many unemployed, there was an air of pointlessness about the whole thing. Why weren't we learning? No one gave a fuck.

Worst of all, I suddenly seemed to be bad at every subject, swamped and drifting along. I became aware that my mind didn't seem to be working as well as everyone else's. In the first maths exam, I spent the fifty minutes trying to work out what number June was in the date-of-birth box at the top of the paper, more afraid of looking like a fool at getting that wrong than of failing the paper itself; trying to write out the months of the year on a scrap of paper, unable to remember all twelve, or the order they came in. The harder I tried to think, the deeper the answer sank from view.

I had always loved school, and my young mind had gobbled up knowledge. I was a 'mine of useless information' as my mum would say. Now I hated school, and felt sick each morning knowing I had another day of bedlam ahead. I wanted a teacher who could look into me and see my potential and help me draw it out, but no one had the time. There seemed to be no future for any of us apart from youth training schemes, dead-end jobs, going on the dole or crime.

I didn't want to sign on. Deep inside me I held the ember of self-belief that I was better than that. I didn't want an ordinary life like the parents of my friends, signing on, doing cash-in-hand jobs, living off the proceeds of goods that 'fell off the backs of lorries', having kids, trying to pay off the catalogue man for their Christmas presents. I wanted to be free of it all. But how?

I went to the careers adviser and told him I'd like to work outdoors, but the only thing he had in his file was working in forestry. I saw a poster for a careers day about being an officer in the army, but was told by the adviser I couldn't go as I probably wouldn't be able to get enough O-levels to qualify for a place. This felt like a slap in the face. I was angry. I wanted to prove him wrong, but knew he was right. I wasn't clever enough.

I began to think about joining the Marines, probably because it was the only option that offered some way out, and maybe because it also offered some way back into the comfort of military institutionalisation that I had felt so attracted to as a child. Robin had applied to the RAF, and had been accepted to join as soon as he was old enough. I understood now why my dad, his dad, and his dad before him had joined. There simply wasn't anything else they could do to satisfy the urge for a life less ordinary and depressing than this. The only problems were that I hated ironing, I doubted I was tough enough, and I feared I was too much of a dreamer to hack it.

The only thing I knew I was good at was drawing. I had so

many ideas in my head, and it seemed that only a pencil offered some way of letting them out. It was this ability to draw that had always pulled me through the hardest times. No matter how bad my maths-test results were, no matter how many red underlinings there were on the pages of my English books, at least I could draw.

There was never any talk of university or college at school. I was so ignorant of higher education, I thought 'Oxbridge' was a university, but I began to focus on trying to get into art college. I had no idea what I would learn there, or how I could possibly make a living, but none of that mattered as long as I had some grace before I entered the crush of the real world.

Exams came and I got O-levels in art, history, technical drawing and, amazingly, English, probably due to a story I wrote in answer to the essay question. Entitled 'The Dream', it was about what the bomb-aimer of the Enola Gay dreamed of as he slept on the way to bomb Hiroshima. My head had always been full of stories but, unable to articulate them in any way that was legible to a reader, I'd stuck to drawing cartoons. On that day, I had somehow shown enough talent, despite my misspellings and poor grammar, to earn a grade.

I failed my maths O-level, but I signed on to go to sixth form, even though my friends told me not to as I'd then become 'overqualified'. Some of the teachers, more realistically, doubted I was clever enough. I also doubted it myself, and so picked my strongest subjects, history and art, for A-level and tried to take my maths O-level again, having been told it was vital if I wanted to go to college. I failed it at the end of the first year, and again in my final exams, along with both art and history, thus proving my teachers right. I really was an idiot, but at least I wasn't going to have the problem of being overqualified.

Then I got an interview for a foundation course at Hull College of Art, a one-year intensive course where you would be taught how to paint, sculpt, take pictures, and see if you were good enough to go on to a full course at the art college. Without an A-level in art, and no maths qualifications, it didn't look good, but I collected up my pictures and went to the interview.

The room was set up with tables where people could show

their work, and the crapness of my schooling became apparent as I looked around at proper canvases, sculptures, framed photos and assorted offerings by trendy-looking kids from all over Humberside. My table held a collection of pencil and pen pictures, mostly on a sci-fi theme, my main source of artistic instruction having come from comics and film posters. The lecturer walked around the room, talking to each person and looking at their work, until eventually she came to my table. You could tell she wasn't impressed either by me or by my work, which looked neither trendy, intelligent nor artistic. This just wasn't my world. Then she focused on a picture that stood out amongst the rest. It was a dark hand-drawn picture on a long piece of white card I'd found, and off-cut. It was a depiction of the inside of a whale, with organs, ribs, intestines. The picture was carefully drawn to look as real as possible, and I'd created a kind of surreal mishmash of shadow and light. What stood out, more in the centre of the picture, was the pure white tip of a harpoon, which created an interesting composition of dark and light, soft and hard lines. It was so different, and frankly so odd, that she picked it up and asked me about it. I told her I'd got the idea after going to the nearby whaling museum and seen the harpoons on display, and imagined what they would look like when they were inside a whale.

For the first time since I'd left junior high school, I felt a teacher look at me and see some potential there. She made a note, telling me it was very interesting, and moved on.

A few days later I got a letter telling me that I had made it onto the course. It was one of the happiest moments of my life.

The one-year course was intensive, and I found myself amongst keen, intelligent and well-educated students, and, more importantly, teachers who seemed to dote on us and would give us more praise than we could handle. The difference was dizzying, and I know in that one year I learned and grew more than I had in seven years of senior school. Most importantly, I was exposed to the positivity of the other students, who seemed to have so many more reference points than myself. Overnight my world of films, videos and science fiction was replaced with one of books, music and the normal things of a teenager's life.

I noticed there were other people like me on the course, who had held onto their drawing skills, found themselves here, and now felt equally out of their depth. Very soon most of them had left, condemning art as being 'up its own arse', but for me life had never been more amazing. My schools had been all-boys, but now I found myself working next to girls, who shone and brought a sparkle and electricity to life.

As the course progressed, so did my work. I had no money for paint, neither oils nor cheaper acrylics, let alone canvases to paint on, so I made do with the contents of the 'free cupboard', painting on sheets of wood with a mixture of PVA glue and powder paint, which, although unconventional, did make them stand out from the other students' work. I began doing abstract paintings on a biological theme, based on what someone had told me: that 'the human body disintegrates at 12 miles per hour'. These pictures were all red fury, often with sand mixed in to give texture, and although odd for me they had a kind of pleasing composition. Very often I would just work by instinct, with no clear idea of why I put paint here or there, and it was only afterwards that I would have to justify it. Sometimes it's refreshing to know that you do what you do just because it feels right.

Around me I would see other students who seemed to have prodigious talents, yet made so little use of their time, whereas I gave 100 per cent, feeling my head strain as my potential, pent up for so long, was drawn out. The culmination of the year was to get into a degree course, something that not only would allow me to carry on this amazing and thrilling adventure, but also to get a grant and move away. The only sticking point was the fact that I had no real qualifications. The course ended and I got an 'Upper Credit With Distinction'. I thought that with this I would wing it at the interview the following week at Sheffield University, one of the most prestigious universities in the country, and, more importantly, in a city I knew had good climbs close by. I was going to fulfil my promise to return.

A few weeks after the interview, I got a letter from Sheffield University. I felt that I was on a roll. I was amazing. I was talented. Then I ripped open the envelope and saw they didn't want me. In that moment my world came crashing down. I was worthless again.

'You'll just have to get a job,' said my mum, 'or sign on the dole.'

I felt sick.

Within a few weeks I did sign on, and then I moved out to live in a squat with a friend, unable to live at home any more, feeling distant, alienated. My stupid dreams of going to art college had been dashed. My only skill had come to nothing.

I threw away my paints and pencils, and my paper and sketch books, and from that moment, for years and years, I didn't draw another thing.

A *very brave man*

Pitch 1 New Dawn

I carried my first load up to the base of the wall in the cool of pre-dawn. The approach was short, a few hundred metres of track leading through forest to the base of El Cap, then up some zig-zagging paths to the bottom of the Dawn Wall.

I walked slowly, picking out the track with my headtorch which cast scary shadows from the bushes and trees as I twisted the beam around, looking for black bears.

One of the most amazing things about El Cap is the way it simply shoots out of the ground without any warning, like Jack's beanstalk, rocketing out of the earth and up into the clouds. In the dark you simply bump into it, its grey granite base looking just like a skyscraper of rock, smoother and more perfect than any concrete. Walking along its base,

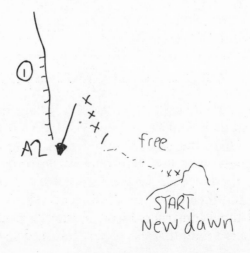

crushed under the weight of a haul bag, hand brushing the rock both to aid balance and because doing so proved it was real, it was only when you spotted an iron deposit or band of black diorite that you would guess this was a natural feature.

I don't believe in God, and intelligent design is only for those who know nothing about either, but when I stand beneath El Cap I always have second thoughts. How could nature be so brash and showy? And if there is a God, he must be American, or the road wouldn't be so close to this glorious wall.

My thighs bulged and strained under the load, the weight causing me to move in a slow painful lurch, using the odd rock or tree stump to help me rest and catch my breath, bag balanced. The weight of what I had brought from England had doubled with a twenty-day supply of water – thirty-two litres in plastic lemonade bottles – plus my food, comprising tins of stew, bagels, cheese, cans of Coke and tortillas. Strangely, although I had plenty of water, I probably only had ten days' food, even though I knew Thomas Humar, one of the best climbers in the world, had taken fourteen days to solo the route in 1998. Maybe subconsciously I knew that being thin would be an asset on such a route, where an extra gram of fat could mean the difference between life and death.

El Cap is one of the biggest ticks for climbers. There were always half a dozen on the wall, and already I could see the odd headtorch springing to life, as climbers woke on portaledges and began preparing to climb as soon as the sun appeared; those at the top were keener to get going than those lower down who still had days to go.

Here and there the base of the wall smelt of toilets, the sign that a 'shit bag' lay nearby, tossed by a team in the last week or so and still not collected or desiccated by the sun. In the past, climbers would collect paper grocery bags from the valley store, crap in them and throw them off the wall. The idea was that, once down, the team would return to collect their shit bags, but many were less than diligent. In order to stop this, it was now the law that climbers must bag up their crap and carry it up and then down the wall, generally in a home-made plastic 'shit-tube' constructed from a drain pipe. Unfortunately, many climbers found this too grim a job, and so still preferred to toss their bags. However, most felt guilty enough to come back and pick them up. I often wondered if the rangers could dust for prints in order to discover who didn't.

There had also been a fad a few years ago to set fire to one's shit bag, creating a 'flaming shit ball' and adding a pyrotechnic edge to the throwing experience.

Of course, the downside of neatly packed excreta was being struck by them while climbing or lying in your sleeping bag. Dawn and dusk were always times to keep your eye out for falling faeces. Luckily I'd only had one close call, when a bag had struck my belay and covered my radio in shit. Fortunately, I had a roll of gaffer tape, which I used to cover the offending areas.

My feet stabbed into the talus as I grew close to the start of the Reticent, sweat already running down my face and back, the burden made worse because I knew I had two more loads to carry up before I would have all my gear in place. I seemed to have spent a great deal of my time carrying haul bags up and down this path, and I passed a few minutes trying to work out just how many that had been, and a rough estimate of the total weight. I wondered if carrying Ella on my shoulders was good training, and tried to imagine the straps that dug into my shoulders were her bouncing legs.

Can you remember being on your dad's shoulders?

I also kept an eye on the ground for wall booty, gear dropped by climbers above. I once met a climber who braved the rain of shit bags by living at the base of the wall, claiming that everything a man could ever want fell there: food, climbing gear, water, even the odd wallet, sleeping bag and fully packed haul bag. He said all you needed was to pray for it, and the next day it would appear. This high-risk but lonely life seemed to work for him, and he lived there for years, until a female base jumper smashed into the ground from half a mile up after her parachute failed to open. After that he moved on. I suppose you have to be careful what you wish for.

I smeared up the final slab to the base of the wall just as the first rays of the sun struck the summit overhangs three thousand feet above me, giving this area of El Cap its name: the Dawn Wall. It would soon be roasting down here, but I rested my bag on an old dead tree and marvelled as the wall lit up.

You'll be up there soon enough.

All big routes are primarily about logistics, carrying heavy gear around, and waiting; but soon all that would be over and the climb would begin. The beauty for me of big-wall climbing is that the moment you step from the ground, your life is suspended – in every sense of the word – with days or weeks of honest hard work, the bizarre joy of struggle, the escapism. Up high, there would be no bills to pay, no emotional demands, no distractions, only climbing, dawn till dusk, and the reward of seeing the sun set at the end of the day.

This was why I was there. I needed to escape from normality. To leave the din of my life, leave my thoughts and troubles behind. The only thing that always seemed to be simple was this piece of rock.

You know you can't escape.

You have to come back down sometime.

Unless . . .

I looked up again. The sun had moved down the wall a few more metres, making slow progress, each minute illuminating more and more of the route, the fearsome and feared Reticent Wall.

The Reticent was climbed in 1995 by Americans Steve Gerberding, Lori Reddel and Scott Stowe, and was immediately hailed as the hardest big wall in the world: fourteen of the most dangerous and difficult pitches possible, climbed from a feature called Lay Lady Ledge six pitches up the wall. This title of super-route came primarily from the fact that Gerberding proclaimed

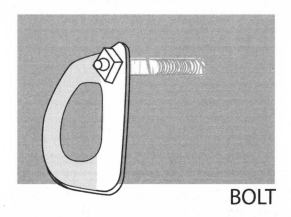

BOLT

it his hardest route, something people took notice of, given his 100 ascents of El Cap, including almost all its hardest routes, in addition to big walls that stretched from Patagonia to the Himalayas. Gerberding was the strong silent type; he had no need to impress. So when he said it was hard we believed him.

The route began with six easy existing pitches, put up in 1975, before branching off at Lay Lady Ledge. From there it took a direct line up the Dawn Wall, the longest and steepest section of El Cap.

This route had acquired mythical status from the start. The second ascent only added to this myth, with tales of 'death falls' and pitches that were so dangerous they were 'unjustifiable'. Each pitch had been at the very limit of what was possible, connecting up minute and fragile features, stretching the rope out in order to drill the least number of bolts. This meant that huge falls threatened on most pitches, with many other dangers lurking: sharp flakes; loose rock; ledges ready to kill or maim the unlucky.

It was said that if you fell, you died. It was 'Pringles' climbing: once you pop you don't stop.

You won't fall.

I pulled out the paper topo I had for the climb, a simple map of lines and crosses that showed me where the route went. Today I would climb the first easy pitch, abseil down, and come back tomorrow with another load and do a further pitch. This would give me a little more time to psych myself up before committing to the route.

I carried on, reached the base of the route, and took off my haul bag. As I set it down, I noticed I wasn't alone. Two climbers were already sorting out gear a few metres away. I said hello and they nodded back, as two more climbers appeared up the trail behind me, also carrying giant haul bags.

So much for solitude.

One of the climbers walking up shouted what sounded like orders in Russian, and the two climbers on the ledge speeded up their gear sorting.

It was obvious they also had plans to climb the Reticent Wall.

Russian teams often have clearly defined roles, with an overall leader, deputy, cleaner, etc., each person given their own job to do. Unlike Western climbers, who share all the tasks – taking turns leading, hauling gear, and cleaning the gear out of the pitches – the Russian system works on putting the strongest climbers up front. The best climber does all the leading, the strongest the hauling, the one with the highest boredom threshold the belaying. It may seem strange to a Western climber, but there is a lot to be said for applying the strongest elements to the task at hand, with the ultimate goal of success coming before the individual's desire to shine.

The leader of the team was older and stockier than the rest, with grey hair and hairy shoulders. Stripping off, he revealed a red 70s-style body-building vest, making him look like an old Soviet Olympic coach. He came over to introduce himself. His name was Seregin, and his team was from Leningrad. I'd heard about these guys, that they'd been travelling around the world ticking off big walls, often with new routes. They looked strong and capable, and seemed to have a jovial and humorous way to them. I had no doubt they were the real deal.

'Tell me,' Seregin asked, 'what do you climb?'

'The Reticent,' I replied, almost embarrassed, as I pulled out my ropes and uncoiled them, dropping karabiners into neat piles at my feet.

Ah yes, we also do Reticent . . . but tell me, where is your friend?'

'I have no friend, I'm going to solo it,' I said, the words seeming preposterous as they passed my lips.

The man raised his eyebrows. 'You are very brave,' he said before saying something in Russian to the other climbers, at which they all laughed.

He turned back to me. 'I have soloed many climbs, and scaled many difficult walls, but I would not dare solo the Reticent Wall. You are very brave.'

'Not really,' I said. 'I just don't have any stupid friends.'

The leader introduced the rest of the team, and told me that they would be leaving tomorrow, their ropes already fixed almost up to Lay Lady Ledge, six pitches higher. I asked him about himself and Russian climbing, and he told me that for twenty years he'd been a quantum physicist, but now he owned a Mercedes dealership.

I liked the Russians and part of me wished I could go with them. It would be fun. However, I knew that even if they offered, I would turn them down. Although the route terrified me I had to do the whole climb myself. I wanted it all. All the rewards and all the suffering.

Life's too short to have fun.

The Russians would be much faster than me, and we joked that I would still be halfway up the wall when they were back down in the bar celebrating, but they promised to leave me presents on the route. It was the Russian way.

'In a few hours,' said Seregin, 'we go up to Lay Lady Ledge and camp before Reticent. We have barbecue. You are welcome.'

I tried to imagine a Russian barbecue: visions of potatoes turning black while the cook lay on the ground with a bottle of vodka.

'Thank you – that would be nice,' I accepted, and carried on unpacking.

We worked together, both teams, their team of four and my team of one, silent apart from the odd question and command, until the Russians disappeared up their ropes, fixing their way up to Lay Lady Ledge.

Are you brave?

I thought about the word. Is it brave to attempt something against all the odds, something you view as being beyond you, yet you try anyway?

Are you just deluded?

Half my water bottles stood in a line against the wall, food in bags sat beside my climbing gear, ropes stacked in buckets were ready to be fed out as I climbed. I put on my harness, rock boots and helmet, and started clipping in my gear and readying myself to climb the first pitch.

Everything was done. Now I could start to climb.

I pushed my sweaty hands into the chalk bag clipped to the back of my harness, wiped off the excess and placed both hands on the rock. The orange and yellow light high on the wall had now made it past the overhangs and was rolling down to where I figured the crux would be.

Will you make it that far?

Most climbs, even the Reticent, where every pitch was said to be harder than anything else on El Cap, have a crux, a pitch you know is harder and more dangerous than the rest. On some routes this could just mean the risk of a big fall, while on the harder routes it could involve easy climbing but on loose features that could snap off and either crush you or chop your rope.

The Reticent crux involved all these things, with the added worry of taking place above a large ledge: hard climbing on loose rock above a death ledge that would smash any falling climber to pieces. No route is assured until you stand on the top, but only when the crux is finished are you really able to believe you can make it and relax. Before that time, the crux is always at the back of your mind and, no matter how well you're climbing, you never relax until it's been completed. The worst thing about this route was the knowledge that its crux came on the last day, pitch thirteen. It would be a real bummer to fall and die on the last day of such a route, especially having taken weeks to get there.

Think how good you'll feel if you get that far.

The reality, even on the Reticent, is that, irrespective of where the crux is marked on the topo, the first pitch, the first move, is always the hardest.

I started climbing.

Windows

I cursed having a broken window beside my bed. All winter long a cold draught blew over me, flapping the brown parcel tape I used to attempt a repair of its fractures before the whole lot fell into the back yard below.

My room was really no room at all. It was a corridor, one wall simply a curtain, the rest hung with my paintings, the paper slowly curling in the damp. I was nineteen, and unemployed. Although far from perfect, this was the first space of my own, a ramshackle squat close to Hull University.

We never knew who owned the flat, and I had moved in as others moved out, the usual hot-bunking you find in squats. For some reason, no one ever came looking for rent, and no bills or final demands ever dropped on the mat. The only gas we used was for frying up chips, our only diet, cut from potatoes bought in a fifty-pound sack once a month for a few quid. I wonder why we never got scurvy.

I lived there with my friend Wayne, and whoever was sleeping on the dirty settees or on the ashtray floor at the time. Life was simple – and wonderfully grim. There were no real jobs at the time, well no real jobs you would risk dropping off the dole for, only picking turnips or packing fish fingers. All we lived for was the giro every fortnight, and so life was a waiting game, eking out our £24 a week by eating potatoes, sitting around figuring out what to do with our lives and attempting to mend the windows.

Wayne had been in the house longer than me, and so had a room with a lock on the door, and spent all his days trying to make the ultimate compilation tape. He was impulsive, and would often blow his whole giro in a day, then spend the next two weeks simply living on chips. Once he lived for a week on nothing but powdered bran and water.

We lived mainly for the nights, getting into cheap nightclubs and stealing drinks from students. I loved dancing, but for me it was simply training. With my eyes closed, I imagined myself far away on a distant mountain.

Each night when I got home I would jump in my mouldy sleeping bag and wrap myself up in blankets from Oxfam, burying myself so deep it was almost impossible to wipe away the feathers that tickled my nose as they escaped from the tired cotton shell of my bag.

The room contained all my possessions, packed tightly under the bed and hidden behind bin bags in case anyone tried to steal them. My curtain wall was no defence against anything, and anyway the flat had no lock on the door. In fact, I'm not sure it even had a door.

Under my bed was all my outdoor gear, each piece more valuable to me than anything in the world. I would lie there, my hat on, listening to the wind outside and inside, and imagine I was somewhere else: Death Bivy on the Eiger, the South Col of Everest, the summit of Fitzroy. The colder the place, the warmer I felt. For me this was all simply training for my escape.

I was dropped off near Kendal, scrambling over piles of snow beside the motorway as my lift sped off, my hitching over. I pulled the rucksack tight onto my back, did up its hip belt and started walking towards the mountains in my army boots. I'd hitched to the hills before, but only with other people, generally with disastrous consequences. The last time had been to the Peak District with Wayne, who'd run a mile when he saw a sheep. He'd never seen a real one before. But this time I'd come alone.

The mountains disappeared into the dark before I reached them, and so I spent the first night under two wooden pallets propped against a drystone wall.

The morning dawned cold, and my trusty cotton sleeping bag was stiff as I packed it away, the feathers that escaped as I pushed it into its stuff-sack blowing away across the snow.

I reached the mountains and began up a ridge, excited to

kick my way up patches of snow, to feel the ground fall away, until I reached the top. There was so much space, and it was all mine.

Moving along the tops I scrambled down to a lake, its surface frozen thick, and put up my tiny orange cotton tent.

I stayed there a week, picking off tops and coming back to the tent each evening, where I'd lie in my bag as my tea slowly warmed on my meths stove, the porch open, looking out into the dark, listening to the crack of the ice, the wind blowing around me.

Each night my tent got frostier and frostier. The foot section of my sleeping bag froze solid, forcing me to wrap my feet in my fleece jacket.

On the last evening, still hungry after a tiny portion of curry and rice, my diet dictated by my giro and the budget constraints of my daily allowance at the 'Scoop and Weigh', I lay and thought about my future, a span of time that seemed as black and empty as the night.

Next day, I stood by the side of the road for what felt like hours until I got a lift to Bolton with a roofer, then to Leeds with a man who ran a mobile disco. After being picked up by the police for walking down the side of the motorway, and dropped at the services, I hitched a lift with a trucker bound for Hull docks, his cab the first really warm place I'd been for a long time.

Hitching always came with risks, and I'd come across my fair share of scary characters on the road, but this trucker was one of the good ones. He was probably in his fifties, kind of unhealthy-looking in a truck-driver way, but stopping at a snack wagon he bought me a cup of tea and told me how, at nineteen, he'd hitched all the way from Scotland to South Africa. He told me tales of being stuck for days on African roads, where lions roamed in the bush, of gun barrels being jabbed into ribs, of sandstorms and sunsets, tsetse flies and bivies in Timbuktu. I listened to him, and envied his stories, the adventure, his guts to just do it.

'Why did you come back?' I asked.

'It was the best thing I ever did, and I enjoyed every minute of it, but when I got to Cape Town all I could think about was going home.'

'What did you do next?' I was imagining further adventures.

'I got married and started driving trucks.'

I was dropped off near the docks and walked back towards the squat, popping in to a friend's house to cadge a cup of tea on the way. The house was full of students, who always seemed to me to have a limitless amount of money back then, and who, it seemed, did no more work than Wayne or me. The settee was full of long-haired students smoking skinny rollies and watching *Taxi Driver* on a small black-and-white TV. Out of the kitchen came an attractive woman with crazy curls of red hair whom I'd never seen before.

'Hello,' she said, surprised at someone new coming in the door. 'Would you like some food?' She spooned out a big plate of veg and rice, the best meal I'd seen for a long time.

I suppose I fell in love with her at that moment.

Her name was Mandy. She was a student at the university, doing a French degree, and had come back to Hull from France where she'd been working in a school. I'd heard lots about her from other people, as she'd been a DJ at a popular nightclub before she went, and was one of the cooler of Hull's many Indie kids.

Trauma was in the air, and I soon found out why everyone was so glued to the TV. Mandy had just found out that her best friend's boyfriend had been two-timing the friend while she was living in London. She'd just told her friend over the phone. Now she had to find said boyfriend and tell him she'd spilled the beans and get him to ring his now ex.

'Who's coming with me?' said Mandy, addressing the room. All eyes were uncomfortably but firmly fixed on De Niro.

No one said a word.

'I'll come,' I said, in an unusual fit of gallantry.

I think I felt obliged after my free meal, and also because I quite liked the idea of spending some time with her, and so we put on our coats and began walking the streets, looking for the boyfriend. Mandy was unlike anyone else I'd ever met. She seemed full of light and ideas. She lived in France, she wanted things. No, she *expected* things. She had the touch of possibility that was missing from most of the people I knew. She also had a sadness about her. Maybe she was just as lost as me.

We tramped through the dark streets, knocking on doors where we thought we'd find the boyfriend, until we knew where he was.

'Stay here, I'll go and talk to him,' I said, leaving her at the street corner – another uncharacteristic act of chivalry, as I'd rather have sat with the rest of them and watched *Taxi Driver*. But I hadn't, and, in that moment, she fell in love with me.

I knocked on the door.

Later, I walked Mandy home and said goodnight, then went back to the squat, up the fire-escape, past the broken door, and into the scruffy kitchen, where a pan of chips bubbled on the stove. The living room was full of people smoking dope and talking about how we were all going to be drafted into the Gulf War. I doubted they'd make very good soldiers.

I went to my room and, pulling back the curtain, dropped my rucksack on the floor. The space seemed darker and more depressing than usual, and I could see the poverty of my surroundings. But then I thought about my trip and the wall with pallets stacked against it, about bush shelters, ditches, and all the other places I'd slept. I didn't live here. This place wasn't me. I knew I wouldn't be here for long.

I pulled out my sleeping bag and threw it on the mattress. The foot of the bag was still frozen, ice coating the cardboard-stiff cotton, but I climbed in and pulled the blankets over it, knowing my body heat would dry it out by morning.

I thought about Mandy, and wondered if I'd see her again before she went back to France.

I just lay there and listened to the wind flapping the tape on the window, and once more imagined I was somewhere else. Only this time I wasn't alone.

Max load

Pitch 2 New Dawn

I pushed the last of my gear into my biggest haul bag and, pulling the lid shut, clipped the bag to the haul line. Two ropes hung down from the belay forty metres above my head, a green climbing rope and a yellow haul rope, clipped to two bolts at the top of the pitch I'd climbed the previous day.

It's been a long time since you've done this.

The first pitch yesterday had been slow, as I worked out how to climb again, but today, hauling these bags up, was where the work would really begin. It seemed almost comical to be feeling so rusty, ropes and hardware awkward and alien,

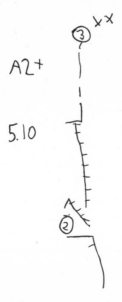

when about to commit to the hardest route of my life. I was aware it would be so easy to make a fatal mistake.

Just take your time.

There were so many things I could do wrong.

Just think everything through.

There is no room for error when soloing a big wall.

You've done it before.

I'd only done it once.

Soloing a big wall requires a complex system of self-belaying, abseiling and hauling, and for years I tried to learn how it was done, spending many days in Derbyshire quarries in the rain perfecting the technique. These days had probably been my most dangerous as I blindly tried out different ways of protecting myself without a partner, several times coming close to hitting the deck.

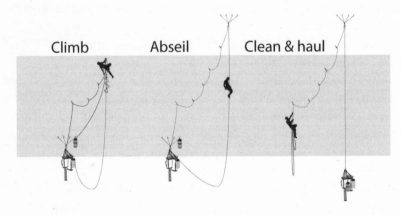

The first lead had been in the slate quarries of Llanberis in North Wales, a thin crack tucked in the back wall of a disused pit. I'd climbed it in the dark after work, and had been so scared of making a mistake I'd climbed about ten feet up before remembering I'd forgotten to clip into the rope; I'd left it neatly stacked on the ground below me.

The next solo had been El Cap by one of its hard routes.

Yes and you did it.

Only just!

I would climb a pitch, paying my own rope out rather than a partner doing it for me, make a belay, then abseil down the second rope I was carrying, my haul line, back to the previous belay. Once there I would attach my bags on the haul line, and return up my lead rope, taking out the gear I'd placed, then haul the bag up after me.

On reaching the belay again, all the protection would be racked ready for the next pitch, and both the haul and lead line restacked, ready for the next pitch, in rope bags designed to stop them snagging as they fed out.

This system is both slow and labour-intensive, with a 1,000-metre route requiring 3,000 metres of movement (twice up the rope, and once down the haul line). It is a well-established and safe technique, but in climbing there is perhaps no bigger test of skill. With no partner to fall back on, or to swap leads, there is also no bigger reward than standing on top of a mighty wall knowing every inch has been climbed alone. There is also no greater weight than to look up at the wall from below, wondering if you have it in you to succeed.

This was what I wanted. I wanted it all. All the good. All the bad. To say it was all mine.

What will it prove?

I slipped off my shoes leaving them sitting neatly next to the large flake at the bottom of the route, and put on my rock boots.

One more night on the ground, and then you'll be on the wall for good. No more coming down.

Using the rope fixed from the previous day, I climbed back up using my jumars – metal clamps that only move up a rope, locking down on it once they are weighted – sliding up the one attached to my harness first, then the one attached to a foot loop next, moving each in turn, slowly progressing up the rope. Climbing rope is dynamic, designed to stretch and reduce the impact force on both your body and the protection, meaning it bounces as you climb it. When you climb one you're mindful of all the people who have died because a rope had been sawn through by the bouncing motion over sharp edges, and no matter how careful you are, your mind will flip into paranoia mode.

Did you do up all the karabiners?

Yes.

What if someone's been up in the night and messed with it?

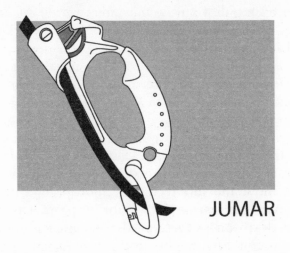

JUMAR

Not going to happen.
I thought about the time I practised jumaring up a rope in a quarry near Sheffield, how one minute I was fifty feet up, and the next I was shooting down. The rope had been running over an edge, and the sheath of the rope, the nylon mantle that protects the core strands of the rope, snapped. Down I slid until, with incredible luck, the sheath bunched up below me and stopped me hitting the ground.

Just trust the rope. Go slow. It's all you can do.
The worst story I'd heard about a rope being damaged involved a solo climber on the Shield, jumaring back up his lead line in a storm, close to the top of the wall. With nearly a kilometre of air below his feet, the sharp burr on a peg rubbed on the rope, cutting the sheath little by little each time he moved his body up. Suddenly the sheath snapped, and he fell several metres, until, like me, the sheath bunched up. Unlike me, however, he was hanging in a storm with no chance of rescue. All he could do was gather up the multiple strands of the core of his rope and jumar up on them, the burr of the peg continuing to saw through them as he went.

Think about something else.
I arrived at the belay and clipped in, making myself comfortable and ready to haul my bags up. I passed the haul line through my wall hauler, a pulley with a toothed cam built in which allows the rope to be hauled one way and then locks

down after each pull. I'd used this pulley on all the routes I'd climbed on El Cap, and I doubted there was any other device that had been the focus of so much expended energy, lifting hundreds of haul bags over tens of kilometres in its life.

Clipping a jumar from my harness to the haul line I began to do squats, using my body weight to draw the rope through until the rope was tight between the pulley and the haul bags. I pulled harder as the rope took the weight. The rope grew thinner under the strain, but the bags stayed on the ledge. I pulled harder. The rope grew thinner. I pulled harder, using both hands now, the strain on me, the rope, and the pulley increasing with each stroke.

I looked down and wondered if the bags were caught on something, or if I'd left them clipped to the belay, but I knew the real reason was they were simply too heavy. I lay back so that my legs were braced against the wall, my head pointing down, and heaved with my arms, the muscles in my thighs bulging as I pressed them out. The rope moved an inch and I collapsed under the strain.

This is fucking impossible.

I pulled again, my kneecaps feeling as if they might pop off as I pressed my legs out and drew another inch of rope through the pulley.

You'll never get them up.

An hour later the haul bags were halfway up the pitch. I

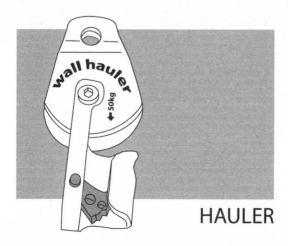

HAULER

was exhausted and despairing. It was pointless, but I was stubborn. I wouldn't give in – even if it took me all day and this was as high as I got, I would have this victory. I inverted again and pulled hard with every sinew. I marvelled at the amount of force the rope, pulley and belay could take. The only thing I doubted was me.

You're going to break something!

Two hours had passed and the bags were almost up, but now I listened to my pulley groaning under the strain. The words 'Max load: 50 kg' stamped on the side caused me concern. My sixty litres of water weighed more than that.

Just get it up quick.

The closer I got the bag, the more the pulley creaked and clicked, as if to demonstrate how overloaded it was. It was an alarming sound. If it broke, the bag would fall straight onto my harness, probably breaking my hips and asphyxiating me in a few minutes. I watched in horror as the cam that held the rope in check also began to deform the alloy plate it pushed against, the weight on the rope far beyond its intended load. There was no way to get the load off the pulley, apart from cutting the rope with my knife, so all I could do was pull and hope it wouldn't break.

Finally after two and a half hours, I had the bags up and lashed to the belay. I looked at the two bolt hangers that held me and the bags, two twisted pieces of steel threaded through the bolts, no thicker or longer than my little finger. What was their breaking strain?

It seemed I was already close to reaching mine and I was only a rope away from the ground. I slumped onto the belay, utterly exhausted and fed up. What was I doing? This was insane. I'd wasted most of the day just hauling my bag up one pitch. How on earth would I ever make it to the top?

Soloing is all about self-confidence, and right then I had zero. I imagined the Russians looking down at me, and thinking what a bullshitter I was, how I couldn't even haul my bags properly.

Why do you always care what other people think?

I put the thought of having to haul the bag again to the back of my mind and began sorting gear for the next pitch, hoping the climbing would make me feel better.

Aid climbing is an odd way of scaling rock, and is designed to make it possible to climb what is impossible to climb with fingers and toes alone. All the hardest walls on El Cap involve primarily the aid-climbing technique. This involves placing a piece of protection – a peg, a nut, a skyhook – then clipping a set of aiders to it, attached to you via a sling called a daisy chain. These aiders are long nylon ladders with steps sewn in, which allow you to climb up and then place the next piece. The physical skill involved, apart from hauling, jumaring, etc., is finding and placing the best protection possible. The harder the route, the less reliable and more hard-won the place for the protection pieces becomes. But what makes aid climbing so addictive is the mental focus required. Very few sports involve the breaking of so many mental barriers.

I started up the next pitch, but my lack of fitness and organisation only seemed to make things worse. The ropes, aiders and gear became a tangled mess.

You fucking fat useless knacker.

The 'easy climbing' also proved harder and more scary than I'd expected, with several pieces of protection ripping out as I moved up on them.

These first six pitches had been climbed since a year after I was born, something I tried to remind myself as I shook my rope clear of rusty pegs and corroded copper heads. I just wanted to get up the pitch so I could abseil off, go to bed, and put the day behind me.

The sun beat down, and a cloud of doubt built with each placement I crept up onto. Even pieces that I knew were good felt more like time-bombs. I was rattled, the reality of the route disintegrating any high ideas I had about my climbing prowess.

And you thought you could climb the Reticent. You can't even climb this piss-easy route.

My hands were too soft and unready for a wall, and the fold of fat that overlapped my harness made me feel far from athletic. I had never felt as foolish and out of my depth. I was a dreamer, a fantasist, a Walter Mitty, an overreacher.

Another piece of protection popped and struck me in the forehead just below my helmet. I sank back in my harness and felt the bump, blood and sweat running into my eyes.

Fucking useless twatting fuck face!

I looked down at the valley, the Merced River twisting below, moving slow and green, people sitting on blankets along its sandy banks. I thought about sitting on the beach at Scarborough making sandcastles.

What are you doing?

Every inch of me wanted to back off and call it a day. There was no way I could climb the Reticent. It would be suicide. I had felt like this so many times – out of my depth, blindingly aware of overreaching myself yet again – but this was the worst ever.

You haven't climbed a wall for a year. You're too fat. You're too weak. You're too scared.

I pushed on.

I arrived at the second set of bolts, about seventy metres up the wall, and, clipping onto them with relief, quickly set up my belay, attaching my ropes to it. I was still very close to the ground. I could still abseil down and escape from the route, and these terrible feelings, for a little while longer. It was too late to haul the bags up this pitch and I didn't have the energy, so instead I set about getting ready to leave. I couldn't wait to get back on the ground.

I concentrated, trying not to be distracted by thoughts of being elsewhere, and transferred from the belay to the haul line so I could abseil back down to my bags. A mistake now would be fatal, just as it would a thousand metres higher, only here I'd have less time to wonder what I had done wrong.

I checked and rechecked that I was attached properly, that the rope fed correctly through my abseil device, that jumars were attached to my harness so I could re-ascend the rope in the morning – countless little things I needed to remember. It had been a long time since I'd done this, and it would be so easy to make a simple mistake.

I unclipped from the belay ready to abseil, all my weight on the one rope, locked in place only by my hand.

I thought how my life depended on that one hand, that if I lost grip I'd slide down the rope out of control and hit the ground. The rope felt hot and stiff in my fingers, my palm was slightly sweaty, my hand gripping imperceptibly harder to compensate. If I let go now I would fall.

I looked down at my shoes, two pin-pricks below, thinking that that would be where I'd land, imagining the air exploding out of me as I slammed into the rock. I thought about them sitting beside the door at home, the image of Ella walking into the living room with them on her tiny feet, pretending to be me.

I looked up at the wall.

The Russians were hauling their bags up onto Lay Lady Ledge.

I looked down.

Carefully, I let the rope slip through my hands.

Alpinists

The storm whipped around me as I clung to the slope, stinging, blowing, sucking, blasting snow and stones at me like machine-gun bullets. I kept my eyes closed and held on, hoping the wind would die, not yet experienced enough to know that it never dies until it doesn't really matter.

It was winter, high in the Mont Blanc Massif, the mountains empty, only me and my partner, balanced on a near-vertical slope of alpine kitty litter.

The wind blew harder, snow stuck to the few areas of flesh not covered by my balaclava, the ice crystals sucked away my heat until they turned to water, more snow stuck to my wet skin with the next blast. Slowly my head turned into an ice pop. My calves stung, their muscles like tight hot fists; my body balanced on crampon points that stuck into mud the consistency of yet-to-be-defrosted chocolate cheesecake.

I squeezed open my eyes and looked at my belay, just a thin sling draped over a nub of flint that stuck out of the frozen dirt, then on down at the glacier a hundred metres below. The snow looked so soft and inviting, the open crevasses snug and cosy, a haven from the storm. I wondered – for the first, but not the last time – what my chances would be if I were to fall now, my body rag-dolling down the slope until it hit the snow below.

If I fell, I'd die. I knew I was close to the line, balanced, the wind about to undo me at any moment. I would have screamed, but I couldn't. I was holding my partner's rope in my mouth, giving the illusion that I had him on belay. If Aaron fell, I'd never hold his weight with my teeth.

This is the overriding memory of my first trip to the Alps and, although I wish I could say I was hanging on the Eiger

North Face or the Matterhorn, in reality I was halfway up a steep moraine slope – nothing but the combined frozen detritus of centuries of glacial rock grindings – having gone off-route in a storm on our way to a mountain hut. This was the pinnacle of my first alpine season, the highwater mark, the closest I had yet got to an alpine climb. I didn't want the indignity of dying on the walk in. I looked down at Aaron, who was climbing up below me, slowly stepping from frozen pebble to frozen flint, moving in between the blasts of wind, unaware that if he fell we'd both end up back on the glacier below.

'Tight,' he shouted, as I struggled to pull the rope up with one hand, saliva dribbling onto the rope and freezing as I locked my teeth around it after each yard was pulled in.

'TIGHT,' he shouted again, his usual calm exterior cracking under the strain of the terrain.

'Argh,' I mumbled back, my mouth full of rope, trying to give the impression that everything was fine.

'Watch me on this bit!'

'Argh, argh,' I mumbled back.

This was not how I'd imagined alpine climbing would be.

I suppose it all started with a book.

It was a quiet Wednesday morning in Hitch and Hike, the tiny climbing shop hidden in the corner of a Derbyshire garden centre where I worked. This was the second real job I'd ever had. It was simple, just selling climbing, walking and caving gear. The only qualifications needed were enthusiasm, the willingness to work for just a hundred pounds a week, plus a strong pair of legs as the shop was a twelve-mile bike ride from home, with one of Sheffield's biggest hills blocking the way. I have never once in my life hated the thought of going to work. I've always had the luxury of poorly-paid jobs that I actually quite liked doing, unlike my friends who had highly-paid jobs which they hated. These friends would often tell me they were jealous of me, doing a simple job, cycling through the Peak District to work every day, while they sat on tubes and trains and at their desks. In fact, the only part I didn't look forward to was that commute, especially towards the end of the week, when my legs had clocked up triple figures. Nevertheless, I did relish the surprise on customers' faces when they found out where I cycled from every day. What I liked most about the journey to work, my thighs straining up the hills, rain spraying up into my grubby face, was the space it gave me to think. Maybe it was an escape or distraction from the boredom of seeing the same road pass below my wheels, but this time alone was full of plans. All my life I had been a dreamer, the dreams changing as I grew from adventures on distant planets, to adventures on this one. These dreams would always grow out of all proportion as they were nurtured in my head, my imagination seemingly boundless. I would think about walking the Pennine Way, then I'd decide I would do it in winter, then dump the idea and switch to the high-level route across the Pyrenees in summer, then winter, then switch to a walk from northern Norway to Gibraltar. Each dream built on the next. The more I became obsessed with climbing, the more my mind filled with climbing dreams, although always of rock climbing. Dreams were all I needed to get through my dull rides to work, and the work itself.

On that morning there weren't many customers, just the gentle tap of rain on the roof. The crags were too wet for climbers, the caves too flooded for cavers, the tea shops too inviting for walkers, leaving me time to focus on some personal retail training, namely drinking tea and reading climbing magazines. People often complain about the low pay of staff in climbing shops – well, climbing-shop staff do – to which I have to point out that really they can't expect high pay as selling boots and rucksacks is hardly assembling cruise missiles.

With all the magazines read I switched over to the guidebooks. For months I had pored over the rock-climbing guides to the Peak District, each one covering only a small area. They were divided into gritstone guides and limestone guides, and every line climbed on every crag, no matter how small or insignificant, was marked. I would thumb through the pages, looking at the climbs I'd done, re-reading the ones I wanted to do, imagining what it would feel like to be up there, visualising the gear, the risks, sometimes the summit. I would obsess about these climbs, each becoming so much more than a line of holds, each route climbed leading on to another.

I had become obsessed with climbing since moving to Sheffield, climbing on my days off, stopping off to do some on my way home on my bike, often even on my way to work. I had no climbing partner, and so soloed everything, slowly increasing the grades as my confidence grew. Gritstone climbs are generally short enough so you can cover a lot of ground, climbing up one route and down another, hands punching and twisting into cracks, palming on rough rounded holds, sticky rubber shoes smearing for all you're worth. At work I would devise grand soloing adventures: climbing all the three-star routes on a crag of a certain grade or linking up one climb on every crag in the guidebook. Climbing alone, I had a few hairy moments of course. As I committed to an exploded arête one morning on the way to work, my hands numb in the cold winter wind, my jacket flapping open as I moved up slowly, a big blast sent my jacket up over my head, blinding me. Breathing hard, all I could do was hang there until another blast blew my jacket back off again and so I could continue. I only fell off twice, once running back down a steep slab as I fell and clattering into a heap at the bottom, winded and vowing I'd never solo anything again if my breath returned, and the second time, slipping off a climb above a shallow pool as I tried to reverse a route that was too hard for me, the water, only a few feet deep, breaking enough of my fall to save any broken bones. Soloing is an addictive activity, the freedom, the self belief, being aware only of that very moment of existence. Someone once said that soloing on gritstone, devoid of heavy ropes and protection and with perfect rock, how could you ever fall? Unfortunately a few months later he did and bled to death, his pelvis broken as he crashed down onto the hard slab below.

For me, these small plastic-bound books, uncommercial but written with care, so British with their love of detail and desire to document a history of rock, were my school books. Reading about the climbs, about the people who had climbed them and the fragments of stories that surrounded them, then actually climbing those routes myself, created the physical and cerebral buzz that made climbing unique. Without these other factors, climbing was no more than pull-ups. I was never a great climber, but I had passion, and was embarrassingly keen.

As Mandy was living down in London for a year, studying to be a teacher, I travelled down on the train when I could, but with neither of us having any money it was hard finding the cash. After our first meeting I had followed her to France, where we lived together. We now found it strange to be living apart, and Mandy missed me, even though she was living in a large house with friends in New Cross. I missed her as well, but was also revelling in the freedom of doing whatever I wanted, with no emotional tie to her, no guilt for being obsessed. I had unlimited freedom to do whatever I wanted. Guilt-free climbing hedonism. My days belonged only to my employers or to climbing.

With all the local guidebooks finished, I picked up a small green-spined guide to the Mont Blanc Massif in France. Alpine climbing had always appealed to me, ever since I read Joe Tasker's book *Savage Arena*, borrowed from the library in Hull. His tales of scaling the Eiger in winter had sounded as if they were set on another planet, but the book had really only taken root in me when I discovered Tasker had come from Hull. I had always thought that mountaineers were a different breed, middle or upper class. The only climbers I'd come into contact with in the shop had been either professionals or students. Alpine climbing also seemed expensive. Rock climbing in the Peak District required only the bare minimum of equipment, with zero spent on travel. Going to the Alps, buying the kit, paying for camping and cable cars – it always seemed to be beyond me.

However, there had always been a part of me, when climbing in the wind and rain, or on a big Welsh crag, that pretended I was Tasker, climbing on a big alpine giant. Every two months the magazine *Mountain Review* would appear in the shop, full of stories of Patagonian big spires, Yosemite big walls and winter alpine climbs. The stories and the people who wrote them were larger than life. They seemed to be addicted to danger and risk, pitting themselves on some of the most terrifyingly committing adventures you could imagine. I read and reread a piece by a UK climber called Andy Perkins, about an alpine attempt on a granite spire in India called Cerro Kishtwar, and how he had spent seventeen days on the face, only to retreat through hunger and fatigue a hundred metres from the summit. I looked at the pictures of him and his partner Brendan Murphy, a team with no chance of rescue, living out there by their wits, and felt envious of such an experience. Andy worked for a climbing company called Troll and I had seen him on their stand that summer at the outdoor trade show in Harrogate. He was shorter than I'd expected, but looked tough, with a scraggy beard and hair that still seemed styled by the Patagonian tempests of his last expedition. I wanted to talk to him, but what could I possibly ask, me a shop assistant who dreamed of being like him. Once I'd plucked up courage and talked to him, my thoughts began to dwell more on mountains than on the local outcrops; my beloved buttresses of gritstone slowly became my training ground for something bigger in the future. Alpine climbing seemed to offer more scope for dreams, the greater ranges of the Andes and Himalayas beyond even more so, and gradually I began to wonder what it would take to get there and who I would go there with, as I had no climbing partner.

The green-spined book was full of small, far from inspiring black-and-white pictures of ice faces, snowy peaks, and towers of rock. Also it was written in some kind of code that made no sense. I thought about my microscopic climbs, so small they wouldn't even make it in as alpine footnotes, and wondered how you could climb routes so huge.

I closed the book and was slipping it back onto the shelf when I saw the back-cover shot for the first time, a picture of a vast wall of ice with a castle of rock standing at its top. Maybe it was because it was the only colour shot in the book that it grabbed me, maybe because it looked like a mountain dreamed up by a sci-fi artist, but for whatever reason the image gripped me like no other. I flicked to the front of the book and found its name: North Face of Les Droites, 1,000 metres, Grade ED (extremely difficult). I imagined what it would take to climb such a face, how you would feel standing on the summit, the exposure, the wildness of space all around you. It must be like standing on the moon, as removed from this world as an astronaut. I flicked through some other books in the shop, and found some more pictures of the face. In Doug Scott's *Himalayan Mountaineering* picture book he had a series of shots from a winter ascent of the North East Spur of the Droites, a vast leaning granite pillar on the edge of the North Face. There was an image of his partner, picking his way across a steep ice field with axe and crampons, a tiny rucksack on his back holding everything he needed to survive. I tried to imagine living on such a face for three or four days, the cold, the vertical world all around you. I tried to imagine something so large; the largest structure in my head was the Humber Bridge, its supporting pillars scraping the sky at 450 feet. I calculated the difference in heights, and my head spun at the thought of the face being eight times higher than that.

Now on my way to work my dreams were of alpine climbs, namely the Droites. My problem was I had almost no real experience for either that face, or anything else. I began immersing myself in as much information as I could get on the techniques and gear necessary, filling the gaps in my knowledge.

Then, in the autumn, I opened a copy of *High* magazine, one of the main climbing magazines, and saw two articles on winter Alpine climbing by Dick Turnbull. Dick was the owner of the other climbing shop up the road, called Outside, and he had a reputation as big as his shop. Hitch and Hike was a hill-walking and caving shop and, like most other small shops, seemed far from glamorous to me. Outside on the other hand was like a temple to cool gear and people, its rafters hanging with portaledges and exotic rucksacks and sleeping bags. When you went in Dick's shop you always had the impression that everyone in there was 'someone', and the staff usually comprised top climbers trying to earn enough cash to keep climbing. Dick was larger than life, rather bombastic, but a true climbing fanatic. He had climbed the North Faces of the Eiger, Matterhorn and Grande Jorasses in winter, a very big tick back then when these faces were considered hard, long and dangerous once you entered the winter season. I had to cycle past Dick's shop on my way to work every day, his staff often beeping me as they passed in their cars, and I had wanted to sneak in and pick his brains for my own climbing plans. Now fate had intervened and Dick had answered all my questions in his article.

My main problem would be the lack of a climbing partner, the lack of any skills, and the lack of any money – but, as I found out early on, if you have the will, ways will always be found.

Aaron came up in jerky movements, palming down on a large cobble that stuck from the slope, his hand joined quickly by a foot, then another foot, then his other hand, leaving him perched like a gargoyle, unsure where to go next, uncertain even if the cobble would hold him.

'Andy, this is crazy,' he shouted up, a small spindrift avalanche filling his mouth before he could make a list of why this was so stupid. I looked at the glacier below and tried to work out what would happen if Aaron fell and pulled me off. The distance was a couple of hundred feet of steep rocky slope. We'd probably survive the fall, but not without breaking many bones and getting badly lacerated by rocks on our way. The snow would help to cushion our fall, that was as long as we avoided the crevasses. Yes, if we fell in one of those it wouldn't be good.

Aaron stretched up and hooked a flint with the pick of his axe just as the cobble broke loose and sent his feet pedalling. 'Take in the rope!' he shouted, 'take me tight!' He screamed as the flint shifted.

'I can't,' I shouted back. 'I don't really have a belay.'

I had met Aaron at a party a few days after deciding I wanted to become an alpinist. He was the boyfriend of a friend and she introduced me as Andy the climber, telling me that Aaron also climbed and that he'd been to the Alps. Great, I thought, someone with experience.

Aaron was doing a Ph.D. in something to do with physics, and looked very hippy with his long hair and glasses. He was also very short on words; in fact I spent most of the party talking to him rather than with him. I found that you could get to the Alps for just one hundred pounds on the bus, and although that was a week's wages, we could camp for free and live very cheaply for two weeks. It was autumn and the summer alpine season was still months away, but I was so impatient to go that I suggested we went there in the winter. Dick Turnbull had said winter climbing was the future – no crowds, perfect weather, the mountains all to yourselves. Being a salesman, I must have been convincing as Aaron said it sounded good, and we agreed to go out in early January.

The only thing I forgot to tell him was I'd never been ice climbing, and didn't even know where the Alps were on a map.

'What did you say?' shouted Aaron, his quiet demeanor suddenly shattered by the news of no belay.

'I don't really have a belay . . . I didn't like to say.'

'Why the fuck didn't you tell me when I was down there at a good belay?!'

'I didn't think I could climb back down again . . . sorry.'

Aaron peered around. It was ridiculous, the two of us strung out on a slope of frozen mud – a rubbish heap from the glacier above. This was far from the North Face of Les Droites, our predicament way short of *Touching the Void*.

I had only been out of the UK twice, so the journey to Chamonix was exciting, from the bustle of Victoria bus station, replete with Glaswegian dossers, on to Dover and the ferry, which I boarded with my new one-year passport clutched in my hand.

This was a big adventure, something to my mind that other people did. For years I had talked to customers leaving for trips to the Alps, and never considered that I would or could go myself. I suppose I finally realised that if you wanted to do the things that you considered only other people did, all you had to do was do them.

It also marked the start of a big change. I had left my job, and would be moving to London when I got back from the Alps to live with Mandy, who was still doing her teacher training course in New Cross. All of a sudden life seemed to be full of expectation, the excitement of a new future of alpine dreams celebrated not with a drink, but with a giant Toblerone, which seemed kind of appropriate with the triangle of the Matterhorn emblazoned on its gold wrapper.

Aaron tried to reduce the chance of falling by taking off his rucksack, and hanging it from a nose-sized pebble so he could climb up unencumbered. He balanced and hopped his way up, several holds ripping out as he moved, until finally he joined me at my stance.

'It's not really worth clipping you in to the belay,' I said, nodding at the flint, which seemed to have shrunk now both of us were looking at it. Aaron grabbed my rucksack and moved up a little higher to a large cobble the size of a football, and half sat on it, proclaiming it far more secure than the flint.

'OK Andy – can you climb back down and get my rucksack?'

I tugged the flake to see if I could use it as an anchor. It popped out like a rotten tooth and spun down the slope into the mouth of a crevasse.

The long dark journey through France didn't end with a picture-postcard Chamonix of gleaming snowy peaks, but a claggy, dull town full of restless skiers. We climbed off the bus and picked up our enormous rucksacks, full with all our begged and borrowed climbing gear, clothes, camping equipment, and also food. We walked through the dirty and slushy streets, the skies above us thick with cloud. The occasional red rescue heli-copter clapping overhead was the only sign that there were big serious mountains above. From town we walked out to the camp site, only to find it was buried under fifty feet of bull-dozed snow. The owner appeared and showed us the wash-room, complete with washing machines and dryers, and told us we could camp there for the same price. It didn't seem like a good deal so we moved on, past rows of millionaires' mansions, until we found a path that sneaked up behind a big house. A hundred yards from the road we made our home, pitching our tent and getting everything ready for the big climbs ahead.

Back in town we visited the guides' building, where Aaron told me you could get information on the weather and condi-tions, routes that had been done, and maps of the range. It was a welcome escape from the damp cold outside, a place of old stone and polished wood. Everything was foreign to me though, the weather forecast, the maps, the climbs. The only thing I was interested in was the North Face of Les Droites. I walked up to the stern-looking woman in the office and asked her if she could tell me where it was on the map on the wall. She walked over and traced a line along a large glacier.

'Yes, we might try it while we're here,' I said, nodding my head towards Aaron.

She lowered her gaze and looked hard at me, standing in my scruffy clothes, my hair a mess from sleeping on the bus, glasses scraped and scuffed. 'It is a very hard and dangerous climb. Have you climbed many other big faces like this?' she asked.

'Not really,' I said with an embarrassed shrug, at which she smiled and went back to her desk. Everything had been said that could be said.

Our research completed, we walked outside to see the sun finally breaking through. I looked up, and again tried to imagine if the clouds I could see towering above me were really mountains, impossibly bold and looming. Then I realised that these visions were not clouds, that the spirals of darkness were minarets of rock, which indeed towered high over the valley.

That first time I saw the Mont Blanc Massif, its scale and grandeur were far too profound to take in. I stood with my mouth open and realised just how much bigger this was than anything I'd imagined, so big it filled my head and blocked out everything else in my mind. I was terrified.

The following morning we woke early, at four, and set off on the snow-choked trail that led up the other side of the valley from the Massif itself, to a range of smaller and far less intimidating peaks called the Aiguilles Rouges. We thought that they would be a better warm-up for us. We were far too overwhelmed to try anything in the proper mountains yet.

The snow was deep, and we sank down to our waists as we tried to make a trail up through the forest, moving with excruciating slowness in the dark, the leader sweating under the toil of breaking trail, the second shivering in the slowness of his wake. The higher we went, the deeper the snow became, until eventually we crept along on all fours, trying to stay on the surface.

By 10 a.m. we had made maybe a thousand feet of progress, when all of a sudden, before we could consult our map, we broke through a gap in the trees and found an unexpected white road of compact snow and a bunch of early morning skiers racing past us. It was a piste. Bugger.

Up the piste we trudged, quadrupling our height gain, until with some dismay we reached a large cable-car station and cafe, complete with hundreds of skiers who no doubt wondered where these two tramps where heading without skis. We saw a tiny ski lift was taking people towards the rock faces above, and so we sacrificed some of our funds in order to make a swifter ascent to the actual climbing.

The man in charge of the chairlift looked at us with a mixture of confusion, concern and dismay, as we moved up with the queue of skiers and jumped onto the swaying seat. The journey was made slightly worrying by the fact we forgot to take off our rucksacks or find the pull-down safety bar. We rode up the mountain clutching each other, with only a few inches of bum-cheek holding us on the slippery plastic.

Getting to the rock from the top of the chairlift was harder than I'd expected, with the deep powder coming up to our armpits in places, but we pushed on. This was what I'd dreamt about for the last few months, winter climbing in the Alps, and, although it hadn't quite lived up to my expectations, it was certainly different from short climbs in the Peak District.

As we ploughed our trench the whole Massif opened up behind, the mighty Dru, the Grandes Jorasses, Mont Blanc. Then I saw the Droites roaring up from the huge river of ice of the Argentière glacier. It stood in profile, the north-east spur like a lowered drawbridge from the castle of rock that formed the upper part of the face. The ice below swept down for thousands of feet, looking steep and diamond hard. I shuddered at the thought of even standing directly under such a face, let alone setting foot on it. What an idiot. What a dreamer. I turned and tried to focus on the easy snow gully ahead.

We reached the gully after a ridiculous struggle and attempted to climb upwards, the snow unresponsive to our will to climb. We were simply digging ourselves further into the slope rather than up it. It was no good. I'd read lots of books about alpine climbing where it said that snow conditions improved in the early hours, so I suggested we dig a snow hole and try again in the morning.

I'd never dug a snow hole before, but there was no shortage of building materials. We shovelled away with our helmets. I'd also read that snow-hole digging was wet work, with the snow melting on your clothes, which proved to be the case. It was dark by the time we finally finished making a tiny cave big enough for us to lie down in. I stood outside while Aaron sorted out his sleeping bag, and watched as ice built up on the shell of my clothing, reappearing each time I wiped it clear as the moisture trapped in my clothes got wicked through to the outer layer. I was fascinated to see this happening, and with the extreme nature of the cold, and with this wild place more alien than I'd ever imagined.

Finally Aaron was ready and I crept into the cave, a claustrophobic chamber only just big enough to sit in, and made all the smaller once both of us and all our gear were stuffed in. Not wanting to get my down sleeping bag wet, I took off my damp clothes, threw them to the end of the snow hole, and lay there naked waiting for my bag to warm up.

So great was our impatience to climb, our alarm clock went off at midnight, and we set about getting ready to climb again. It was now that I regretted not placing my clothes in my sleeping bag to dry. I picked them up, now as stiff as boards, and prised them apart so I could put them on.

Outside the temperature was positively arctic, forcing us to cover up every inch of skin as we followed our tracks back up to the gully. Aaron sank back up to his neck as soon as he tried to move further above our high point. There was no change.

The daytime temperature had probably been −10 Celsius, the night-time temperature −20. My grand plan was based on summer conditions where the daytime temperature would be above freezing, with the lower night-time temperature freezing the snow. We turned around and went back to our snow hole, feeling no ill will to the mountain or each other, still simply exhilarated at being in such a wild place.

I moved down slowly, my crampon points searching out tiny little features in the slope as foot holds, kicking hard into the mud itself when nothing could be found. The rucksack was getting closer as the wind picked up again, and I tried to tug it free of its perch. If we lost it we'd be trapped up here, far from the valley, unable to reach a hut. I'd never felt so exposed in my life. I was utterly terrified, but with the terror came that incredible feeling of being more alive and focused on the moment than ever before. Past and future, even the minute before and the minute to come, dulled until they blacked out, leaving me here in the very moment of action, climbing down a frozen heap of mud and stones for a rucksack.

Balanced on one crampon, I grabbed the rucksack, carefully slipped its straps onto one shoulder and then the other, then started back up the slope. With the weight of the rucksack, climbing back up was twice as hard as climbing down, and four times as hard as climbing up the first time. Finally I reached

Aaron and told him that this was the hardest thing I'd ever climbed, which, although true, wasn't saying much when you considered my winter-climbing CV.

Going on seemed to be a recipe for disaster, but with no real belays so was abseiling back down. However, going down was all we could hope to do, and so we set about hooking the rope over Aaron's football-size boulder.

He set up the ropes while I balanced without any protection, then watched as he slipped both ropes through his belay device and prepared to abseil down. I swapped my gaze between his eyes and the boulder, as he started to weight the rope. 'At least if the anchor pulls and he falls I won't be pulled off,' I thought selfishly. 'Go on Aaron,' I said. 'It looks good,' I lied, thinking that if it held Aaron it should also hold me.

Down he went, totally dependent on the rope, yet trying not to weight it, slithering down until finally he reached the snow at the bottom of the face, where he stopped and waited.

I shifted over, clipped into the rope and set off down after him.

I reached Aaron after a scary ride down the slope, and with relief pulled down on one of the ropes, but brought them both down in the process. It would soon be night, and without shelter we wouldn't survive long. Zig-zagging through the crevasses we headed for a large boulder, hoping we could hide under it, only to find the house-sized block seemed to form a wind trap, curving the snow around it into crazy waves. The only option was to use our new-found snow-holing skills and dig some shelter.

Kneeling down we took turns, shovelling like crazed animals, desperate to get out of the wind and the storm. After an hour we'd dug a coffin-shaped cave, just big enough as long as we left almost everything outside. I was putting the finishing touches to our temporary home, scraping any irregular lumps in the roof so water wouldn't build up on them and drip onto us, when, as I was leaning against one wall, my hand shot through and I fell onto my shoulder. I rolled away and realised we'd dug through into the side of a crevasse. It was so late that I just filled in the gap and climbed back out into the storm. I said to Aaron that he could sleep on that side, neglecting to tell him why. He was lighter anyway.

Inside, we got the stove going and tried to warm up, both of us seriously chilled by the storm. As the temperature rose in the hole all the snow and ice that clung to us began to melt, until puddles had formed on our sleeping mats. The air became a thick moisture-filled fug. After half an hour the stove went out, and refused to light. Then the lighter stopped working. I felt dizzy, and looked at Aaron lying beside me, already asleep. I flicked the lighter again and wondered why it wouldn't work. My head began to throb. I looked at the doorway, it was full of snow. I punched a hole in it with my ice axe and, as the spindrift flew in on the draught, I flicked the lighter and it sprang back to life.

That night I slept badly, imagining we would either suffocate, fall into the crevasse below us, or be buried alive. I thought my nightmares were coming true when we woke and tried to get back out again. I had to dig for several more feet than expected until thankfully I thumped through into fresh air and squeezed out on my stomach.

The storm had cleared. It was cold. It was colder than cold. My clothing went stiff immediately, and all the gear we had left outside was frozen together in a big lump. Aaron's Gore-Tex jacket stood stiffly to attention. The mountains all around us were magnificent, perfect, immaculate. Terrifying. We had no right to be here. They knew that. We knew that. These giants didn't suffer fools. It was time to go. We went.

We staggered up the trail back to the ticket office and cafe at Montenvers later that afternoon, looking as if we'd just returned from some mighty north-face success, not a frozen-mud-pile failure. It didn't matter to us what we had done and what we hadn't. We had been somewhere amazing and, more importantly, we had found our way back to tell the tale.

Leaving our rucksacks outside, we shuffled into the cafe, the tables empty because all the people were crowded outside to photograph the mountains. We would be going home in a few days, and we thought we deserved to splash out on an expensive cup of coffee. After all, we had made it into the mountains.

Leaving Aaron at a table, I walked up to the counter where a large bearded Chamoniard stood, his blue jumper with white stripe signalling him as a climber.

'*Deux cafés au lait s'il vous plaît,*' I said, proud of my only words of French.

Silently the man made the coffees, then slid them towards me.

I pulled out a plastic bag with our francs in, ready to pay.

The man looked at me and shook his head, pushing the coffee forwards.

'There is no charge for Alpinists.'

Solo

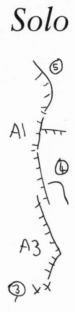

Pitches 3, 4 and 5 New Dawn

Climbing a wall takes commitment, but once you are committed this becomes less important, as the steepness of a big wall, together with the difficulties of being alone, generally mean retreat isn't an option. I knew that once I started up the Reticent from Lay Lady Ledge there would be no turning back. It would be like jumping from a great height into a river. It takes balls to jump, but once you've stepped off, all you can do is see it through. On a route like the Reticent the only way to escape was to climb the route, a terrifying prospect.

This was my first thought, as I woke in Camp 4, and knew that I couldn't put it off any longer. Today I would have to cast off and begin the route. It had been good having this time on the horizontal, sleeping without wearing a harness, treating myself to pizza, Coke and ice-cream, having people to talk to, shade, all the things I would miss.

(*Above left*) Who would have thought
I'd become a climber?

(*Above*) Two decades later and little
has changed, well, apart from the rope.
The author on Lost in America, A5.

(*Above*) Aaron learning it's best not
to play with strangers – about to abseil
off a thumb-sized flake of rock

(*Right*) The Boss – as in, he *was*
my boss, the inspiring and loud
Dick Turnbull on the approach
to the Dru Couloir

Aaron trying to smear in crampons on day two of our Frendo epic

Big and bad, the North Face of Les Droites and the North-East Spur

'Men working overhead' – rescue on the Dru Couloir

El Cap – the second wonder of the world,
the first being the Humber Bridge

(*Inset*) Paul Tat sky-hooking on A4 terrain
and loving it. Pacific Ocean Wall.

A storm hits us on
the Shield headwall.
The only way out was up.

he author reaching the top of El Cap for the
st time, a thousand metre drop at his heels

Andy Perkins, a bit of a hero

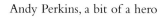

Just about hanging on, but never been happier. My shadow (right) on Lost in America

Jim Hall, Paul Ramsden and Nick Lewis, on our way to Fitzroy. All strangers –
I couldn't have asked for better partners for my first expedition

'Like sheep in a haunted abattoir.' Nick's eyes say it all. Two a.m. on Fitzroy

(*Overleaf*) Thin fragile ice, no protection and nowhere to run. Super Couloir

Time away from the wall had been good for my morale, making me believe it was possible. The fear and the difficulty of those easy pitches receded and were easily rationalised as stage fright. Of course it felt hard, I hadn't been climbing for a long time, but I would get back into psychological and physical shape quickly. I'd have to.

The one thing that had turned my mood was that I had thought of a strategy for hauling, which I knew would make or break the next few days. I had had a choice: either to dump water and hope I could make it to the top sooner, or create a new pulley system that would increase my pulling power. The first option was high risk, as running out of water could be fatal. Dehydration had contributed to several deaths on El Cap. The second would be slow. Then I thought up another option. I had a spare rope that I planned to carry in case my haul or lead line became damaged, and I could use this to split the load, hauling twice. I'd used this system in the past when climbing in a three-person team, and knew it would work. Using my red and yellow haul ropes, I knew I could do it.

I walked back up to the base of the route, to my rope, where I had tied jumars and harness to the end of it so that the wind didn't carry it off onto a distant flake, and started jumaring up, my only load being my sleeping bag. At the haul bags I dug out my spare rope and rearranged everything, then carried on up to the second belay and hauled the two loads. The difference was remarkable. Both bags jerked up the wall at twice the speed, and soon I was ready to climb the next pitch, knowing that this was it. No going down.

The pitch went slowly, but smoothly, and so did the next, my body and mind finding a little more rhythm, the hauling in between hard but do-able.

It was late in the day by the time I reached the final pitch below the Lay Lady Ledge, hauled up my bags and readied myself to lead. I was feeling pretty done in, hands cramping from dehydration, my harness leg loops digging in, sunburn on my neck throbbing away. The next pitch was a wide overhanging slot which proved strenuous and claustrophobic, the back choked with several kilos of bat shit which drifted down into my eyes

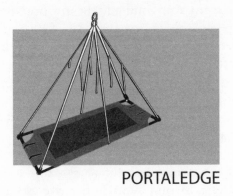

PORTALEDGE

and mouth and stuck to my skin. Sweat stung my eyes as I fought and kicked and battled my way up, half aid climbing, half free climbing, pushing my largest cams ahead of me as I went. My mood began to sour. The vast amount of energy required just to move up an inch sapped the last of my strength.

This is hopeless.

Just keep going, you always feel like this at the start of a climb.

I pressed on.

As is often the case, darkness came while I was far from the next belay and my headtorch was still below in my haul bag, leaving me to finger my way up the cast of the shit-choked crack. As I squirmed and whimpered I could hear the voices of the Russians, high up, drifting down the crack. The image of their smiling, welcome faces pushed me on rather than allowing me to back off. It would be good to spend the night with them, and take away some of the frustration that had got hold of me.

The last few moves saw me reaching blindly over a small roof, feeling for a set of bolts and, I hoped, the edge of the ledge, but when I followed my fingers round, instead of a ledge full of smiling Russians, I found yet another soaring crack.

I'd made a mistake and had another pitch left to go.

I wouldn't be able to make it to the ledge.

Tying off my ropes, all I could do was abseil back to my bags and sleep there.

Once I had found my headtorch, and after hanging a while

feeling sorry for myself, I pulled out my portaledge. With no ledges to sleep on, this contraption of nylon fabric and alloy tubing provided the only way to get a rest. Unfolded and fitted together to form a narrow bunk just big enough to lie on, it could be attached to the wall via straps leading up to the bolts.

After some aggressive tube bashing, taking my frustration out on my portaledge, I had it up, and fell onto it despairingly, a millimetre of nylon suspending me above the black drop below.

To say I felt low was an understatement; I'd made mistakes and I felt useless, incompetent and far from ready for this route. I was also crushingly lonely. With companions, when things go wrong, laughing about your failings often takes the edge off your incompetence. In fact, for British climbers, incompetence is all part of the game. But when you're alone, laughter is harder to come by, and it only makes you feel closer to insanity.

I lay there and felt the pulse of the bats as they swooped down out of the crack, clicking. The chill of the Sierra night enveloped me now I'd stopped, so I reached into my haul bag and pulled out my fleece to put on top of my black T-shirt. Next I pulled out a tin of stew, opened the lid and sat watching the headlights of cars leaving the valley, going home, and the constellation of big-wall headtorches beaming down the wall round about me. I found Ella's toy in my pocket and held it in my hand.

I wanted to go down.

I wanted to go home.

Then I smelt something, something amazing, mouthwatering, the smell of meat being cooked. It was the Russians' barbecue, the aromas wafting down the crack from the ledge above.

My cold stew suddenly didn't seem very appetising.

Then I heard them begin to sing to the twang of a balalaika. I wondered if taking musical instruments was part of the 'Russian way'. I switched off my headtorch, lay in my portaledge and listened to them sing. I thought about them above me, having fun, strong, well fed, confident, a team, sharing the load of such a hard climb. I thought about me, alone, out of my depth, the hardest climb of my life stretching on for weeks ahead.

How will you ever do it?

Snow gets in your eyes

Dick, my new boss, entered the boot room and began pacing backwards and forwards. Then he came and stood over me. He had something on his mind. I knelt at the feet of an old lady, carefully fitting a pair of lightweight leather walking boots, doing my salesman patter, double-checking myself, in case Dick was just making sure I was following the party line.

I'd come to work for Dick Turnbull in Outside, a stone's throw from my old job, after moving back north with Mandy who had now finished her teacher training. It was odd to be working for the author of the article that had propelled me to the Alps in the winter. No doubt having that experience on my CV had gotten me the job.

After the woman had paid for the boots and left, Dick came over and told me what was on his mind. 'I need a partner for this winter. My regular partner can't go to the Alps, so I was wondering if you wanted to come instead.'

I could hardly believe it: the man who less than a year ago had inspired me to go on the greatest adventure of my life, was asking me if I wanted to go back with him.

'I want to try a route on the North Face of the Dru – would you be interested?'

My excitement suddenly went cold, as I imagined the reality of what this would mean. I would be lashed to this God of winter alpine climbing who had scaled the North Face of the Eiger and the Matterhorn in winter, with me having failed to climb even a lump of frozen dirt. And a route like the Dru North Face in winter – that would be seriously hard, long and dangerous. Dick obviously imagined that I must have a vast amount of experience, with my one winter trip being the culmination of several years of hard climbs in summer. Only I didn't. I was still a novice. But I was incredibly keen. Maybe that was enough.

'Well?' he said.

'Yes, that would be great,' I replied, too scared to say anything else.

Dick lay beside me in the reclined driver's seat, snoring away under a giant duvet jacket while I sat shivering in a thin fleece. I was frozen, the cold seeping into the car from the icy French car park beyond, but sleep didn't escape me because of the chill. What bothered me were the images of being with Dick on some winter north face in a few days' time.

I had spent the last few months gradually getting more and more worried about the trip. The greater the excitement on Dick's part, the deeper my concern. He would come up and tell me about some horrendous icy crack high on the face, too wide for hands and feet, and too narrow to slide your body into, only to be climbed by desperate lay-backing, hundreds of metres from the ground. As he described what he'd heard about the pitch, he'd act out the moves, the rest of the staff standing around looking from him to me. 'Yes, it'll be desperate,' he'd say, 'but it'll be OK, because you can lead it.'

I beefed up my training for the trip, walking the twelve miles to work several times a week carrying a forty-kilo rucksack. I tried to get out climbing as much as possible, going to the climbing wall when the weather was bad, traversing backwards and forwards for hours, trying to strengthen my fingers, wondering if they would survive the Dru intact. Wondering if *I'd* survive the Dru.

Friends who knew how little I knew shook their heads when I told them what was planned. 'You'll fucking die, Andy,' they would say, and I knew they were right. This was no game. People did die. Or worse. Yet somehow I found the strength to believe I could do it. The route was first climbed in summer in 1935, so how hard could it be? This was only let down by the fact the Eiger North Face was climbed in 1938 and was still, by all accounts, desperate.

Biking to work I would ponder every eventuality, every possibility. I would imagine the pitches, the bivies, the descents, building up a model of the climb that I believed matched the scale of the real thing. This went on for months. Every mile I cycled, or ran, or walked under the yoke of my murderously heavy rucksack, I worked to reduce the climb by another inch.

The problem was now, lying in the dark and cold, I felt the mountain topple under the reality of finally being en route. One part of me told me it wasn't too late, that I could tell Dick the truth, but another part of me didn't care about the risk, the danger and the fear; this was a once-in-a-lifetime opportunity. I had to take it.

And just imagine if we actually got up the climb.

Dick woke as the dawn broke, pulling off his duvet jacket to light up a cigar and turn on the engine to get the heater on.

'Sleep OK?' he asked gruffly.

'Not really . . . I was a bit too cold,' I replied.

'Fucking hell, you're not one of those people who complain about the cold all the time are you?' he shouted angrily.

'No,' I said meekly.

I wasn't.

The snow was up to our knees. Amazing rock faces hung above me, walls of ice, granite buttresses, high jagged summits, but I kept my head down, too terrified to look up at the Dru.

A pillar as high as the Eiffel Tower loomed over me, black and sinister. It was very cold, and only the pumping of my legs as I made slow headway through the snow kept me warm.

Dick followed me, both of us tied together in case of crevasses. Every now and again he would shout about how amazing it looked, how much bigger it was than he'd imagined, how we'd probably take at least a week to get up it, and that he hoped we had enough gas. At this last comment I stopped and asked if we did, praying we might put off execution for a few days by going back for more. 'I think we've got enough,' he said, stamping his ski poles into the snow and carrying on.

A few hours before dark we reached the bergschrund below the route (a crevasse that forms between the mountain and the moving glacier), and decided to bivy there rather than risk being caught out on the steeper ground above.

Chopping out a long flat spot below the bergschrund, we

lay toe to toe in our giant sleeping bags, Dick melting water for tea, while I prepared for the first couple of pitches above. All my confidence had left me, and now it was only blind fear of embarrassment that kept me going. Dick chattered away as he piled snow into the pan, seemingly oblivious to the seriousness of what lay in store for us tomorrow. It occurred to me that he was actually looking forward to it. He was mad. I was mad. I felt as if I was sitting in a hospital ward waiting to go under the knife, my stomach so knotted I doubted I'd ever get it untied again.

Dick vomited up the first mouthful of food and passed me the rest, saying he couldn't eat anything due to the altitude. He pulled from his rucksack a packet of ginger biscuits instead. I sat in the dark and shovelled down the food, a rehydrated mush in a thick plastic bag. I shone my headtorch inside every now and again to see if there were any choice bits left. There weren't. I could tell why Dick had puked it up.

The warmth of our sleeping bags, the light from our torches, were now making me feel immune to my surroundings, perhaps because they were hidden from view. I finished the last of the food and folded up the packet, slipping it into my rucksack. I lay back, only my eyes and nose protruding from the sleeping bag, and for the first time in days felt relaxed. The stress of the last few hours, days, weeks and months suddenly left me, as the magic of the place began to play across my mind.

I imagined that I was lying back amongst the tower blocks in Hull, the silence of the space between filling my mind. I felt a bolt of excitement race through my body when I thought about tomorrow. I had passed through a maze of doubt, countless turns that should have stopped me dead, but now I was here and I would live up to expectations.

A snake slithered up out of the bergschrund, its body wide, wet and cold, coiling on top of me, slipping into the cowl that covered my face, and settling down on me, its skin icy cold, plastic, sweaty, its tongue hissing in my ears. Hissssssssssss. Hisssssssss. Hisssssss.

'Andy,' it said.

'ANDY,' it repeated, this time louder. Strange, I thought. It sounds just like Dick . . .

'AAANNNDDDYYYY,' Dick shouted.

'What?' I mumbled, coming round to find a faceful of frozen sleeping-bag fabric smothering me, the snake hiss still ringing in my ears.

'It's fucking snowing!' he shouted.

I pulled open the zip in the cowl that covered the head of my sleeping bag, designed to keep snow out in just such circumstances. I had borrowed the sleeping bag from Dick for the trip. The twist of light from my headtorch illuminated a world of large feathery snowflakes drifting down, every few minutes joined by the rumble of a mini-avalanche as it poured down the walls all around.

'Yes, it is,' I said rather pointlessly.

I looked at Dick, just the top half of his body protruding from the snow, the look on his face telling me he was not amused.

'Might clear up later,' he said. 'The route is so steep, we don't have to worry about avalanches,' he went on, lying back down.

I lay back myself, suddenly filled with disappointment. I hoped the weather would pass. The weather forecast had been good. Alpine climbing seemed to be full of hope, fear and disappointment.

Sleep came back to me soon, only this time without dreams of snakes. The protection and warmth of my sleeping bag insulated me from the reality of where I was; that was until, some time later, I smelt something unfamiliar. Smoke. Was I dreaming again? No, I could smell smoke. My brain tried to work out what it was, but the only thing that we had that could start a fire was the stove.

'Shit!' I thought. 'The stove's set Dick's sleeping bag on fire.'

I sat up with a jerk, and for the second time ripped open the cowl of my sleeping bag, ready to dive on Dick and put out the flames. Only instead of finding a mass of flames and smoke, I saw the small red glow of a cigar sticking from a tiny gap in Dick's sleeping bag. I twisted on my headtorch.

'Dick?' I asked, his name combining every question I needed to ask.

'Yes,' he said, the cigar disappearing, replaced by one eye. 'I always smoke a cigar at night; it helps me sleep.'

I lay back down and tried once more to get to sleep.

This time I fell into a seriously deep, deep sleep, exhaustion weighing me down. Then yet again something tried to wake me up. A muffled voice tried to prise me out of my slumber. I rebelled against the words and tried to block them out, only for the noise to increase. Someone was shouting my name, but the words sounded as if they were coming from a loudhailer wrapped in a blanket.

'Andy,' the voice said. It sounded concerned. I thought I'd better get up. Only I suddenly found I couldn't. The weight of sleep pressing on me wasn't imagined, it was real. I was buried.

Shifting and fighting inside my sleeping bag, I eventually forced my head up out of the snow to find Dick shouting my name and the snow pouring down in torrents directly onto us.

'Bloody hell – I thought I'd lost you then,' he shouted over the hiss of the cascading torrents of snow. 'This is shit,' he carried on. 'We can't climb in this.'

Resigned, we crawled up out of the snow and sat on our rucksacks for the remainder of the night, snow blowing its way into our sleeping bags and melting, leaving us pathetic, cold and deflated.

As soon as we could go, we did. Dick stamped around in a bad mood, stuffing his gear away. I packed mine, worrying about the dangerous sugary snow on the descent, knowing we had no choice but to go down.

'Never mind,' I said cheerfully. 'We might get another chance before we have to go home.'

Luckily for both of us, that chance didn't come.

Robbins's peg

Pitch 6 New Dawn; Pitch 1 Reticent Wall

I pulled up onto Lay Lady Ledge the following morning, just in time to watch the Russians disappearing up the wall with a wave.

The ledge was large, triangular and sloping, set within a deep corner, around 200 metres up the wall. A small barbecue was stashed amongst some boulders at its back. The New Dawn route, which I had followed up to the ledge, and which was first climbed by Charlie Porter in 1972, now carried on upwards, while the Reticent headed off on the right-hand side.

Charlie Porter was a Yosemite legend who tackled many of the hardest walls in the 70s, often solo, redefining hard aid climbing. This ledge must have been welcome to him after the steep pitches below, although it came at a high price. Porter had set down his haul bag containing his food and sleeping bag but he had neglected to clip it in, no doubt because of the size of the ledge. Unfortunately, the ledge has a slight angle to it, and Porter turned to see the bag rolling away. Giving chase, he thankfully stopped short of the edge as the bag went over and crashed down the wall below. Most climbers losing their sleeping bags and food would have retreated, but not Porter, who carried on and altogether took seven days to complete another first ascent.

Porter had long been a hero of mine, both for his toughness and for the quality and vision of his routes, climbed at the limit of the gear used at the time and at the limit of what was imagined to be possible. He took this ability to suffer from Yosemite to the Arctic, climbing a big new route on Baffin Island, then on to a mind-bending solo ascent of the two-kilometre-high Cassin route on Denali, the highest mountain in North America and considered one of the hardest mountain routes in the world. Always reticent about his achievements, Porter gave up climbing at the top of his game, swapping his haul bags and ropes first for a kayak, making the first solo circumnavigation of Cape Horn, then a yacht. The last I heard, he was still active down at the tip of South America, a well-known skipper sailing out in the harsh South Atlantic and the fjord-lands of Patagonia and Tierra Del Fuego.

What would I do if I gave up climbing after this?

I hauled up my bags, and then, pulling out my hand-drawn topo, I tried to work out how to do the first pitch. The first pitch of the Reticent.

I'd been told that the Reticent was so hard that even the easiest pitches were harder than the hardest climbs I'd done. Looking up the blank sweep of granite I could understand why. It looked impossible. There simply didn't seem to be anything there at all, no cracks or edges to use to ascend, let alone places to protect myself. Worse still, the pitch stepped off the ledge, so within a move you were suddenly faced with having a huge drop, six pitches of vertical rock, beneath your feet.

Impossible.

I looked harder.

There was no way.

I sat down on the ledge, feeling despondent. I'd been an idiot. What had I been thinking? All I could do was go down.

Down.

My mood lifted. I suddenly felt relieved. The doubt was over. I could only go down.

At least you know now that it's too hard for you.

At least not many people know what you wanted to do.

I felt foolish, it should have been obvious that this would happen. I was so out of my league. I should have listened to my instinct lower down.

At least I could still retreat from this point.

I looked down at the valley, people setting up picnic blankets in the meadow, ready for some climber-watching.

I could be down in a few hours.

Maybe I could just go home.

A mouse scuttled across the ledge at my feet, and stopped for a second, perched on the lip of the ledge before darting up a crack and up the wall.

Even a mouse can scale a big wall.

I wondered how much bigger a big wall was to you if you were a mouse.

Maybe you can *do it?*

I thought about Royal Robbins and his ground-breaking first solo ascent of El Cap in 1968. He'd started the climb knowing that only a handful of teams had ever scaled El Cap, teams comprising the cream of North American climbing. Robbins had made many of these early ascents, but now he stood alone, with 3,000 feet of climbing above him – the route, the Muir Wall, hadn't even had a second ascent. It was a giant step into the unknown, both in terms of climbing, and in self-belief, but perhaps Robbins knew there was no one else in the world who had the experience or skills to pull it off. In terms of world climbing this would be equivalent to landing on the moon.

Several days later Robbins was not sure if this was an attempt too far. His confidence and belief were leaving him bit by bit, metre by metre, peg by peg. The work involved, leading, cleaning, hauling, combined with the difficult climbing – not to mention the loneliness and self-doubt caused by having no one to share the experience – had convinced him that it was beyond him.

'I dug into the rucksack of my soul and found it was just an empty husk.'

Robbins decided he would abseil off the following morning.

Yet when morning came he decided to place one more peg. Just one. In it went. Perfect. He clipped his aiders into it and stepped up. It didn't seem right to place just a single peg, and so he placed another, then another, never thinking any further than the next.

Ten days after leaving the ground Robbins reached the summit, his hardest climb over, a turning point in his life.

All soloists think about Robbins and his ascent of the Muir, his antiquated gear, no portaledge, only pegs, no chance of a rescue. What he wanted was more than just a first, or to break a record, or to be famous. He wanted something deeper and more meaningful than that. The closer he came to failure, the closer he came to finding what all soloists are looking for: to break themselves apart on the wheel of a climb, to know what they have chosen to do is beyond them, to discover they are empty and wanting, yet somehow to find the strength to push on regardless. To dare and try their best. To overcome every instinct and rational thought. To push on. To travel alone to the height of themselves. To believe such a thing is possible.

I thought about Robbins's peg.

I stood up and ran my fingers up the wall, looking for something, anything, a reason to carry on, an excuse to go down. The Russians had passed this way: there must be something.

With the tip of one finger I found an edge no bigger than half a fingernail. I had my first move.

I sat back down and looked up the wall.

Just do one move, that's all.

I racked up all my skyhooks, hanging them from my harness like the tools of a torturer, spiked curved hardened steel, clipping a small one to my aiders, its point no bigger than the tip of a Biro.

I went back to the hold, and placed the skyhook. I gently

tested it, half expecting it to spring out and bash me in the face. It flexed. It held. I slowly stepped up.

I clipped my harness into the hook, which was now at waist level, and sat there a few minutes, trying not to think about the drop below, even though a fall now would only be short.

I moved up the aider until the hook was above my knee and, balancing, felt for a second hook and my next move. My fingers touched an edge only the thickness of a matchstick.

I placed the second hook, smaller than the first, and, clipping in my other aider, slowly stepped up after again gently testing it. The ledge was only six feet below, but my heart was beating. It was high enough to bust an ankle, with the drop below the ledge adding to the feeling of exposure.

I tried not to think about the fact that I was actually climbing the Reticent Wall. Somewhere above were two bolts, but between us lay 200 feet of the most difficult climbing, and beyond them two thousand more feet. As in a game of chess I couldn't allow myself to focus on winning, or even on a few moves ahead, but only on the next move and no further.

I stepped up and felt for the next placement.

The knot

Chamonix, France. February 1996

For two years Aaron and I had been planning another winter trip to the Alps. On our days off we climbed together on the tiny gritstone crags around Sheffield, starting early and climbing and soloing as many routes in a day as we could. Generally this was midweek, so Mandy would drop us off before going to her teaching job, and then pick us up on her way home. That summer seemed to be full of long days and sore finger-tips. Aaron became my first real climbing partner, and we progressed through the grades together, willing each other on as we went from easy classics to harder, more scary routes, leap-frogging up the grades past one another. He was never a talker, and so we climbed with mainly me talking, scheming our return to the Alps that coming winter.

Aaron was coming to the end of his physics Ph.D. in Sheffield, and his thoughts were primarily about things that made no sense to me: particles of matter, equations and computer models. He was working towards a career as a professional, either academic or commercial, his big analytical brain in demand in an analytical world. I on the other hand remained a simple shop assistant at Outside, my thoughts only of mountains and hard routes, kara-biners and ice axes. Aaron was more cautious than me, always thinking things through methodically, aware of his limitations and areas where his skills were lacking. I on the other hand thought I had made strides to becoming a great alpinist, and had big plans for that winter. Even though these strides were purely in my head, my ambition was boundless, unconstrained by reality. I seemed to have perfected the art of visualisation, a technique much used

Frendo Spur

by sports people and athletes, who imagine themselves as winners and record breakers long before whistles or start-lines are crossed. I spent my days thinking of nothing but climbing, doing pull-ups on ice axes in the boot store, making plans, tinkering with gear, an alpine version of *Billy Liar*, a fantasist using his imagination in order to get through the boredom of work.

Mandy was bound up with her work, teaching children about their bodies, touring Sheffield in a mobile classroom. She was a great teacher, and loved children, and many would say at the end of their morning or afternoon in the mobile classroom that it had been their best-ever lesson at school. She threw herself into her work, and at times we seemed to have separate lives. She dreamed of hotel-holidays with me, and the normal things that couples do, while I dreamed of hard climbs and big walls in foreign countries. Often when we lay in bed, she would ask me what I was thinking about, to which the answer was generally something like 'crampons' or 'ropes'.

I felt the pressure that she wanted me to get another job, as I was forced to work most weekends, but I could think of nothing else I could do. The only qualification I had was my obsession with climbing, and the only place it was valued was at Outside. However, I knew that working in a climbing shop was not a long-term option, something Dick Turnbull had told me on my first day.

Increasingly, Mandy had also been dropping hints that she wanted to have a baby, but my mind was only full of ice faces, so I didn't really think too much about what she wanted, or what having a baby would mean. All I could think about was going back to the Alps in February, and making who I thought I could be, and what I could do, a reality.

For the first time in my life I sat at a computer. It was old, slow and second-hand, a cast-off from Mandy's mum and dad, but a computer nevertheless. Mandy said I might find it useful, as she'd been researching and discovered that people with dyslexia often found it easier to get their thoughts down via a keyboard rather than with pen and paper. I was excited at the possibility that it could help me write, because the older I got, the more I wanted to describe how I felt, my thoughts, my ideas, the things you can't say to another person, the secret things you can only write and then run away from before they are read.

People think that for dyslexic people a computer is needed simply for its spellchecker. Spelling mistakes don't ruin lives. For me it was the fact that the ideas I had to communicate seemed trapped and broken, they were non-linear, and would need digging out one by one and reassembled, something impossible to do with pen or typewriter. This computer was the tool required to fit the mosaic of my thoughts together again, even though I didn't even know what the pieces were. All I knew was that perhaps this computer could help me tap into something that needed to be released.

I switched it on, and listened to it hum into life, watching as it slowly woke up. I'd only ever sat behind computers, never in front, generally wondering what was being typed in by housing benefit or DHS officers, glad I didn't have to sit in a grey-green dimly lit office like them. But now I was prepared to do that.

I opened up Microsoft Word and looked at the screen, all grey on the tiny monitor, and placed my fingers on the grubby keyboard as you would if you could actually type. The screen wanted to be filled, like one of those pieces of wood I'd painted on at college. My mind was as full of images and ideas as it had been then, but it had been so long since I'd written anything more than a cheque. How could I translate these thoughts into words when words always failed me? But I knew that nothing else would do.

I wrote my name.

Where would I begin? Why would I even want to try? I wasn't a writer. I always said that when you think about taking a photograph, you should ask yourself if anyone would ever want to look at it. I asked about my story, the first I would write about a climb, 'Who would ever want to read this?'

But this wasn't just a climb. It was an event that I had thought about every day since, maybe even every hour. This climb had changed me. It had made things make sense. It was more than just a climb. I just had to write something. I looked for the letter W on the keyboard and began to type with one finger.

After a while, I ran the spellcheck, and the page came alive with red lines, each disappearing one by one as I went back over the text until it was all black-and-white again. I scrolled down and marvelled at the words, how perfect they seemed, forming up to be my thoughts. Alone with this computer, I had all the time in the world to craft my story, to get my thoughts in order. I could hide my inadequacies behind the words.

I printed it out and felt a thrill at seeing my name at the top, the words I'd written placed on the page, my thoughts and experiences now expressed as I had imagined them. The words looked so neat, so much more perfect than my dunce handwriting. I read it again and thought it was perfect. I couldn't wait for Mandy to read it.

Mandy groaned. 'It's terrible,' she said, having read only the first paragraph, wincing as she read on. 'It's sort of sub-sixth-form angst.'

I was crestfallen. What was I thinking?

'There are loads of spelling mistakes,' she went on, proving that although a computer can check for the right spelling, it can't check for the right word. 'It needs lots of work.'

I returned to the computer. It frustrated me that I could get it so wrong. I didn't have an ounce of talent. I was deluded. I had conned myself I had something to say. I switched off the computer, clicking 'No' when it asked if I wanted to save my untitled document, grumpy with my first rejection.

February finally came and we arrived in Chamonix on the bus, stepping down to high pressure and good conditions. As we walked through town, I pointed up at the Rouse-Carrington route on the Aiguille du Pélerin, a hard and scary ice smear, and suggested we warm up on that. Aaron took it as a joke, not realising I was serious.

We got to the chalet we were sharing with a group of climbers and skiers from Outside, and after dumping our gear started looking through the guidebook. My route choices were outlandish and ridiculous, while Aaron's were feasible and sensible, if a little pedestrian to me. I had two weeks to realise my potential. I didn't have time for warm-up climbs or easy classic snow plods.

'How about the Frendo Spur?' I suggested, knowing that on paper this might look like a suitable compromise to him.

The Frendo Spur was a jagged buttress of rock, a spine of shattered pillars and stepped walls that terminated at a steep ice arête as it neared the Midi *téléphérique* station at its summit. It was first climbed in 1944 by Edouard Frendo and René Rionda, with its first winter ascent coming in 1967, and had become a plum classic introduction to the longer and more committing summer routes. As a winter route there wasn't a lot of information about it, but on paper at least, the moderate climbing gave the impression it wouldn't be too hard. There was a cable car that went up from Chamonix to a small free hut close to the start of the route, making the approach simple, and once on the route it looked objectively safe if we ignored the hanging ice cliffs on each side. Once we'd summited we'd be able to ride the cable car back down to town. It would be a perfect warm-up.

In reality the route, even in summer, was way beyond our capabilities or experience, and was no easy tick. It seemed to generate a great many epic tales, perhaps due to its attraction as a stepping stone from easy to hard routes. One of the best was of a solo climber who had fallen close to the top, and been seen shooting down the ice arête and then down the gully on one side. The following day, the rescue helicopter could find no sign of his body at the base, but they found him alive as they flew up the fall line. He was hanging from his jacket hood which had snagged on a spike of rock.

In winter the difficulty would be massively increased, the easy rock climbing transformed to difficult mixed climbing, with snow and sub-zero temperatures requiring axes and crampons to be used the whole way. In summer the route usually took two days, with climbers racing up the rock spur and bivying below the ice arête, climbing it in the morning when it was well frozen. In winter the speed would be halved.

I put it to Aaron and after reading the description he simply nodded. He was really clever but on this occasion not quite as clever as I'd assumed.

'We could sort out our gear and head up there after tea, and get on the route in the morning?' I suggested, ignoring the facts that we were unacclimatised and still tired from our twenty-four hour bus journey, and that leaving after tea would mean missing the cable car and breaking trail until midnight to get to the hut, zig-zagging up the steep, snow-covered paths that led up the valley.

I sat at the computer again. All week, biking to work, I had thought about my story, and why it hadn't been any good. Maybe it was because I hadn't read enough books, but books had never been a major part of my life. Outside school, I'd only voluntarily read one book in my youth, and James Herbert's *The Rats* was not the ideal material for a young writer's mind. My childhood had mainly been full of comics, ideal material as I didn't start reading until much later than everyone else at school. Comics had been good in many ways, their visual story-telling perfect for my visual brain. I thought in pictures, so stories in pictures work well. I wondered if my lack of story-telling skill was that I tried to provide too much detail. Maybe the trick was to paint the story rather than write it, use the words lightly, to provide the colour as in an impressionist painting, and allow the watcher room to feel what it was like, perhaps to know why this was more than just a climb.

'It doesn't look very easy,' said Aaron, planting his axes at the bergschrund, the moat-like crevasse formed between the base of the Frendo and the moving glacier. 'It looks really difficult.'

It was dawn and we had arrived below the hardest climb of our lives.

'It looks great,' I said, panting as I moved up the steps Aaron had made on the approach slope, feeling utterly done even before we'd begun.

'It doesn't look like fun . . . like I said, it looks massive and hard.'

I joined him, rested on my axes, and looked up. I had never stood below such a huge wall of rock and ice. The climbs we had been doing all summer had been ten or twenty metres at the most, not such great training for a wall over a thousand metres high. Also, it now didn't seem to be objectively safe, with huge overhanging ice cliffs on either side of the top of the Spur, the ice blocks we'd passed on the way evidence they were active.

We'd had very little sleep. The walk up through the woods,

with the trail buried under deep snow, meant we hadn't made it to the hut until 2 a.m. Another party had been asleep when we arrived, and I woke them again a few hours later when I had to run outside and be sick, the combination of a thousand metres of altitude gain and a belly full of half-cooked potatoes scoffed down before we'd left. After only a couple of hours' sleep we'd woken again and started up towards the Spur.

I had spent a year thinking of nothing but climbing a route like this, of putting myself against something hard and proving that my faith and passion for climbing weren't misguided, but now I was here, the rock cold, the face silent, the air stinging, my mouth still tasting of sick, my bowels churning, thirsty, all I could think of was the valley. The climb dwarfed me.

Part of me still revelled at the scale of the climb, a part that grabbed at the opportunity it provided and told me I could climb it, but there was just so much unexpected fear. I had forgotten just how scary this all was.

I looked at Aaron. Our friendship was strong enough for me to say that I was scared, but that word could dissolve our climb before it had even begun. I knew he really didn't want to climb it either. But to say it, and fail now because of my fear, would betray the dream I'd had, this opportunity I had been given.

The weather was good. We were fit enough. We could climb it. We simply had to try. I had to give everything I had. And so we began to climb up the Frendo Spur.

I printed out the story again, and reread it, spotting countless mistakes I'd missed. I had been rewriting the story for months, yet I never seemed to get any closer to finishing it. I made my changes once more and printed it out again, the thick stack of paper I had started with now down to a few tatty sheets.

Mandy had continued to prove a hard critic so I gave a copy to my lodger Jon, another climber, who said it was good.

'Don't listen to him,' Mandy said, later that night in bed, 'he's a climber, he doesn't know anything about writing.' I watched as she read my story again, wondering if we were both wrong and she was right, and I knew she was as I looked at her grimaces and raised eyebrows, the objective teacher in her coming out. I'd given her books to read by the climbing greats, Joe Simpson, Jim Perrin, Greg Child, writers I aspired to be like. She'd sometimes stop after a chapter or even a single paragraph and say, 'Oh I can't read this; it's introspective rubbish.' Every time I gave her something of mine to read, she would give me a low mark. Sometimes I'd lose my temper and unfairly accuse her of being a terrible critic or teacher, giving nothing in the way of praise to nurture the tiny bit of talent I might have. 'Well you want to be a good writer, don't you?' she'd ask. She was right. I did. I wanted this story to be perfect, an impossible task I knew.

I had always thought of myself as a wimp, simply wanting an easy life, but through writing this story I discovered something inside me that I found surprising: not my ability to write, or the depths of despair when I was rejected – something I was used to – but my unending ability to try again, and again, and again. No amount of rejection or criticism, both external and internal, seemed to quell this spark within me. Was I just deluded? Was I simply blindly stupidly stubborn?

I wasn't sure, but the next day I started again.

We climbed slowly, the rock either buried under deep powder or steep and strenuous. We took turns belaying each other, growing cold through lack of movement, watching the cable cars moving up and down high above us, seeing the Day-Glo blur of tourists and skiers through their windows, wondering if anyone had spotted us down here at the toe of this climb. It was a surreal experience, struggling on this route while tourists passed overhead, probably not even aware we were there.

We hoped to make a summer-style ascent, and climb the first eight hundred metres in a day, so moved as fast as we could – but our plans had assumed summer conditions, clean rock, and no bivy gear. As the day drew on we realised our pace was pitiful and the plan unrealistic. We barely ate into the distance we needed to cover.

As we climbed I saw that Aaron was slowing down, as if his mind didn't want to leave the ground, probably aware that the higher he climbed the more committed he was. We had only one sixty-metre rope, having left the other in the valley in order to save weight. Two ropes would have meant we could make full-length abseils, using one rope to pull the other down at the end of each rope length we descended. With one, we would only be able to abseil thirty metres at a time, thus requiring more anchors and making slower progress.

It was Aaron's lead. He eyed the difficulties for longer than was necessary, so I offered to carry on leading before he had the chance to persuade me to retreat. We were silent with each other, only communicating when we needed slack on the rope to move up, or to say when it was safe to follow. The tension grew throughout the day. We both knew that we didn't really have a chance, that our one-day supply of food and gas wouldn't last the route, which at our pace would take three times as long as we'd planned. I knew we should go down, but part of me wouldn't let go. This could be our only chance.

'It's not bad,' Mandy said, handing it back, 'but it still needs a lot of work.'

I had poured my heart and soul onto the paper, written and rewritten it dozens of times, analysed every word and sentence to eradicate any fat and gristle. 'Not bad' was not enough for me. It had to be great.

'There are still quite a few spelling mistakes,' she added, as I pulled it from her fingers. I had no satisfaction. I felt I was simply grinding her down. I wanted to write something she would think was good. That was all that mattered. I wanted to show her that although I just worked in a shop, and had no trade, or skill, or degree, I had talent.

I kept writing, and the thing that drove me on was my need to prove her wrong. I believed she didn't think I had it in me to write something good enough for her, and people like her, people with degrees and good jobs. I was trying to prove something, never realising that she needed no proof from me.

'Aaron!' I shouted down into the dark, my body wedged awkwardly in a steep flared groove, feet scraping as they tried to stab into a thin vein of ice that trickled down the back. 'Watch me, I might come off here.'

I tried to relax and pressed my crampon points into the ribbon of ice. I couldn't tell if they were well placed, their security blocked from view by my body. I felt as if I could fall at any moment. My shoulders were wedged against smooth-sided walls – if any single part of me slipped, I was off. I breathed hard and tried to stay calm.

It was late, it was dark, it was incredibly cold, and Aaron was pissed off. The afternoon had been squandered as I'd wrestled up a fantastic icy crack, the evening lost break-dancing around in a mixed couloir, and now the cold Alpine night arrived abruptly, without the decency to let me put on my headtorch, as the real climbing began. Aaron hung below me on a large spiky flake as I began fighting my way up the groove, hoping we would find somewhere to sleep at the top.

The higher I climbed, feet stacked one above the other, the more noticeable the weight of the rope became. It hung, unhin-dered by protection, down to Aaron, who silently shivered as the temperature dropped off the end of our cheap thermometer, the halogen bulb of his torch tracing out my flight path above his spike belay. He remained silent.

I pressed on, promising myself I would climb just one more metre, each metre leading to another. I was hoping to find some gear so I could lower off, getting to the top now replaced by the need simply to get down in one piece, but after each metre there was none. Attempting to stay calm, focused and in balance, I tried to step carefully back down into my last crampon placement, but as I reweighted it, the ice buckled and fell away, sending my crampon screeching and sparking down the granite, until it miraculously caught a blob of stubborn ice. As I pressed my head into the groove, my tired, hungry body tried to puke up with fear, only managing a pathetic dry heave.

'How's it going?' shouted up Aaron, code for 'What the fuck are you doing?'

'Won't be long,' I croaked, lying.

I climbed across into a secondary groove, close to losing control and falling. I scraped away the snow to find a crack, placed a peg, and lowered back to the belay, defeated. I was exhausted, desperate for water after a day where there had been no time to drink. I could make no decisions, so Aaron took charge. All I wanted was a pan of cold water and my warm sleeping bag, but there seemed little chance of either.

Aaron scanned around with his headtorch until he spotted a blob of snow below, the size of a wheely-bin lid.

'OK, we'll abseil down to there and use this spike as our anchor,' he said, preparing the rope as I just hung there pathetically.

What seemed like aeons later I was squirming, pulling, pushing and grunting as I tried to get my sleeping bag out of the rucksack without dropping anything important or falling off my narrow perch. Aaron was in his bag, boots off and stove on, long before I'd even had time to find my headtorch. It would have been easy to imagine we were in the Himalayas or Antarctica, if it hadn't been for the lights of Chamonix twinkling up at us. My tired mind imagined the friendly laughing groups huddled around warm crêperies, wandering from bar to bar, then returning to beds warmed by blonde Norwegian goddesses, and wondered what I was doing here.

'Andy!' Aaron woke me up from my cold daydream, 'Are you OK? Get in your bag.' With great difficulty I removed my right boot's plastic outer shell, leaving just the foam inner boot on my foot, and clipped it into the rope. Then I proceeded to wrestle with the other. For some reason my mind wandered for a moment to the implications of dropping a boot so high on a winter route. I had heard of climbers doing this and shuddered at what such a fumble would mean on such a cold route.

The shell refused to budge, probably due to a thin layer of ice building up between inner and outer, and my hands were too cold to take my slippery gloves off, forcing me to push harder. All I wanted was to get the boot off and get into my sleeping bag.

The shell shot off my foot and disappeared into the dark below.

I was dumbstruck, uncomprehending. Aaron remained silent beside me, looking down into the dark. My first thought was about how we could carry on with just one boot. I'd not yet grasped the reality that this was it.

'Fuck!' I shouted.

'I suppose we'll be going down now,' said Aaron, as calm as could be.

'Fuck, fuck, fuck,' I repeated, hardly believing what I'd just done.

I put my head in my hands and tried to pretend I'd just imagined what had taken place. This couldn't really be happening, it had to be a nightmare. Different emotions shot through me. I couldn't accept we would have to give up all the ground we'd just made. It seemed so unfair, and yet there was no fighting it.

Aaron, seeing I was in distress, tried to comfort me. 'Never mind,' he said.

All I could think about was how would I get down without getting frostbite as I had only my inner boot, and how were we going to retreat with only one fifty-metre rope and a minimal rack? I sat there for a long time, shaking my head, vowing that once down I'd give up climbing for good. This was it. I'd sell all my gear, return home to Mandy and go somewhere sunny for the rest of the holiday instead. If this was winter alpinism I didn't want any of it. I'd wasted three years dreaming about it, but in reality it was just grim, and I was far too weak and useless for it.

Just at that moment a huge spotlight came on, shining up from the building beside the hut we had started from that morning, illuminating the whole of the North Face of the Midi for the tourists. Aaron shifted in his sleeping bag.

'Bloody great! How am I going to sleep with that shining in my eyes all night?' I said, wondering how things could possibly get any worse.

A moment later the answer came with a boom that shook the air all around us. A serac weighing hundreds or thousands of tons had carved off the glacier above our heads. There was a long roll like thunder that rose as the avalanche smashed its way down the side of the Frendo, blocks of ice the size of houses breaking apart and exploding into a whirring wave of debris. The noise grew into the roar of a train, freezing us with fear as it rumbled closer. Both of us shrank onto our already tiny ledge, sure we were going to be hit, as giant blocks of ice shot past and ice and snow filled the air.

All of a sudden, my lost boot, and being denied this route, didn't seem all that important.

I sat at the computer every night for an hour making changes. The story grew to five thousand words, then to none as I accidentally deleted it. At the time, I didn't realise you could simply undo the deletion. I cursed my bad luck and felt like smashing the computer to tiny pieces: six months of hard-fought work simply blinked out of existence. I screamed at the computer, rather than myself, and cursed not backing up. The last print-out had been months ago.

Later, however, when I'd calmed down, I found I could tell myself that this was an opportunity to make it right. The best pieces of my story remained in my head. As with any good story, being retold would be good for it.

And so I started again, the strong sections coming back to me, the weaker sections remaining lost. The story grew even larger. Every word, every paragraph became sacred. My work became a work of art. It was perfect.

No. It was shit. I cut it down to a thousand words; my long rambling detailed account, written in a code only a climber could translate, was transformed into a Haiku poem. I began to be my hardest critic and to see my mistakes. I had tried too hard to make people understand how difficult climbing was. I had too many similes, everything was like something else, when simply being what it was was good enough. The story was swamped under a landfill of unimportant details. Lines like 'The cold white snow fell down' suddenly jumped out at me. 'Of course it's cold, it's snow, and snow only falls down, plus we know it's white.' The line would be deleted and replaced with 'It snowed.'

A year went by, hundreds of hours, tens of thousands of single-finger keyboard taps, the story ebbing and flowing, as slowly I learnt how hard it is to write, how bad I was, how published words would be there forever and had to be perfect. I had to trick the reader into thinking these words had come easily, and hide the work in the spaces between the words. Yet the more I wrote, and the more I thought about what I wrote, the further away the end seemed to be.

The avalanche crashed by until the roar finally slid into a long and deafening hiss.

Coughing up ice crystals, we opened our eyes and found to our surprise that we were still alive. Stunned, we sat and watched in amazement as a great cloud of ice particles and debris rolled across the glacier far below, fanning out for hundreds of metres, destroying our tracks, shimmering spectacularly in the beam of the spotlight as it swirled slowly in the air, forming a galaxy of halos. My heart beat hard. It was the most beautiful thing I had ever seen.

I felt more alive than at any other time in my life. I forgot about my boot, which would now be buried under the ice. I knew in that moment we would be able to get down in one piece, and, more importantly, that alpine climbing wasn't for me.

The following afternoon the rope slithered from our final abseil. We had made it down. All my socks were on my boot-less foot, which was further encased in a mountain mitt and had a crampon strapped on with abseil cord. I ran for my life across the glacier, praying we'd be spared any more trundling seracs.

Three hundred metres from the face I stopped dead and rubbed my eyes.

There before me, standing upright on a pile of ice debris, was my boot.

As I picked it up I instantly forgot last night's thought of selling gear, sunny holidays in Spain, and the stupidity of winter climbing. I'd got myself down alive and in one piece. I felt stronger, mentally more able to cope with the stresses of winter, plus now I had two boots again. I was back in business.

Dick came into work and I asked him to read my story. He promised he would at dinner time.

All day I waited nervously for his opinion. He was well read *and* a climber. Who better to give the nod to my talents? No doubt he'd be shocked that such genius had gone unnoticed in his shop.

'I just don't understand what you're trying to say,' he said, handing it back, the paper covered in question marks and corrected spelling mistakes. 'It can't have been as hard as you make out. You seem to be trying too much to impress. It's only the Frendo Spur.'

I told him it *was* hard, and that difficulty was relative to experience anyway. Dick was an old-school climber and his climbs were simply climbs, not metaphors for life. I knew he thought I was bullshitting, laying it on thickly. I just wanted to tell it how it was, how the route had affected us. Yes it was just a climb, but I had thought about it every day since then. It was more than that.

'Maybe read a few more books,' he said, 'instead of climbing magazines.'

'My arse will never be the same,' I groaned, shifting in my sleeping bag. It was another alpine dawn, and I sat with my back against the Frendo, the lights of Chamonix thousands of feet below me still shining as I shifted my weight from bum cheek to bum cheek. It was our second night on the Frendo since our return a week after retreating that first time. I wondered if the crux of alpine climbing was getting a good night's sleep.

'How's *your* arse?' I asked, directing my question to the half-sitting, half-lying sleeping bag beside me. It looked like a misplaced body bag. I knew full well what the answer was, but this was a nicer way to ask if he was awake.

'I think I'd just managed to fall asleep,' came the reply.

It was hard to understand our keenness to hike back up and have another go at the Frendo, but something had clicked last time, and through the fear and trepidation of that first day and night, I'd felt a powerful force stir within me. As soon as I'd found my boot I knew I had to go back. Failing and then getting down under our own steam had proved we were strong enough to succeed, but now we had spent another night on the Spur, with more than half the route left to do, I wondered if it had just been youthful testosterone, mistaking the relief at getting down for belief we should go back up.

I moved carefully on our tiny chopped-out ledge, ropes feeding in and out of my sleeping bag, trying to dig out the stove and get our breakfast brew of lemon tea started. I scooped up a pan of snow, careful to dodge the yellow patches close to our feet.

I lit the stove and sat with my head bowed looking into the pan, hypnotised by the slow breakdown of the snow crystals which turned from white to grey, grey to transparent, a pan full of snow slowly shrinking down to a small puddle of water that warmed, then bubbled, then boiled and steamed. I dropped in another handful of snow and watched again as it transformed into water.

Aaron unzipped his bivy bag, sticking his nose out to sniff the air. 'Did you sleep?'

'No, I don't think so, I needed a piss all night but couldn't work out how to go without getting it on myself, my sleeping bag or you – and I was gripped in case I fell off the ledge.'

'Do you still want one?' he said.

'No, I went in my cup.'

'In *your* cup?'

'Yes, I think it was my cup.'

I passed Aaron the pan to drink out of, the metal warming his hands for a minute or two before the air chilled it. I took a sip of the tea and felt nauseous, and wondered if I'd poisoned myself with fumes from the stove. Then I munched my small muesli bar. Once the snow is melted breakfast is a short affair.

Aaron craned his head and looked above us. 'I hope we get to the top today, I don't think I can last another bivy like that.'

'I think it's good,' said Mandy, and my heart leapt. 'There are a few spelling mistakes, but I really liked it.'

I gave it to Dick at work. 'Not bad,' he said, 'much better than last time.' His praise, although not glowing, was good enough.

I passed it on, and tweaked it as each new reader found things they didn't understand, or thought it too over the top. The story shrank to an easy-to-handle two thousand words: long enough to tell the story, short enough for people to complete it before they switched off. I deleted all the other versions from my computer, dozens of foldersful, the result of nearly two years' work. Two years of work just for one short story about a climb! But what next?

I thought about sending it to a UK climbing magazine, but part of me wanted better than that. I knew the best in the US was called *Climbing*, a publication that set the standard for climbing journalism, with articles written by the very top outdoor writers. It was a long shot I knew, and by sending them my story I was setting myself up for yet more rejection, but what if . . . ? After scribbling work's fax number on top with the words 'Wondered if you like this piece I've written.

Andy K', I tapped *Climbing*'s number into the fax machine and pressed Send.

One week later I cycled into work, by this time already convinced I should try another avenue, but as I walked into the office I saw a fax with my name on it sticking out of the machine. The *Climbing* logo was clearly visible.

'Hi Andy, love your piece. Would like to publish it. A few spelling mistakes, but almost perfect, what's your number? Michael Kennedy'

It was the greatest news I'd ever had.

We climbed as fast as we could, up grooves and along steep arêtes, the climbing hard enough to be fun, but easy enough not to be scary. I revelled in the height and position on the Spur, the knowledge that every move made put us closer to the top and success. I wanted this climb so much. I would be lying if I said I was completely enjoying myself, as the stress and tension of being there was intense, and I was in no doubt I was overreaching myself, but that was what made it so exciting. Here I was, on the Frendo Spur, and in winter, the only other mountains I'd climbed just those in my head. I began to realise that mountains are climbed just as much in the head as with the hands. We arrived below the crux.

Promising not to be long, I set off up the pitch, a vertical wall. We didn't know it, but we were off route, the pitch above us much harder than we knew, harder than we had ever climbed, a compact vertical wall that barred the way to the easy climbing above us.

It started with difficult hooking with axe picks and crampon points, each move feeling irreversible, each move unprotected. I pushed on, Aaron belaying me from a huge sword-like flake that promised to spear me if I fell.

Twenty feet above Aaron I mantled up onto a narrow ledge no wider than my boot. It crossed the wall, leading to a corner that looked like the way on. With no hand holds or protection I began shuffling my feet along, my crampons scratching as I went. It felt as if I was traversing along a thin balcony on the side of a sky scraper, a suicide jumper with second thoughts, a daredevil, a cat burglar. I was surprised at my boldness, but it seemed the only way. Each step felt more insecure than the one before, but each step put me closer to the corner where I would gain the security of the facing wall. There was no going back.

The last few steps were hurried, I felt as though my rucksack was about to pull me off. My hand shot out to steady me against the other wall just before I fell. I stood there in balance and tried to calm down before looking for the next move, mindful of the time, hoping I could find some protection and climb the next section quickly, just several metres between me and easy ground above.

Using a shoulder pressed into the opposite wall, I pulled back my mitt and looked at my watch. I had already been climbing for an hour.

'Not long now, Aaron,' I shouted down, trying to convince us both I was nearly there. Once this pitch was in the bag it would be plain sailing.

The corner was full of snow, so I raked it clear with my axe, and found, with dismay, that instead of a narrow crack that would take some protection, there was only a wide four-inch crack. I had nothing that big.

I looked back at the way I'd come and knew I couldn't get back. I also knew that without any protection I could neither climb up, nor be lowered back down. I leaned into the corner and tried to think what to do. No ideas came. My biggest pieces of gear were only about two inches wide.

I had a thought.

I took a hex 7 and Rock 10, my two largest nuts, and placed them side by side. As I'd hoped, together they spanned the crack. I placed one nut, then slid in the second and hammered it into place. Mechanically it looked as if it could work. Emotionally it didn't. I gave it a small tug to convince myself, then clipped it into the rope. It was all there was, but it still wasn't enough.

I began making a check list of items that might fit: helmet, too big; pan, in Aaron's rucksack; plastic boots, yes, but not really an option.

I ran my fingers on my thin rack: nuts, a few cams, pegs. I pulled off a long thin angle peg and, instead of inserting the tip, turned it sideways and saw that it fitted from tip to eye instead. I hammered it into place and clipped it into the rope. It was far from text-book, but again it should work.

'How's it going?' Aaron shouted up, his words slightly slurred with cold.

'Nearly there,' I shouted back, knowing I wasn't.

Another hour passed and I hadn't moved from the spot.

'Come on. Come on. Come on. Come on,' I shouted. 'Fucking DO SOMETHING!'

The corner above was too wide to climb. The gear was too bad to lower off and find an alternative line. I'd climbed myself into a dead end. The word 'dead' seemed highly appropriate. The only option was to see what lay around the corner.

I held onto the gear I'd placed, trying to put as little weight on it as possible, and peered round. I could see a steep wall, with what looked like a good crack running up it, leading to a ledge maybe only seven feet higher. The crack was too far away to reach with my hand to place some gear, but close enough to hook my pick into. I pulled up my axe and tried. The pick slid in. I pulled down on the shaft and it lodged tight, probably on a jammed pebble.

I couldn't imagine trusting it, so slipped it back out and returned to the corner. I knew it was the only option, but I was in no doubt that if I fell off I would rip this gear and fall onto the jagged rocks below. But I had to. I had no other choice.

I leaned out and slipped in my pick again, then got cold feet and slipped it out once more, repeating this several times. I knew I was too weak for this, too timid, but I also knew that this was my only option. I was more afraid than I had ever been before. This was life and death. This wasn't a game. This wasn't climbing.

Do it, said a voice in my head. It startled me. It was stronger than I was. *Do it*, it repeated. I felt panicked, the voice pushing me to the edge. *Do it*. The words were impossible to ignore. I leaned out and slipped the pick into the crack again, then to my horror and surprise felt my body follow it, swinging out onto the axe, everything I was or could be hanging from this blade of steel wedged on nothing more than a jammed pebble. I was doing it, but it wasn't me, it was someone else. This was beyond anything *I* could do.

I hung one-armed from my axe, crampons pedalling against the rock for purchase, the smell of granite and steel filling the air around me. *Move*, the voice shouted. I hooked my other axe over the pick of the first, pulled up and locked off. I tried to move it up and slot it higher up the crack. It slid out. I tried again, my bicep burning under the strain. It slid down the crack once more. 'Climb back to the corner,' I told myself, but I knew I couldn't, I was committed. All I could do was give this 100 per cent. *If you want to live, climb*, shouted a voice. My arm screaming, my hand losing its grip, I slammed the pick in again. Sparks shot out as it wedged against something. I pulled down on it. It held. I pulled up on it and locked my arm on the tool, trying not to dwell on what it was actually hooked on. I manipulated the axe out below it, then hunted for the next hook. I could see the ledge above, perhaps four moves away, but yet again I could not get my higher axe to stick. I screamed out as I tried and tried. There was nothing. My arm was unable to stay locked off with my shoulder beside my pick, and slowly began extending. Without the height I wouldn't be able to find a good placement. I bit down on the wrist of my sleeve to help me retain my position. I could have been biting my hand off for as much as I cared as I almost threw the axe into the crack. The pick stuck with a twang.

Without testing it, I pulled up, pushing a point of one crampon onto a crystal in the crack, desperate to take some weight off my arms. *Find some gear*, the voice shouted. *No, keep going*, contradicted another. If I had been stronger in body and soul I knew I'd have been able to make it, but I wasn't. I had to find some gear. My whole body was shaking with the build-up of lactic acid as I grabbed a karabiner with some nuts racked on it, sized from small to large. Without the time or mental capacity to find the correct nut and place it, I stuffed the lot into the crack and fumbled the rope into the karabiner.

I screamed again, hoping some primal rage would get me up the last couple of moves. Hand shaking, I pulled out the axe from below and reached back to smash it into the crack once more.

BANG.

The axe I'd been hanging on sheared out of the crack and smashed me in the face.

Unconscious I fell.

I came round with a start, finding to my disbelief that I was hanging from the rope, not crumpled on the ledge below. I was alive. I looked up and saw that a single nut had held me. The rest had ripped out and were dangling uselessly from the crack. I noticed I couldn't see properly out of one eye, and that my face stung. Lifting my fingers to my face, I could feel a hole in my cheek, and that one lens of my glasses was missing. It had deflected a blow that would otherwise have blinded me. I felt a power race through me, adrenaline mixed with fear. I was alive.

The magazine came in the post a few months later, printed after a few weeks of editing, which introduced me to the luxury of someone being paid to make me look as if I knew what I was doing. Feeling like Charlie Bucket looking for his golden ticket to the chocolate factory I opened the thick airmail envelope and slid out the magazine. I flicked open the glossy pages, and found it: my story, my name, my words. 'Broken Promises' by Andy Kirkpatrick. I wondered what I was more proud of, that climb or this story, the climber or the writer. I thought about all the hard work and doubt that it had taken for both, and it had been worth it! I had believed I could climb that route, and I had believed I could learn to write, and tell my story. I had learnt that belief was in me, and now I would find it harder to doubt myself again.

I arrived at the ledge and collapsed, utterly exhausted. I saw a black bird close by, and wondered if it was real. Surely birds wouldn't be able to survive up here?

Aaron jumared the pitch, swearing at the stupidity of mixed climbing, until he saw the stacked gear and then the blood. He was silent after that. Pulling onto the belay, he looked tired, cold and as strung out as I was. He knew this was beyond us – but so was the ground. We had to push on. I realised that this route was changing us both. After every pitch I felt stronger and more confident in myself, confounding what I thought was possible, feeling more and more in my element, whereas Aaron seemed less sure. I knew after each pitch he became more and more convinced that this wasn't for him. It suddenly struck me that this was going to be the last route we'd do together.

An hour later, I mantled onto the summit of the last tower.

The oppressive blackness and complexity of the lower rock spur finally gave way to the simple white landscape of the upper ice field. The relief at arriving at the ice arête was indescribable. We stood together, and for the first time in three days, relaxed a little. I smiled, not because I knew we'd make it, but just because I was happy. I wondered for a moment whether I'd shake Aaron's hand or hug him when we reached the Midi, imagining this would make everything all right. All the pushing, anxiety and resentment of being dragged onto such a route would have been worth it, wouldn't it? Anyway it hadn't been all that bad.

'Your lead, Aaron, a nice bit of ice to see us home.'

'Maybe this isn't such a bad route after all,' he said, giving a laboured smile. He looked out of place here. I wondered if I did too.

Letting down our guard, thinking it was almost over, Aaron led off up the ice arête as the first flecks of snow fell and a major storm blew in from the east, warm Mediterranean winds clashing with Arctic cold.

With the last of our energy, we bashed against the ice-coated door, the entrance to the high mountain *téléphérique* station. The north face we had climbed dropped away behind us into the darkness and the storm. Snow spun around us, caught in the eddy where the door appeared out of the mountainside. We smashed into it again, knowing we wouldn't survive unless we got inside quickly.

It remained solidly closed.

I dropped to my knees and tried to prise it open with my ice axe, its pick already bent and blunt after the kilometre of hard climbing it had taken to get here. I twisted it hard into the metal reinforcing on the door, but it snapped and I fell back defeated. After all we'd gone through, we were going to die because of a fucking locked door.

Frustrated and too frozen to care, Aaron flung himself at the door and disappeared inside with a bang. I crawled in after him.

The door blew shut as we rolled onto our backs, sealing out the storm and putting a loud full stop to the strain of the last three days. Both of us lay there for a long time, staring at the icy ceiling, neither of us wanting to speak and spoil the over-whelming return of peace and safety.

My hands were frozen and dried blood covered my face. The rope lay at our feet; new a week ago, it was now a frozen torn mess, its core strands bursting out like loose intestines. Most of our climbing hardware was gone, left strung along the final section of the 1,200-metre face, left without a second thought as we battled to reach the top through the violent storm. If we had reached the last pitch an hour later we wouldn't have made it.

Slowly we began to move, knowing we had to find some-thing to eat, something to drink, and we had to tell people we were still alive.

Standing carefully, creaking like old men, we looked down at the knot that joined us and began to untie ourselves, our fingertips starting to throb as they warmed. The rope, our rope, the one we had climbed on all these years, which had kept us alive, kept us together, at first simply as partners, and then as friends, was now only fit for a washing line.

I haven't seen Aaron for many years. He works in IT and has a nice house, a wife and children near Bradford. I know he doesn't climb any more because I've still got his gear.

After our climb his girlfriend told me he'd realised that alpine climbing wasn't for him. On the Frendo he'd realised it just wasn't worth it. He'd grown up, she said. And me?

Sitting on some god-awful ledge, hungry, cold and nervous of what is to come, I often think about Aaron and our ascent of the Frendo in winter, my first climb. I think about him spending his holidays on beaches, in forests, having fun – happy, healthy, relaxing in the sun and sleeping with the woman he loves, while I cuddle up to some rock.

I wonder what life would be like for me now, if, below the Frendo, I'd failed to find my boot and just walked away from it all.

It's all easy until you fall

Pitch 2 Reticent Wall

I woke and for a moment couldn't place myself. It was dark. A small triangle of stars hung above me. I sat up and, removing my arms from my sleeping bag, felt around. I touched something rusty and metallic. A barbecue. I settled back down. I was on Lay Lady Ledge, sleeping on the flattest spot, tucked in right at the back, the rest of the night apart from the triangle of stars obscured by the soaring walls on both sides. Somewhere close, my ropes hung, arching up out of sight, up to the next belay. The first pitch of the Reticent Wall was in the bag.

The sky began to grow pale. Dawn was on its way.

I closed my eyes, rested my head on my fleece jacket, and felt almost satisfied. I had climbed the first pitch. I had overcome my fears and doubt.

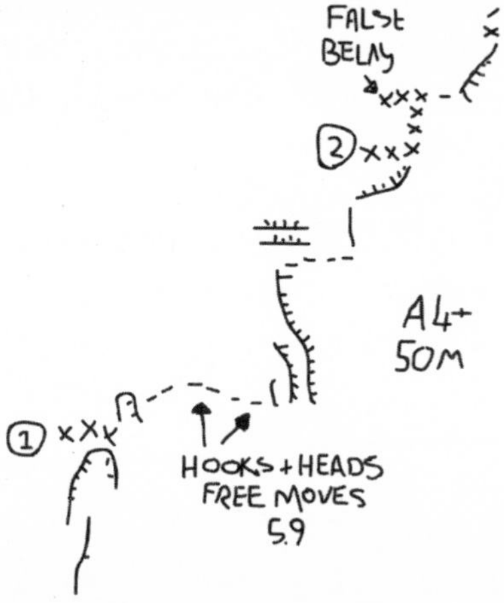

FALSE
BELAY

②

A4+
50M

①

HOOKS + HEADS
FREE MOVES
5.9

The sky began to turn from black to dark blue, the sun edging up slowly somewhere beyond the Sierras. I could make out my ropes gently swinging, drifting in the early morning breeze.

For the first time in a long while I felt calm, the voice in my head silenced by my action.

Although itself out of sight, the sun touched the wall.

The idea of carrying on, actually attempting to climb the Reticent, made me giggle inside. It was crazy. Impossible. Maybe I could do it. I felt buoyed by my little taste of success, even if the pitch had been graded as relatively easy.

It had felt pretty damned hard.

Lying in my sleeping bag, I thought back to all the mornings I had lain like this on other routes and felt uncertain about what to do, what the future would hold. There was always the knowledge it would be better to fail without doubt, than to fail because of doubt, that to turn around because of what I imagined, not what I knew, would leave me regretting my own weakness far more than my folly.

Yet the overriding draw was the thought of actually climbing the route. Just imagine it, me climbing the Reticent Wall. It would be unbelievable.

Yet what if I couldn't? What did that actually mean? There was no way of retreating once I committed to the next pitch. There would be no way down, the only escape option was to climb the route to the top. What about rescue? On such a steep and vast wall a rescue would be a huge undertaking that would take days. Don't think about it.

The sun began to creep into view, moving light down the walls on either side of me.

What to do? Go up or down? Do I carry on or call it quits?

All my doubts returned as new.

I had maybe ten minutes until the sun reached me. I snuggled down and put off the potentially life-changing decision until then.

I was falling.

It came so fast I had no time to be scared. One second I was stepping up on a copperhead, the next I was falling.

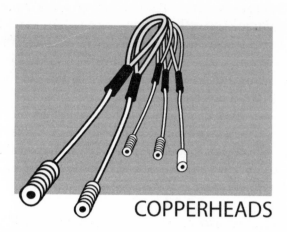

COPPERHEADS

I felt the next piece – a small birdbeak – rip out as easily as if it had simply been Blu-Tacked against the wall, and I carried on down for thirty feet, my fall slowing as a piece held and the rope stretched out. I stopped.

Fuck!

I hung in space, breathing hard, my heart thumping so loud it rattled in my ears. I was OK. A fixed peg – probably one left by Tomaz Humar in 1998 – had stopped me.

I gripped the rope and looked up, feeling strangely proud to measure the distance of the fall now it had been taken. Then I felt angry with myself for having fallen in the first place. This time I'd been lucky and only gone thirty feet. Next time I might not stop.

I clipped my jumars to the rope and headed back up until I reached the peg, clipped in and set about reclimbing the fifteen feet of crack, taping in the birdbeak I'd pulled out, and replacing the copperhead I'd ripped.

Maybe it's good to fall. Maybe it takes away some of the fear of falling.

I climbed on. Suddenly, the heat of the day receded as the sun passed into black cloud which was scuttling without warning over the rim of El Cap, catching me out in just my T-shirt and shorts. It looked like a storm.

Storms are rare on El Cap, but when they come they spell trouble. They have killed several climbers over the years and forced the rescue of many others. Often the victims are plucked off with moments to live, rain, ice and snow having sent them into hypothermic comas.

I knew I was exposed. My storm gear – fleece and water-proofs – were back down at the belay in my haul bag. I had to move faster to finish the pitch, fix my ropes and abseil back down before the heavens opened.

On most climbs you can tie your ropes off at any point to a collection of pieces of protection, but here I couldn't trust anything. I was forced to carry on. Luckily I could see the belay only fifteen feet higher, the two bolts promising a quick turn around, allowing me to clip in my lead rope, and abseil down one of my two haul lines, which stretched back to the safety of the belay below.

Just get to the belay, I told myself. Block out the storm. Concentrate only on the climbing.

By the time I was below the bolts, the sky was almost as black as night. I could hear people shouting around the wall: teams that were still low enough to reach the ground were bailing back down their ropes; those too high were setting up their portaledges and attaching their rainflies, battening down the hatches for what looked as if it was going to be a major storm.

The first hailstones hit me as I clipped into the bolts, pelting me, piling up on my shoulders, running down my back, hammering off my helmet. In seconds my body temperature began to drop. I made heavy, mannered movements, over-tensing my muscles to generate heat as I tried to set up the belay as quickly as possible. I couldn't afford to waste one second, nor make one mistake. I felt the goosebumps rising all over my body as it tried to stave off the cold. I might as well be naked.

I clipped in karabiners and attached my ropes, knowing that any mistake or miscalculation would be fatal. In less than a minute I had my lead line tied off, ready for me to climb back up the following day, and my red and yellow haul lines were fixed – my escape route back to the safety of my portaledge and storm gear. By the time I was attaching my abseil device to the yellow rope, my body was beginning to spasm with cold, my hand muscles becoming stiffer, fingers growing less respon-sive. I knew it wouldn't be long until I lost all dexterity, and that would be it.

I clipped the yellow rope into my abseil device, checked and rechecked in the blink of an eye, then unclipped from the belay and committed my life to the single strand of rope. I looked down at it disappearing below me into a galaxy of falling hail and swirling mist, the belay lost from sight.

You'll make it.

I started down, slowly for the first metre, then with barely controlled speed, thinking I should have clipped into both haul lines, instead of the one, thus doubling my security.

It's too late. Go!

The wall was overhanging, with the previous belay way over to my left, leaving me dangling out in space once I was level with it, forcing me to lock off my abseil device and begin pulling myself in with the rope. Each pull should have been bringing me nearer to my storm gear and safety. Yet each time I pulled, I simply pulled more and more rope out of its sack, forcing me frantically to gather in the seemingly endless rope. It was a comical scene, and the effort warmed me a little.

I knew that all the rope would have to be pulled out of the sack before it would come tight to the belay, the other end being clipped in with a karabiner. On I pulled, metre after metre, my body temperature now dropping fast. The rope came tight, allowing me to get some traction and pull myself closer.

The closer I got, the harder I had to pull, but then, with only a few metres left until I was safe, the rope snagged and ripped out of the bag, sending me swinging back into the storm.

To my horror I saw the end of the rope whip from the bag as I swung out.

I had forgotten to clip the haul line into the belay.

I had no fear, just the knowledge that all I could do was jumar all the way back up, and abseil back down on the second haul line.

Did you leave your jumars at the belay?

Did you leave the other rope untied?

One fuck-up and I was dead.

My hand shot to the back of my harness and with relief felt the shape of my two Petzl jumars. Removing them, my hands already beginning to cramp and lose control, my body shaking with the onset of hypothermia, I clipped them in and set off back up the rope, just as the first bolt of lightning shook the wall.

NE Spur

North Face

Droites

The last time

Chamonix, France. February 1997

Three simple words slipped out of my dream into the darkness of the room, three simple words that stained the night: 'Please don't go.' They hung in the cold air, a plea, an ultimatum, until by opening my eyes I scrubbed them out, until there was only the hum of the wind on the cracked window beside my bunk, and Rich's fitful breathing beside me. I moved my eyes like a blind man, unable to see anything except the receding images of my dream.

I moved my hands under the pile of blankets, each one thick like an army greatcoat, unwashed perhaps for a decade or two. They reminded me of my grandmother and her house with its tiny bedrooms and the thick heavy layers of crushing blanket – more like being buried then being put to bed. I thought about her thick hands. Her stubbornness, how she told us we all had our own lives to live. She had died ten years ago, and I tried to remember her as she was the last time I'd seen her, sitting in a hospital bed, her IV incorrectly set, fluid filling and bloating her skinny arm. It's a shame we have to die with so much indignity.

The dream and those three words came back to me in the dark, insinuating themselves like a ghost through a wall.

I ran my hands down over my body, unzipping my fleece so I could touch my skin, now warm. My body felt different. It had changed so quickly – out of sight, buried beneath thick winter layers for the past five days – that it didn't feel part of me. I hadn't had time to acclimatise myself to myself. I felt my collarbone, my ribs, moved my hands down to my flat rumbling belly, to my pubic bone, down to my cycling thighs. It was erotic, like feeling the body of a stranger. Comforting.

I closed my eyes and tried to remember what had created this change, filling my mind with memories, to push away those three words.

I stood in the doorway, swaying with a fatigue so deep and overwhelming that only good manners kept me from falling flat on my face.

My partner Rich sat slumped down at the end of the table, smiling with relief, four concerned French skiers seated around him. He looked like a picture of Jesus, unshaven, the skiers his companions at our first supper for days. We both looked tattered, torn and emaciated, as if we'd climbed up from hell, while they looked well fed, healthy and surprised at us stumbling into this mountain hut late one winter's night. I steadied myself against the wall and breathed in the warmth of the room. Its walls were illuminated by messy candles, and a pan of water boiled on a coal stove in the corner.

Cheese, bread, sausage, everything we'd dreamt of for the previous five days, lay spread across the table. The rich, vital smell of coal, wood and food mixed with the hot moist air and made my head spin. There are no smells out on the mountains in winter.

A tall, smiling skier stood up and walked over to me, helped me with my rucksack, sat me down, and passed us both some cold water. We looked into our cups, neither daring to drink or to believe. The skier sat back down and they all looked at us, at our faces raw and gaunt, at our ragged frost-nipped hands which were visibly shaking, and waited for us to tell them about our climb.

That night I woke up several times, scared out of my wits, panic gripping my brain, grabbing for something to hold me on to the world. Then I'd remember I was safe, and lie back down and listen to the sound of the wind, Rich's fitful breathing, the blood pumping through my head, telling myself everything was OK, we'd made it. Each time, I'd close my eyes again and think about getting back to Chamonix, back to Sheffield, back home, lying next to Mandy, feeling companionship and warmth with someone who wanted me to be there forever.

In my dream we're in our bedroom while the sun casts its light through yellow curtains onto sea-blue walls. My arms are round her, and her curly red hair is in my face. She hugs me tight, as if she thinks she can hold on to me forever. I hug her back and whisper a promise into her ear, a promise that will unwind her arms. 'This will be the last time, Mandy, *the last time.*'

Then my dream changes as I open my eyes and find myself back on that face, pressed tight to Rich's frozen corpse with the wind howling and the black clouds boiling up to engulf me and set me like stone upon the mountain . . .

Panicked, I woke again and listened to the wind outside. I knew she'd be worried, we were a few days overdue – but everything would be fine once we got down.

It always was.

Mandy's mother died when she was six, but her father and family had kept her apart from her mother for a long time before her death, hoping this would make her loss less devastating and traumatic. She told me she couldn't remember her mother at all; all she remembered was the loss. She told me once that she couldn't lose someone that close again.

We had lain in bed together, the last time before I left for the Alps. She had asked me what I was planning, asked me why I had to go. She worries about me. She hates it. If I loved her I wouldn't put her through this. I know the pain it causes, but I have to go. Without this I have nothing. She had made me promise not to take any risks, and I had agreed. Both of us knew it was a lie.

I lay in the hut with Rich and thought about her, pleased to be alive, but knowing she was alone at home fearing I was dead. I thought back to all the other times. After I'd come back from the Frendo the year before, she would find me asleep, cradling the alarm clock as if I was trying to tie myself into the electric lead, dreaming I was back sleeping on the spur.

She'd wrestle the clock from me, only to find me safely re-belayed into the electricity system by morning.

'You're losing it, Andy. What happens to you up there?'

'Nothing.'

Later, she had sat next to the bath as I told her about the climb and watched my frost-nipped fingers shedding dead skin. Forgetting myself, I gave her the hardcore version of what had happened: near-death and near-disaster. Instead of gasping and looking impressed, she'd had tears in her eyes.

Now, at home, she gave in and located the number of my friend's house in Chamonix.

'Is Andy there?'

'Hello, Andy's not back yet,' the voice said, unaware of who or why anyone was asking.

'It's Mandy, Andy's wife.'

'Don't worry,' the voice said, telling her that the weather was good, and that there had been no rescues, that the route was really long and hard, but safe. 'I'll ring you tomorrow, I promise,' he reassured her.

Things hadn't gone to plan from the start.

I had been all set for the North Face of the Eiger, hoping to try a winter ascent, a ridiculous objective considering my single alpine climb. However, the months that had followed that climb had allowed me to digest the Frendo experience. The failures, successes and mistakes were mulled over and lessons learnt, until I believed I could make that giant leap from novice to Eiger warrior. The Frendo had been simply a stepping stone. For a year I trained: biking, walking, running and climbing, testing out gear and visualising myself on the White Spider, the Hinterstoisser Traverse, moving across the Traverse of the Gods.

Aaron no longer climbed, but that summer I met Paul Tattersall who, although almost ten years older than me, shared the same rabid obsession with climbing. He had begun working in the shop part-time, raising funds for an expedition to Greenland, big-wall climbing. He was the archetypal free spirit, with no fixed address, only a collection of climbing gear. He travelled around, climbing with his German girlfriend Angela; he'd met her while living in a cave in Spain. On rock he was world class, soloing up and down routes I couldn't even top-rope, sometimes in mismatched boots, very often with holes in. To me he was a god, fit, strong, and able. We climbed together a few times, generally with me struggling to lead on my routes, then struggling again to second on his. Paul was hoping to become a guide, but wanted more alpine experience, so we decided we'd go out to the Alps that winter. The Eiger was chosen because I knew Paul had the ability, and I had the ambition.

That summer and autumn I thought of little else.

As the trip drew closer, I became more and more nervous, imagining the Face, thinking of everything that could go wrong, always falling back on the knowledge that if Paul was there everything would be OK. The idea of climbing the route, of coming back with it in the bag, was dizzying.

Then, with a week to go, I got a call from Angela telling me Paul had contracted some kind of heart virus, and that he'd been told not to do anything. I made the right noises and I was sorry for him, but all I could think about, as she explained how serious his condition was, was who could replace him at such short notice. Before she'd had time to put her phone back on the receiver, I'd started to dial for a new partner.

I'd met Rich Cross only once before, when I had gone out after work a few weeks previously to do some winter climbing on Kinder Scout, the highest mountain in Derbyshire – well, the highest hill. That night Rich, myself and Jon my lodger had squeezed into his car and driven up snowy roads for an all-night climb, getting back from the hill just in time for work the following morning.

Rich was the same age as me, but exuded a quiet physical confidence. He was tall and built like a brick. He had been pushing his climbing grades through three years at Leeds University, both in Scotland and the Alps, and had returned the previous summer from a bold expedition to the Ogre in Pakistan. His experience was far beyond mine, but we had got on well that night, sharing dark belays and tramping through the snow. So I dialled Rich's number first.

He was also the only person I knew who could leave at a few days' notice.

* * *

We drove over in a van lent by my friend Pete the Grocer, the back full of climbers and skiers rather than bananas and oranges.

The Eiger had been put on hold, so we were bound for Chamonix, and needed a new objective. I thumbed through the guide, panicking that I had had no time to climb any potential route in my mind beforehand.

'Why don't we try the North East Spur of Les Droites,' suggested Rich, his raised eyebrows and wide eyes showing that even he thought this would be a bold leap in both our grades. I scanned my memory banks for data on the route, thinking of that 1,200-metre face on the back of the guidebook, the awesome spur running up its left-hand edge, steep and hard, a big tick in summer for any alpinist, a very rare tick in winter. I remembered an image from one of Doug Scott's books of Aid Burgess tiptoeing out on a big ice field on the Spur. The picture had stuck in my mind at the time as particularly vertigo-inducing. I had tried to imagine how it would be possible to go on day after day for such a long and sustained climb, a route as hard as the Eiger North Face, a route that made the Frendo look like a bike path. My brain whirled at the possibility. I imagined that with Rich as a partner we could do it, not knowing that Rich was under the self-same misguided belief in me.

'The stove's fucking fucked,' said Rich, twisting the tiny control knob. The flame, no bigger than a dying match, remained unchanged and certainly unable to melt any snow. We sat in our thick sleeping bags, one day up the climb, and looked at each other.

We'd started on the route hoping to storm up it in two days, but the climbing had proved much harder than expected. On one lead I'd backed off, finding it too scary, the hardest climbing I'd done. I left it for Rich to complete. A pitch higher I'd found myself on the same type of terrain, only this time I had pushed on, not wanting to seem weak in front of such a strong partner.

Reaching the snowy notch in the spur, a third of the way up my hardest climb, had been immensely satisfying. A good weather forecast, and feeling strong, had given me the confidence that I could do it. But now, with a broken stove, that dream was over. The only thing to do was retreat and hope we could get another weather window long enough to return.

'Fucker, fucker, fucker,' said Rich, as he continued to fiddle and shake the stove.

'If we climbed fast enough, we could do the rest in a day, and get down to the hut on the other side,' I said, and both of us craned our necks up at the colossal black mass of the spur above.

The North East Spur is famous for getting harder and harder as the climber progresses, with the crux situated near the very top. Today had been one of my hardest days' climbing ever, but tomorrow would inevitably trump that. To carry on, with no ability to melt snow for drinking or cooking our dehydrated noodles, would be madness. Yet it was easy to convince ourselves that we could. Blind youthful confidence, if nothing else, was on our side. So we continued.

Two days later our recklessness was becoming all too apparent as I pulled into a snow-choked chimney, and, digging above my head, inched upwards. Having drunk less then a pint of water in the past three days, I could feel my body shrinking by the hour. Luckily, the climbing had been far too hard and scary to worry about such trivial matters. Too high to retreat, and too British to ask for rescue, we felt we were climbing for our lives, unsure whether we had the reserves to make it.

The feeling of being so strung out and exposed both terrified me and made me aware that this was the greatest adventure of my life. In that moment there was nothing but Rich and me.

It was only while belaying that we could dwell on our crazy position, near the top of this huge north wall in winter, hands pumping to stave off frostbite, worrying about frozen toes, Frankenstein feet, hoping they would rewarm once we began to move again. Standing there, head bowed, only looking up as the rope was drawn out by Rich's slow progress, I became acutely aware of the tiny dot I was, a speck of lichen on this tombstone. How misguided I had been even to dream of such torture.

Twisted awkwardly in the narrow slot of the chimney, I desperately swung my axe above my head, searching for purchase, until with momentary relief I felt it sink into a solid lump of snow the size of a TV. Trying to relax, I pulled down on it as I wriggled my body up a few inches. The axe ripped and the block of snow smashed down on my head, the force transferring down my body to my feet. My crampons slipped on the granite, a sharp steel point tearing into the back of my leg. Snow tumbled down around me. Somehow I held on.

I looked down, panting, and saw a blotch of red grow below me on the snow, not realising at first that it was my own blood dripping from my leg. It was at my temperature of course, vivid, alive, but it quickly cooled and then froze. I didn't think then of the beauty of the white and the red, the hot and the cold, the alive and the dead. All I thought about was a blood-flavoured slushy drink.

I wriggled up further, where the snow blob had been, until my head butted up against another barricade of snow. I set my feet in case of another impact and began to punch and hack until this block also split and crashed down, once more nearly dislodging me. My crampons screeched as they slipped, then held.

I wondered where my courage and strength were coming from.

Almost at the top of the chimney, I hooked a loose flake that protruded like a petrified giant's ear, knowing that this was all the chimney had to offer. It groaned with a cold, terrifying grinding sound, shifted in the crack and pinned me to the wall. Nonchalant with fatigue, I wrestled it out and heaved it over my shoulder.

Only when I heard it crash below did I think of the damage it might have inflicted on my ropes or on Rich.

I hung there and looked down, and saw with relief that both Rich and the ropes were still intact. I felt my head throb with dehydration, and my belly painfully squeeze itself tight with hunger. For a moment a sense of hopelessness came over me, a sense of utter despair. I wondered how or where I would find the energy to push on to the top. It seemed I was living from second to second, without the energy to achieve anything more than a heartbeat. I could not dwell on what the next pitch would bring, or the following day, or my life beyond this climb. All I could hope to do was string together these separate moments of brief activity.

Two hours later and one pitch further up the buttress, I woke up, blind, terrified and startled, as a piece of ice ricocheted off my helmet. It was cold and dark and I felt like a drunk as I fumbled with my headtorch with thick-gloved fingers. I was lashed to three pegs, my body suspended in a hanging chimney above some blackness. Then I heard Rich high above me, panting in the dark, moving slowly up the steep smear. There was only a bad nut in an icy flared crack between us. I remembered where I was and checked I was still holding on to Rich's ropes.

I scanned up with the beam of my headtorch as Rich shouted something – it sounded as if he were at the belay. I hoped this was the last hard pitch. I hammered out two of the pegs at my belay, then waited for the ropes to go tight before knocking out the last. Then I heard his voice again, clearer this time: 'Watch me here, Andy, I might come off.'

I turned off my headtorch, and closed my eyes again.

Some time later that night we finally broke away from the top of the buttress onto a long corniced ridge that led to the traverse across the huge North Face and then on to the summit. Any relief here was short lived as I soon found myself in a nightmare of vertical crud, bad snow lying over bad ice. My arms were buried up to the hilt, my feet pedalling, and all the while I was conscious that Rich was probably asleep at the belay below in the darkness. I knew I didn't have the energy for this, but somehow the flame kept burning as I fought my way upwards.

It was way past midnight when I found a place big enough for us to lie down. We cut it out of the snowy ridge, working in slow motion until we had a space big enough. Even so, our feet hung over each side. We crawled into our frozen sleeping bags, boots and all, and lay shivering, too hungry to sleep, too tired to talk. I tried to find some relief by imagining myself soloing on gritstone on a fine summer afternoon, the smell of the heather, piecing those familiar moves together, the smooth stroking curve of the rock, and its texture.

I woke up to the sound of my Gore-Tex bivy bag flapping. Wind. I sat up. It was light, but the sky was grey and overcast, black clouds filled the valleys, wind and storm boiled over the highest mountains. I looked to the east, my heart racing, and saw a huge weather front coming out of Italy, just as one had on our last day on the Frendo. In our extended condition, a storm this high on a route could kill us easily, the wind putting us beyond rescue.

'Get up, Rich!' I shouted. 'Let's get the fuck out of here!'

We madly stuffed everything into our sacks and set off immediately, forgetting about such things as food and water as survival instinct suddenly took over.

Unseen by us, the ground had changed as we had climbed in the dark, the Spur kicking back to an easier angled ridge that could lead us to the top in a few hours. After so long on the route it was almost impossible to believe that such a place could even exist.

We moved as fast as we could, yet remained slow and methodical, aware we were so extended it would be easy to make a mistake and plunge back down the Face. We moved off the Spur onto the sweeping kilometre-high North Face, the steep ice making our calves burn. Halfway across a long traverse, Rich slumped down on his axes, his helmet pressed against the ice.

'I can't do it, I can't do it – I need some water,' he said.

For the first time since I'd met him he was showing weakness. Not knowing what else to do, I pulled the rope tight. The moment passed and Rich looked up at me, shook his head, then carried on again.

The summit was a trick. We had to keep going, and going. Maybe we had died days before and this was our vertical hell. Starving, thirsty, for us the climbing would never end.

I saw a strange piece of yellow ice. A hallucination? A piss stain! We had joined the regular North Face route. I turned and shouted the good news to Rich, who looked a little bemused, but I knew no climbers would take a piss until they felt they had time to stop and relax. The summit had to be close.

Up we climbed, ice giving way to deep snow, which in turn gave way to windslab that broke away and fell into the gloom, and then . . . nothing.

I collapsed onto the summit, dry heaving with pain. Rich

arrived grinning, full of a new-found energy, enough to get us both down. We shook hands and slapped each other's backs, then sat down and savoured the knowledge that there was no more 'up', only 'down'.

The Mont Blanc Massif stretched out all around us, panoramic-postcard perfect. Rich pointed out the Matterhorn in the distance, and said we should climb that next. We sat in silence. We knew we should get a move on and abseil down the other side of the mountain, in order to reach the glacier and the long walk to the hut, but we couldn't help waiting for a moment on this pyramid of snow. The Frendo Spur had meant so much to me, and I had thought about it every day since I had reached the top, but now my world had changed. This was my second route, but it was my first real summit. Ten metres below, I would have bet all I had that I would never climb another mountain in my life. Now all I could see was possibility all around me.

Inside the hut, I listened to the wind outside. Rich was having a nightmare beside me. It would soon be light.

Get down and ring her, tell her you are all right, tell her this is the last time you'll put her through the pain.

The phone rings, a stranger answers. After a while I get her to speak to me, but she seems stronger than before. She's changed.

I start to cry but she's made up her mind.

'No more, this was the last time.'

'Don't go, please,' I hear myself say, but she's gone . . .

I wake up with a start, shaken, heart beating fast. I've been dreaming again. The silhouette of the Grandes Jorasses has grown darker, it'll soon be dawn.

I lie back one more time and listen to the wind.

Black bites

Pitch 3 Reticent Wall

The storm raged all night.

I was alive.

I knew I could just as easily have been dead, hanging frozen on the end of my haul line.

I lay in my warm sleeping bag on my portaledge, the flysheet clamped down tight around it, listening to the hail rattling on its taut skin, knowing I'd been lucky.

In the morning I emerged like a mariner from his crow's nest. My home, now suspended from two bolts, was a shipwreck of storm-battered rigging, ropes, bags, hardware hanging from every portion of my camp, clipped on in haste last night. I found a food bag of bagels and cheese, climbed back into bed, and waited for the sun to take the post-storm chill out of the air.

From now on every night would be spent in this bed. My harness would stay on until I reached the top – slept in, climbed in, even worn on the toilet.

I ate a bagel and thought about how close I'd come to hypothermia the previous day. The reality was that I could have died.

I also thought about my past close calls – avalanches, falls, crevasses and falling rocks – and how each time, because the outcome was positive, the experience was simply shrugged off.

Perhaps what worried me was the fact that yesterday the outcome was black or white: either get back to the belay and live, or be stuck and die, first by losing all motor skills, then by swift hypothermia as my core temperature dropped until I lost consciousness. The significance of yesterday was not that it was any worse than other close calls, it was that it was experienced alone. I had been a victim of my own incompetence, but also my own saviour.

I had to start taking this more seriously, and that was best achieved by not wasting my mental energy or thoughts on useless doubts and fears. I had to keep a cool head and stay rational. I had perhaps two weeks of climbing left, and countless opportunities to make a mistake that could cost me my life. Next time I would probably not get a second chance.

The sun was getting close, so I sat up in my sleeping bag and started to warm-up my aching muscles. The tightness and stiffness in my back and biceps felt good, but it had been a long time since I'd felt so wasted. How would I feel a week down the line? Could my body and mind take it?

My fingertips were already looking pretty ragged, my fingernails scratched and sore around the edges. I wore fingerless leather gloves to protect my hands, but whatever you did your fingers always got hammered. I also had a few mosquito bites from my time in Camp 4, that had turned alarmingly black. I thought for a minute about blood poisoning, lying on my ledge slowly dying of septicaemia, waiting for a rescue that could take too long. I shook the vision from my head, knowing that fear of dying was almost worse than dying itself. If I got blood poisoning then I got blood poisoning. I'd worry about it if it happened.

I swung my legs over the edge of the ledge; the drop below was now over a thousand feet. I could see people moving around, carrying haul bags slowly up the trail to start other routes, oblivious to my presence.

I looked up and tried to spot the next belay. All I saw was seemingly blank rock, but I knew that somewhere up there I'd find bolts.

Bolts are 12-millimetre steel rods with a plate screwed into the end for a karabiner, and they provide islands of security in what can otherwise be a desert of fear and anxiety.

On any climb you have to trust that you, your partner, maybe even three or four of you, plus all your monstrous haul bags weighing hundreds of kilos, can hang solely from two steel rods no thicker or longer than your little finger. Such bolts gave the only security on a climb like this. They provided the comfort of knowing that although you could potentially fall and rip every piece of gear out, taking maybe a 400-foot whipper, at least the belay would hold.

The numbers of bolts drilled on a first ascent is often used as an indicator of how brave the first ascensionists were. Most climbers, running it out on terrible gear, and looking at a death fall, will eventually reach for the drill and place a bolt for protection mid-pitch, or place two bolts in order to make a belay and a shorter pitch. The Reticent has very few drilled holes, the belays are far apart, the team had pushed their skills and mental fortitude to the max. The result was pitches that went on seemingly forever, often longer than the length of a standard rope. The mental weight of the climbing built with every metre until the leader would be a gibbering wreck, praying to get to the bolts before his mind snapped.

The sun was only fifty feet away now, so I pulled on my shoes, being careful not to drop them. Next came my knee

pads, then my helmet and leather gloves, the material stiff with
cold until I flexed it back into life. I pulled myself up and stood
on the unsteady portaledge, the thin fabric holding me above
the void. I strapped on my chest harness, used to hold all my
gear, and began clipping on nuts, pegs, cams, hooks, copperheads, each one making me feel heavier and heavier. Next came
the ropes, tied to the belay I'd escaped from last night in the
storm, stacking them ready for the next pitch. Lastly I set about
dismantling my portaledge and stuffing my sleeping gear away
in my haul bags, each piece fitting into its own stuff bag, each
stuff bag stowed in its set place in the haul bag. Finally I was
ready to move.

The sun was now two hundred feet further down the wall.
It was already getting hot. I clipped in my jumars and started
up, back to the next belay where I'd haul up my bags and
begin the next pitch.

I still couldn't see the belay bolts.

My brain throbbed, my head felt as if it was on the boil. I
took the last sip of water from the bladder attached to my
back. It was hot. Grainy granite dust and sweat covered my
face, stinging my eyes and finding its way into my cut fingers
each time I tried to wipe it away. I could taste the wall and
my fear.

I'd been climbing for four hours; the wall was the blankest
section of rock I'd ever climbed, smooth and almost faultless.
The only way to progress was to follow a braille of tiny geological flaws: a scab of iron, a crystal standing proud, a fingernail edge, revealing themselves one at a time, more often than
not at the very limit of my reach. This route must have been
climbed by fucking giants!

I hung from a single hook, a few millimetres of hardened
steel clawed over a tiny crystal that stood proud of the wall.
The last piece of protection was several metres below; my rope
snaked in the wind down to its winking karabiner. If I messed
up here I'd be in for the biggest fall of my life. I'd be falling
into space. I wouldn't hit a thing. The thought brought little
comfort.

The hook was called a pointed Leeper, designed by a climber
called Ed Leeper back in the sixties and still one of the best

hooks around. I looked at it, and thought it amazing that all my weight could be held by such a small piece of folded steel. I knew Leeper had been a rocket scientist once, with climbing hardware as a sideline. This hook had been made by hand in his forge in Colorado. It was a work of minimalist art. On the scariest placements I would often repeat the words 'Leeper was a rocket scientist, Leeper was a rocket scientist', a mantra that for some reason seemed to help.

I'd hung from the hook for fifteen minutes, trying to find the next tiny hold, repeatedly stepping up high in my aiders, each time fearful I'd pull the Leeper hook off. The blanker the rock, the higher I had to step; the higher I stepped the more unbalanced and insecure I felt; the higher I went the bigger the chance I'd fall. I felt on the edge of control, tasting, hearing, feeling the drop below. Being so close to disaster was like falling itself, that stomach-lurching drop on a roller-coaster. I could feel the taunting pull of gravity.

I tried again, moving up the steps of the aider, one at a time, until the hook was at my knees. My sweaty hand fingered around for anything. My stomach muscles tensed as I held on to the hook with my other hand, every ounce of physical control used to avoid a slip.

There must be something.

My fingertip brushed an edge no bigger than the thickness of a tooth.

Too small. There must be something else.

Trying to stay calm and breathe evenly I felt around further, my body stretching out, looking for anything, a matchstick edge or matchstick flake.

Nothing.

I pulled up my other aider and clipped on a pointed Black Diamond hook, its tip filed sharp for the tiniest of edges. I clipped in a daisy chain and aider, stretched up and carefully placed it on the minuscule edge, trying to set it in the optimum position, difficult when I could only work blind by touch. The hook was placed and, careful not to disturb it, I crept back down on the aiders below and psyched myself up for the test.

You must calm down, be methodical, test the hook.

On hard aid, where falling has to be avoided, the only way to proceed with any degree of safety is to test everything. This

SKYHOOK

is a rule I live by. No matter how poor, no matter how fragile, everything must be tested. By testing everything with your body weight, giving it a little bounce, then a few harder shocks, you know that the piece can hold you – it's a psychological aid more than a physical one.

I eased my weight onto the Black Diamond hook in increments. Small jolts, slowly. My left hand held onto the Leeper hook below, my foot lifted off the aider by only a centimetre, ready in case the hook above popped.

I watched it flex, wobble, but hold. It defied all reason to hang on the edge. I rested back on the Leeper.

It must be the one.

I didn't want it to be the one. I thought about the other climbers who had passed this way, tried to imagine what they had felt and thought.

Were they as scared as me?

I looked down at the rope, flapping in updraught, the fear of the fall rising in my throat like sick.

It must be the one. You must test it one more time, then get on it.

I began testing again, counting out the number of jolts.

One.

Two.

Three.

My body shock loaded the hook with increasing force.

Four.

Five.

Six.

Seven.

I pulled hard. I wanted it to fail. I wanted an excuse not to trust it.

Eight.

Nine.

Ten.

The hook held.

Eleven . . .

PIIIIIIINNNNNNNGGGGGGG!

The hook sprang from the edge and smashed into my helmet, sending me back into the Leeper hook below. Instinctively I caught myself with my hand, slowing my impact onto the hook, my foot falling back onto the aider, with a jerk.

I was off!

I let out an involuntary yelp, but my mind was screaming.

The whooshing fall didn't come. I was hanging from the Leeper hook.

Calm down, you haven't fallen.

I clipped back into the hook and tried to pull myself together.

I thought about a friend who'd made lots of hard and scary rock climbs, and whose advice on how to overcome fear had been, 'Just imagine you're someone else.' This was the perfect time to find out if it helped. It didn't.

I pulled myself up and searched once more for a better edge or flake, stretching up as far as I dared. All I could find was the same tiny edge. My head hurt. I wanted it to be over.

Keep focused. Don't get sloppy. If you fall you'll only have to climb all the way back up and do all this again.

I blindly placed the Black Diamond hook once more, and began a second bout of testing. It held. I tested it again, counting the jolts out. Ten. Twenty. Thirty. Again and again, until I had no excuse.

There was no way back, I had to commit to the hook.

Go on.

Holding my breath I transferred across. It felt as if my heart was shaking.

Go on. Go on. Go on.

I accidentally caught the Leeper hook with my foot and saw it tumble off its perch.

I was now totally committed.

No going back.

I hung, unable to move, waiting tense, for the whooshing fall, feeling that any movement would disturb the fine balance of hook and steel. My whole weight and future were focused on one square millimetre. I couldn't imagine how it could be so strong, or the structure of granite be so resistant to my enormous and concentrated weight.

I hung there for ten minutes without moving, every second giving me hope.

You can't get any heavier than this.

With bomb-defusing slowness I began to move up the aider, feeling the nylon stretch and shift, my eye never leaving the hook's point, the fulcrum of all my hopes and fears.

On fire

Chamonix, France. January 1998

I crouched alone at the bergschrund and waited. Flicking the beam of my headtorch upwards I studied the wave of ice above me, and wondered how much it must weigh. It looked like an Arctic tsunami, just hanging. I looked down into the darkness and considered the gap I would have to jump before I could begin. I shivered. It was cold.

I sat on my rucksack and waited. The night was growing pale, the snow grey, the mountains around me developing slowly.

I looked down into the bergschrund and tried not to imagine what it would mean to fall down there, to be trapped between rock and ice, to be smothered by the snow that fell with me, arms and legs twisted and wrenched back.

No one knew I was here.

It wasn't good to think about death. Not now. I shivered again. I sunk my head down and shrugged my shoulders to warm me up, then watched the far summits begin to light like slow candles. This is it, I thought, it's time to go, it's time to do it.

I stood up. My legs felt tired. I hadn't even started yet. I flicked my torch upwards again, and was glad of the bergschrund's overhang. It hid the face above me. I felt utterly terrified.

I picked up my axes and slipped a spare into my harness in case one broke, then clipped in the trailing rope already uncoiled at my feet.

It was light enough now to turn off my headtorch.

It was light enough to start.
Everything was in place.
I thought about dying.
I thought about him.
I thought about him falling.

I first met Thierry one cold winter's morning high on the Dru Couloir. It had only been a few days since Rich and I had stumbled back to town after climbing the North East Spur of Les Droites. Now, although we were wasted, good conditions on one of the plum hard alpine ice routes had been too much of a draw.

Staying true to form we had been slow on the route, our bodies aching as soon as we'd set off through deep snow to the base of the climb, an 800-metre helter-skelter of hard blue ice that spiralled down the North Face. The Dru is one of the most iconic mountains in the world, a true skyscraper of rock that overhangs the village below, its plummeting faces devoid of easy lines or safe descents. To climb the Dru in winter is a true test of an alpinist's mettle, and the Dru Couloir, once hailed as the hardest ice route on the planet, a rare climb to come into condition.

As we left the warmth of the *téléphérique* station and went into the cold alpine night, I regretted my eagerness to return, missing the luxury of being back on the flat, not yet having washed away the hunger for food, warm baths, or nights spent without a harness on. My body stung with the cold, almost bewildered and disbelieving that I'd brought it back so soon. We climbed as a three, me, Rich and a friend called Steve Mayers. I remember thinking it was funny having Steve along, because, although he was in fact one of the UK's strongest and boldest rock climbers, he appeared to my inexperienced eye a novice. I was forgetting that this would be only my third alpine route if successful. It seemed slightly crazy to have made the big leap from nothing to the Frendo in winter, and then the even bigger leap to the North East Spur, and now this. I wondered if I had just been lucky. How had I managed to find the courage for such a scary and fraught learning curve? I viewed myself as weak both in body and mind, timid, useless, almost still a child, and yet, somehow, deep inside me something was driving me on. But what?

The climb had started with a race, a two-person French team appearing out of the pre-dawn as we neared the route's bergschrund, and overtaking us as Rich's bowels overtook him. Forced to climb a few pitches below, we had to deal with a shower of ice as they hacked their way up above. Then they slowed when they reached a barrier of overhanging rock that had to be aided. Once they had disappeared up over the fifty-metre wall I started up behind them, aiding up on rusty pegs which were shrunken by the cold, wobbling as I clipped in and crept on by. Rich and Steve were tied to the wall below me, eager for me to climb the pitch quickly and get up the route before nightfall.

The climbing was slow and scary, made all the harder by the fact that I chose to climb it with my rucksack and crampons on, rather than haul them up afterwards. My world shrank down to just the peg I was hanging on – and then the next, my heart in my mouth. I had only aid climbed a few times in a local quarry on wet-weather days, and although cheating – hanging off your protection rather than using fingers and toes – it seemed monumentally terrifying and strenuous.

Only a third of the way up the wall, my attention was suddenly drawn away from the peg I was lashed to, by the sounds of shouting from above, a panic shout, a warning, then a blood-curdling scream mixed with scraping rock, as if the mountain were grinding the climbers to death. Then I saw a body falling, mixed with rock. The body disappeared out of sight onto a ledge, but the rock carried on, straight at me. I was in the fall line, there was no way I could duck or even move, I was a dead man, my body about to be cloven in half by a spinning meteorite of granite. I looked up, knowing I was about to die, and was surprised at my reaction: not fear or anger, nor a lifetime passing before me, only a deep sense of sadness. Of loss. It was the same as I had felt when my father hadn't come home.

The rock slipped by, a degree or so saving me as I hung, and smashed down the gully below. The feeling passed.

We shouted to each other, myself, Rich and Steve, making sure we were OK, then shouted up at the French guys. All we could hear were groans.

'Get up there and see if they're OK,' shouted Rich.

I wanted to call it a day. My body and mind were in agreement that we'd pushed it far enough last week, and this was just taking the piss. Yet at the same time I knew I was in the middle of an epic, it was my duty to climb up and help these guys, and also, I hoped, climb the route.

On I went.

A few minutes later, the helicopter appeared and began making its way into the enclosed couloir.

The three of us sat on a tiny ledge, our feet stuffed in our rucksacks, tied off to the remains of the French climbers' ropes, left after their long and dangerous rescue. I slept and woke, and slept and woke, the space for my bum no bigger than a loaf of bread, only not so soft. The rescue had left us sitting at the top of the rock wall, the darkness of the North Face all around us complete, a black hole that sucked starlight and climbers deep within it.

When dawn came, so did Thierry.

He and his partner, living in Chamonix and not wanting to sleep out on a mountain when their beds were so close by, had chosen to climb through the night.

Shivering and tired after a horrible night out, I felt inadequate and embarrassed for being so British, for being so crap, as he mantled onto our ledge, cramponed past me with a grunt, clipped in, shouted for his partner to jumar, then began rolling a cigarette. I tried to smile, the stove balanced on my knee, brewing up a cup of tea, hoping to show that I may have been slow but at least I was having fun. But I expect he saw through my chapped grin. He just ignored me, no doubt cursing his bad luck for being held up by a bunch of bumbly Brits on a camping holiday. At the time I just dismissed him as yet another 'French climber', but, looking back later, I was impressed by his skill and motivation: he had climbed up in a few hours what had taken us all day. He had an efficiency and ease that I lacked. He was in his element, while I was out of my depth. I watched him, standing there in his one-piece Gore-Tex suit festooned with sponsors' badges, smoking. I think I was both jealous and inspired. I could see a fire burning inside him, a fire I wished I possessed, impelling him to succeed and powering him on to bigger and harder routes, whereas I was resigned

153

to climbing at my limit on pedestrian routes put up before I was born. I could see it in his eyes, he was driven, he was hungry for success and he approached his climbing as a professional. More importantly he believed he could do it. Maybe he could have learnt to play the guitar, joined a band and found what he was looking for, but instead he chose a pair of axes to carve himself a niche in the world.

His partner arrived, out of breath, carrying their single rucksack, and then they were gone, moving off our bed.

Packing up, we followed them, and as the day progressed and the climbing grew harder, we kept at their heels. At one section, they stopped to aid up another rock wall, and Steve overtook them, hooking his way up with his axes, running it out, while they stopped to place gear. I could feel an air of competition grow, the climb becoming a race. Near the top, they argued for us to let them pass, saying we were too slow and were holding them up. Behind the armour of Gore-Tex and youthful bravado, I could see they were now as concerned as us about this route and just wanted to get to the top, so we let them pass, our own pace slowing as ice crashed down from their axes and crampons. But as I watched him climb into the gloom, I felt that maybe I was at a turning point in my climbing, realising that all I had to do was believe that anything was possible – and of course it is. Hadn't this been proven by my climbs so far, which on paper were impossible for such a climber as me to pull off? Although I had so little confidence in myself, somehow, somewhere, there was belief.

As night fell once again, with the summit passed and abseiling now down the back of the Dru, I felt a warm stirring inside, a hunger.

A few months later I was asleep in the dirt of Camp 4. It was my first visit to Yosemite, in fact my first real climbing trip beyond the Alps. I was there with Paul Tattersall, who had recovered from his virus, and was keen to climb big walls. After my struggle on the aid pitch on the Dru Couloir, I had decided I wanted to learn all the skills necessary to climb the hardest routes – not just free climbing, but aiding, jumaring, hauling, everything I would need when I went back to the Alps.

That was my goal, this novice alpinist, to return and, in the space of three climbs, repeat the hardest winter routes.

Paul had climbed El Cap twice before, and I wondered at the time why he would go back with a novice, but I suspect he saw my wild ambition, and ignorance, as a sign that I had the right stuff to fulfil both our ambitions.

I woke to shouting, a French voice asking where his bread, butter and cheese had gone. His corner of the steel bear box, designed to protect food, was empty. I unzipped the tent and looked out at him, as he stood there furious, surrounded by sleepy climbers. A dirty climber told him a bear had run off with his food in the night, which in fact was true, as this man had been so drunk he had gone to bed leaving the bear box open.

'All is left is my coffee,' the Frenchman shouted.

'Aye mate,' he said, scratching his head. 'Bears don't drink coffee.'

I recognised the Frenchman immediately: it was Thierry.

We had arrived a few weeks before and, being ravenous to climb, wanting to squeeze the most out of my precious and expensive four weeks off from work, we started climbing immediately, making a five-day ascent of the Shield on El Cap, a 1,000-metre climb where each pitch was harder than the last. It was a perfect introduction when we really knew nothing about climbing big walls. Our first mistake was that our haul line was too short, with Paul being unable to get to the first belay as the rope twanged tight to the haul bags. Not wanting to fail for such an oversight, I tied on a length of rope we'd found at the base of the wall. Although this necessitated passing a knot every time we hauled, and gave us a few raised eyebrows when we passed other teams, it did allow us to continue. The next mistake was a lack of toilet roll, again remedied by scrounging a patch of gaffer tape found stuck to a sharp edge a few pitches higher. Although it was not ideal – the smooth side being far from absorbent, the sticky side being far too painful – Paul made do, and I just didn't go.

Our ambition was painful. The route had only been climbed once before without placing any pegs. We decided we would climb with a hammer.

Fiddling in bad wires where a stonking peg would go, and leapfrogging our precious cams where a solid peg could be hammered, we climbed for three days.

I could hardly believe I was actually on El Cap, hanging out on our portaledge, hauling, jumaring. We joked as we sat in the dark, tired and content, buzzing still with the day's climbing, that we were living the dream. We weren't. It was the first part of a nightmare.

On the fourth day we woke to a storm, and I started up the crux – the triple cracks – hoping we could get to the big ledge three pitches higher before it hit hard. The triple cracks, first climbed by Charlie Porter in 1972, were once hairline cracks that necessitated dozens of tiny RURP placements, each one going in no further than a fingernail. Now, decades later, these cracks were full of big holes that took big wide pegs, the tips sawn off so they fitted snugly against the wall. Without pegs, we were forced to make do with sky hooks and 'just in' cams, reaching up to clip old fixed gear, broken pegs, twisted nuts, and rusty copperheads. As I climbed my fear grew, the mind-bending drop sucking at my confidence. This section of the wall barrelled out, with nothing but air below for seven hundred metres. I moved with total concentration, aware that no matter how scared I became, this pitch was down to me, no one else. I had to climb it.

Then, halfway up, with virtually no gear clipped below me, I made a long reach for a tiny fixed copperhead, taking out the bombproof cam below me as I moved on up, in case I needed it again.

Hanging there, the rope whipping around in the storm below me, I suddenly felt something was wrong. My body suddenly flushed with cold, the hairs on my head stood on end. The wire of the copperhead, swagged together maybe decades ago in a tight alloy sheath, was slowly creeping apart under my weight. I froze with panic. The terror of the inevitability of my plummet was indescribable.

And then I fell.

It was the first big climbing fall of my life. And it was BIG. The fall was long enough for me to think: *Shit, I'm falling off a big wall!*

Then slowly, as if caught by the hand of a caring god, the

rope stretched out and I stopped, and looked into the eyes of Paul, tangled and shocked at my unexpected plummet from above.

'Pass me the pegs,' I said.

A few days after the bear box incident Thierry came up to me in the campsite while I was sorting some gear.

He was short and looked very French, with his sunglasses balanced in his hair. He asked if I could give him any information on the Shield, as he wanted to climb it hammerless. I asked him what else he wanted to do and he told me, 'I come to climb A5s.' I knew he didn't recognise me, but why should he? My face had been hidden by a balaclava on that occasion.

He stood a while and talked to Paul and me, told us how he had failed to climb the Moonflower Buttress on Mount Hunter in Alaska a few weeks before, after the death of another climber. I wondered if his failure in Alaska had caused some doubt in himself. How long can you believe everything is possible, how far can you push it? I could see that fire burning inside him though, as strong as ever, but this time I understood how he felt. I could feel the energy building in me as well.

The next time we met was at the base of Zenyatta Mondatta, a tough and dangerous El Cap route with a reputation. A soloist had fallen to his death a few months before when his rope had snapped when it had run over an edge. We had climbed the Pacific Ocean wall the week before, the route steep and hard, the climbing at our very limit. Once we'd reached the top, instead of thinking of getting down and eating pizza, of going home to Mandy, all I could think was 'What next?' We were both worn down, but even so I wanted to climb an A5 before we left, and so I'd talked Paul into it. One more route.

I sat belaying Paul on the first pitch, harder and more run out than anything on the Pacific Ocean Wall. Thierry walked up and began sorting out a tiny rack of half a dozen pegs, two hooks and three aliens, and lowered himself to ask me if it was 'enough for A5?' I said it was, knowing it wasn't. We sat and watched Paul, his fear of being on such hard rock, so close to the ground, passing down the rope to me.

'I've met you before,' I said to Thierry, my head craned up checking Paul's progress, 'on the Dru Couloir last winter.'

'Oh?' he said, looking surprised.

He asked me if I was going back to Chamonix that coming winter. When I answered yes, he asked me what routes I planned to climb. 'New ones,' I heard myself say, watching his expression. Then I went back to watching Paul.

When he reached the top, the longest lead of his life, he just looked down and said, 'Stick a fork in me and turn me over – I'm done, Andy.' And that was the end of my dream to climb my first A5.

I heard a few months later that Thierry had also failed to climb Zenyatta Mondatta – but had soloed the Shield instead.

That winter we met again. I was wandering around Chamonix, depressed after two failures in the mountains. I had had such hopes for that winter, but was now partnerless. Paul had come out to the Alps with the same dreams as me: big alpine winter walls, mixing winter climbing with big wall climbing on the biggest alpine faces. I knew we would be an unstoppable team, and had planned and trained all autumn. Berghaus had been impressed with our Yosemite trip and had sent us a big box of fleece and Gore-Tex for this winter expedition, thinking that we might in fact be able to climb something hard.

However, my dream quickly unravelled. Paul, the hardest person I knew, left after two weeks and two big failures, declaring alpine winter climbing 'too cold, too frightening and too expensive'. I was staying in a gîte with a bunch of climbers, but no one wanted to climb anything hard. The well-known Sheffield climber Andy Cave was staying there with his girl-friend Elaine, still recovering from his fraught ascent of Changabang a few months earlier on which his partner Brendan Murphy had been killed. Andy was famous for being an ex-miner who'd learned to climb during the miners' strike, and both Andy and Brendan had been heroes of mine since my Hitch and Hike days reading *Mountain Review* magazines. I'd expected Andy to be full-on, like me, ready for anything. But he wasn't; he seemed to be hesitant, stand-offish. I was disappointed, my obsession clouding my ability to see that this man's love of the cold, of high mountains, was crushed under the weight of the avalanche that had taken his friend.

One night, as I was complaining about my lack of success, someone asked if maybe it was because the routes I chose were too hard for me. I felt the words strike into my well-shielded heart, the thought that it might be true almost overwhelming the illusion of who I thought I was.

I bumped into Thierry in the street.

We shook hands coldly and each asked what the other had done. Both of us seemed to be at a loose end, maybe a bit down. The weather was bad: rain in the valley, and grey clag blocking out our dreams above. Nevertheless our fires were still smouldering. In that instant we could have planned to do a route together, we should have, we wanted the same thing, to climb hard routes, to stand out, to do something amazing. To amaze even ourselves. But we didn't. I didn't like him. He was competition. And so we wandered off with our own separate plans.

That night my inner fire got out of control as I tossed and turned in bed. Losing all rational thought, I got up and left the house early the next morning, leaving a simple note saying, 'Couldn't sleep. Gone to Chamonix, back tonight.'

It really began to burn as I waded to the bottom of the North Face of the Midi Plan a few hours later, towards the 600-metre ribbon of ice of Fil à Plom, an ice route to the left of the Frendo Spur. The fire was driving me forward, stoked by my recent inactivity. In the background, almost driven out by the white noise of my mind powering up, was a tiny rational voice asking what I was doing, and for whom I was doing it? I thought about Mandy, and about the chances of dying, but then I thought about those words, 'Are these climbs too hard for you?' The lack of belief in me hurt, both from the outside – teachers, bosses, friends – and, worse still, from inside. There was a shard of unhappiness in my heart that undermined everything I wanted to believe about myself. No matter what I did, no matter how good I felt, it would be there, bringing me down again. Now I would do something that would remove it for ever.

I began climbing.

Right axe. Left axe. Right crampon. Left crampon. Up I went. Metre by metre. Steeper and steeper. No rope to slow me up. No hope if I fell.

As I gained height, I noticed footsteps in the snow, leading off to another climb close by, and wondered if I wasn't alone. Then I turned my attention back to the ice.

I kept climbing, hoping that the higher I went the saner I would become, but it was only once I reached the top of that dark icy face, and collapsed into the sun, that I felt some peace and control return.

I sat there for a long time, one leg hanging down the face in shadow, the other in light, thinking hard about what I'd done, going through the motions of asking why, knowing I didn't need to ask. I thought about my father, always observant, telling me for the first time ever 'to be careful' before I left. Maybe he saw in me what I'd seen in Thierry.

A few hours later I was back in Chamonix, now walking tall and proud, feeling that maybe I was finally beginning to shake off the mediocrity that dogged my belief. The shard seemed to have gone. I felt the heat of the fire inside me, the possibilities that it opened up. I could do anything.

Walking down the street I kept an eye out for Thierry. Now I felt that we could do a route together. Maybe now I could accept I was more like him. In the Patagonia shop I overheard two people discussing an accident on the North Face of the Midi Plan, then as I left I watched a helicopter buzz the face. At the time I thought maybe someone was looking for me.

Two days later I stood below the North Face of the Droites.
Alone.

I looked at the face as the sun lit up the glacier, and both rocky buttresses of the North East Spur. We'd climbed it only a year ago, that vast ice field topped by a castle of granite. I thought back to looking at this face and imagining the impossible, of climbing it. I thought about Dick Turnbull telling me how he took two days to climb it in the 80s, and how Doug Scott had phoned to congratulate him. And here I was. Nothing but my axes and crampons, a helmet, a water bottle, a single rope to abseil down the back, a thousand metres of ice between me and the summit I had stood on a year ago.

I thought about what had brought me here.

I thought about what I could be about to lose.

I thought about what I could be about to gain.

I felt empty and lost. My fire had been extinguished the night before by a late telephone call from my friend Andy Parkin, an artist and climber who lived in Chamonix: 'By the way, did you know Thierry?' he'd asked. The word 'did' was enough to know he was gone. He'd fallen, alone, on the North Face of the Midi Plan.

Now I felt cold, crouched by the bergschrund, waiting for the right moment, savouring who I was, thinking that after this, whatever happened, I would never be the same.

I wondered if I really knew where the line was, if I could control the fire inside me, forgetting that just being here meant I knew neither. I didn't want this to be so complicated. I wanted to be in love. But it seemed to be something else. I wondered if I could be strong enough to climb this face and never tell a soul, to prove my motives were pure.

I took one more photo for my sponsors, and started climbing.

Expando

Pitch 4 Reticent Wall

The pitch began like all the rest – from the end of my bed, a shallow corner stretched up for several metres.

I stood on the edge of my portaledge and placed the first piece of the puzzle – a thin knifeblade peg. The peg slipped in easily, prising the rock apart with a dull thunk instead of its usual rising tone indicating solidity.

Expanding.

The crack was expanding – elastic. Any piece of gear placed in it prised it further apart, then it snapped back again once the gear was removed. This in itself was worrying enough, as it's a fine line between an expanding feature and a loose one, especially when the feature in question weighs several hundred tons and hangs, unstable, above your belay.

The problem with an expanding crack is that even if the first piece holds your weight, as soon as you begin tapping in the next piece, this will expand the rock further, causing the piece below to loosen its grip and rip out. It's not unknown for every placement to fail as the leader plummets down, snatching all the hard work out and often leaving a sole peg to show the high point.

The only technique to employ on such terrain is to clip yourself into the peg as you drive it home, hammering it in as fast as you can so that the moment the peg you're standing on rips, the peg above may hold. This of course isn't rocket science, but is rather a terrifying ordeal of nerve and concentration. Climbers push both the limits of protection and their own mental stamina. It is without doubt the most terrifying technique employed in big-wall climbing. It was all I could do, however.

I stepped up on the first peg, clipping the eye of the peg to my harness, which allowed me to stretch up as high as I could to place the next peg. This I tapped in slowly at first. Then, clipping it into my harness, I tapped it in faster, feeling the peg I was on shift with each blow. They both held and so I crept on up.

As I pegged my way up the crack, my heart was in my mouth. I tried to make every placement, every movement, perfect, yet I felt that at any moment I could fall, knowing that nothing would hold me if I did. I would smash into my haul bags and ledge, then carry on down an equal distance below. Apart from the chance of breaking or spraining something in such a fall, this wasn't so bad as the whole flake ripping off with me. If this happened, that would be it.

I carried on. Tap . . . Tap . . . Tap. Each blow was designed to get the peg to stick, but without causing any tremors which would disturb the pegs below. Once I felt I was getting close to a good fit I would step up the tempo, stopping the moment I thought it would hold me. My hands tingled with fright, and my head began to thump as I climbed, knowing I was hammering on the brink of disaster with each blow.

On I went.

I stopped repeatedly and tried to calm my nerves.

An hour had passed since I'd set off, but time meant nothing. Everything was an irrelevance apart from each placement, a lifetime's worth of worry and contemplation spent on each one, each forgotten in an instant as soon as I moved on.

Finally, I came to the top of the crack where it pinched down and became part of the wall itself, the peg I placed there singing a rising song of security and life as I struck it hard with my hammer until it wouldn't go in another millimetre. The feeling of safety that washed through me was indescribable.

I clipped into the peg and looked for the next feature to climb.

Surely that had been the hard part of the pitch?

The wall above seemed blank, apart for a loose fin of exfoliating granite, seemingly stuck to the wall to my right. This was six feet long, finger-like and only a finger's thickness. It was terrifying to look at, defying gravity. Any climbers would steer clear of it, knowing that, if they touched it, it would instantly break away and crash down.

The climbing below had only been a warm-up. This was the next piece of the puzzle. I had to climb out along the flake.

I tapped it with my finger. It moved.

I tapped it with my hammer. It made a sound like a giant cup being set down on a saucer.

It only seemed to be attached at my end, the rest being totally detached. It was insane to climb onto it. It was impossibly dangerous. There was no way I could do it.

But I knew there was, because other climbers had thought the same, yet carried on and it had held them.

You have no choice. It's the only way.

I thought about the people I knew who had lost fingers when such flakes broke off; an image of four pink tips sitting on a ledge came into my mind. If it broke it would be more than fingers I would lose.

I tried to think more positively. The flake had hung here for ten thousand years, through winter cold and summer heat, earthquake and continental drift.

It will hold you.

I unclipped my sky hooks and carefully placed one on the flake, the steel scraping on granite making me feel sick, sounding like fingernails on a blackboard. I crept onto the hook, and stood there, proving to myself it could hold me.

It did.

I placed my second hook further out, clipped in my aider and moved over onto it, trying to transfer my weight as lightly as possible.

My skin tingled with fear again. Goosebumps rose along my arms as cold sweat crept up my spine. This was the most stupid thing I had ever done.

I pulled the first hook off, moved it over, and placed it and the aider on the flake.

What are you doing?

Go back.

I stood between both hooks. The flake was perched directly above my belay below. If it broke it would sail down and chop clean through my ropes. We would fall together, a thousand feet, to the talus and trees below.

Go back!

I *wanted* to go back. It was *all* I wanted right then.

Please don't break, please don't break, please don't break, I muttered, but I knew that this was not a place for prayers, only movement.

Go on. Go back.

I had never been as terrified.

My legs began to tremble, shaking so much I thought I would dislodge the flake. I had the peculiar feeling of tunnel vision as the world began to turn grey, then grow black at its edges.

I wanted to go back more than I'd ever wanted to do anything in my life, but I knew the fear came from the knowledge that I wouldn't.

I moved over and stepped onto the hook.

Fly or Die

Yosemite, USA. September 1998

I devoured books on climbers and their epics, wanting to know what made them tick, and more importantly what skills they had that brought them back from the brink. My days sat reading *Mountain Review* magazine while working in climbing shops had left me with many heroes, but one that stood out was a climber named Andy Perkins, a northern climber who always seemed to be pushing the limits. He climbed hard on rock, ice and in the mountains, from the Alps to the Himalaya, Patagonia to Yosemite. I'd seen him on the crag a few times, always looking strong and in control, his body and demeanour unlike most climbers, neither lithe nor athletic, but more akin to a tight knot.

The first time I actually got to talk to Andy was in North Wales, on a training trip out from the shop. Andy worked for a climbing company called Troll, a manufacturer near Oldham. Paul Tattersall and I had travelled over the night before we were due to meet up with Andy and the rest of the staff, wanting to get some bivy practice on the thousand-foot face of Llwidd on the flanks of Snowdon. We'd driven over after work and arrived at the car park late that night, Paul's tiny Bedford Rascal van buffeted by the wind, the snow racing through his headlights, barely lighting up the lonely patch of hillside in front of us. It would have been easy just to head down to the valley, go to the warm pub and camp, rather than head out into the storm to climb and shiver the night away in a damp sleeping bag on the side of a rock face. But we didn't, and that's why Paul was always a great partner. He was as stupidly keen as me. Life was too short for soft options.

We set off, our plastic boots scuffing up the snowy path, arriving at the bottom of the face around midnight, and started climbing, keen to get to our beds. The ground was fairly easy, snow and frozen springy turf and grass into which axes could be thunked, but there had been no protection, so we kept climbing, hoping to find a nice ledge to sit on round the corner. But none came.

On we climbed until about one in the morning, when all of a sudden, and with combined surprise, relief and disappointment, we found ourselves looking down the other side of the mountain. Forgoing a mountaintop bivy we stumbled down instead, soaked and tired, and slept among the bins in the car park.

We arrived in the cafe only a few hours later, where everyone was waiting, Andy sat with the rest of the Outside staff drinking tea and working out what to do on such a foul day. Most of the people I worked with weren't interested in mountains, and no doubt we looked quite comical wandering in late, still drenched after our night-time jaunt.

We all sat and talked about climbing, excited to be out of the shop, going climbing yet still being paid. The usual climbing stories were told as tea was drunk, Paul and I sitting next to the gas heater trying to dry ourselves before getting wet again. Andy didn't say much. I studied him, his giant forearms folded, his face crinkled and lined by what I imagined were years of facing up to starlight and storm, looking more like a salty sea dog than a climber with his black beard and streaked hair.

Then in a quiet moment in the conversation Andy spoke. 'What's the biggest fall any of you have ever taken?'

The question silenced the room. Someone said he'd once taken a huge lob with just the rope tied around his waist and had pissed blood for days, and a few others had some small fall stories of half a rope length. 'Well . . . I once fell five hundred feet' said Andy.

'Did you survive?' I asked; everyone laughing and somewhat defusing the tension Andy had just built up.

Ignoring me, Andy went on. 'We were climbing on Creag Meagaidh, on a grade 5 ice route and my partner was climbing above me, with a snow belay. All of a sudden he fell off.' The room was quiet now. 'He fell past me and I knew I had to reduce the load on the belay, so I let the rope slip through my hands, hoping I could slow him down before his weight came onto me.' I tried to imagine what it must feel like to know you're about to die, how you could have the mental control not to just freeze and let it happen.

'And then I was ripped off the belay.'

Andy described how they had plummeted down the face, over steep bulges of ice and near-vertical snow, until with two thuds they landed at the bottom.

'We were both pretty smashed up,' said Andy, straightening. 'My mate got an ice axe stuck in his chest, and I injured my ankle, but we were very, very lucky.'

The training had been great, with Andy limping around to remind us of the story, showing us the ropes, the whole shop thrutching its way up a snow-covered crag. Andy seemed to have a very professional approach to climbing; he was solid, which was perhaps how he'd survived the close calls that go with his kind of climbing. Only the year before he'd been climbing a hard route on El Cap called Sunkist, when he and his Norwegian partner had been trapped in a storm for several days, ice-cold waterfalls striking their tent directly, bringing them close to hypothermia. They had only survived by getting into the same sleeping bag for two days until a rope could be lowered to them and they could jumar out.

On the last night of the training we had a slide show by a sponsored Troll climber called Adam Wainwright, who gave us a talk about climbing a route on El Cap called Aurora with two top American climbers. The route had been put up in 1981 and graded A5, and was the hardest climbed by a Brit at the time. I found it hard to imagine climbing anything that long and difficult, listening to him describe ladders of copper heads stretching into space, tiny hooks gripping fractured crystals, and the never-ending fear of the drop.

Then Andy gave a slide show about his near ascent of Cerro Kishtwar in India in 1991, with Brendan Murphy – days with minimal food, equipment failure, going to the edge, and just getting back again. I was in awe of anyone who could combine all the climbing skills, rock, ice and mixed climbing, then project it onto a big wall, in the Himalayas, and push on for days and days. I think that night I decided that of all my heroes,

I most wanted to be like Andy. I wanted to devote my life to climbing wild big walls.

A few years passed, and on my return from Yosemite and then the Alps, I began to send Andy some feedback on Troll gear I had been using, though it was probably more like pestering a hero then actually doing anything of any value. After soloing the North Face of the Droites I sent him an email about the climb, and how I'd done it in six hours, but misquoted the route's height as 10,000 metres rather than 1,000, to which Andy responded, 'You must be a very fast climber, youth.'

I began planning for a return trip to Yosemite that year, and was looking for a partner as Paul had moved to the far north of Scotland. At the time you could probably count on one hand the number of climbers in the UK who were up for hard big walls and so when I heard Andy was also planning to visit the valley, somehow our plans converged and we ended up going together.

To meet your climbing heroes is one thing, and to climb with them another, but to climb with them on El Cap is something else altogether. With Paul it was always so easy. Even though Paul is a phenomenal climber, we just kind of wrote each other off as being crap and useless and took it from there. We could only get better. With Andy I felt he had an image to keep, he was a solid and competent climber, very old-school in some ways, not quick to show weakness or incompetence, whereas weakness and incompetence seemed second nature to me. I found this hard to begin with, and felt very much the apprentice, but as such I was keen to learn everything I could about climbing from Andy.

Things didn't start well. Andy rang me on the Wednesday night to ask if I was packed. I replied I hadn't started yet, believing we were flying Friday morning from Manchester, only to discover we were flying the following morning. I was fitting a parquet floor in our new house while Mandy was away on holiday. I hated DIY, believing that it stood for 'don't involve yourself'. I was suddenly forced to pack and finish the job. My haul bags, when emptied a few days later in the dirt of Camp 4, contained dozens of pieces of wood parquet, with glue sticking everything together. Several pieces ended up stuffed in cracks on the wall, no doubt confusing many of the climbers that followed.

Sitting sorting gear in Camp 4, we realised that we'd forgotten to bring a 'shit-tube' for the wall, and started asking around if anyone knew where we could get one. The Camp 4 camper is either a climber, a walker or a nut, and as it happened we ended up sharing our site with one of the latter, who appeared to be a Vietnam vet who was into survivalism. He had no tent and chose instead to set out all his gear on a tarp beside our picnic table; knives, bed roll, camo clothing, more knives. He had a hard time understanding our northern accents, but when Andy asked if he knew anything about 'shit-tubes', he quickly departed, asking us to keep an eye on his gear as he scuttled into the woods.

Eventually a guy rode up on a bike with the unlikely line 'Hey dudes, I hear you're looking for a pipe bomb?' He produced what looked like a well-used piece of white plastic pipe for us. 'Be careful though, dudes,' he said, as he passed it over. 'It's still loaded.'

Unscrewing the cap on one end, we found it was indeed still 'loaded', the stench of the contents enough to make you want to turn and run. I came up with a plan, and boiling a pan of water, Andy poured this in while I held the tube at arm's length. Sticking the cap back on, and still holding it as a man holds a shitting baby, I gave it a big shake to dislodge the contents.

BANG. The end shot off, and a long spume of brown water and paper shot out of the tube, turning to a cloud of vapour that descended, to our horror, down onto the survivalist's neatly arranged tarp, covering all his gear.

We decided it was time to get on the wall.

The route we chose, Iron Hawk, was a jump up for both of us. The first section had a bad reputation for looseness, and Paul and I had tried it the previous year, but had got lost, confused and a little scared by the black, intimidating lower half. Yet again things didn't go quite to plan. The black diorite was a magnet for the hot Californian sun, reflecting off it in waves, the heat hitting us both back and front. Andy started acting a bit oddly in the heat, his black helmet contributing to his overall heat exposure. He flaked out under the only tree on El Cap, aptly named 'El Cap tree', while I led the lower crux. It was obvious that Andy had heat stroke, but although I was worried he might pass out while holding my ropes, my full attention was on the climbing. The pitch was a horror show of loose blocks and shifting flakes, danger everywhere you looked or touched. I felt as if I was making my way up an earthquake-wrecked tower block: pull on the wrong hold and the whole lot could come down. The only way to progress was by a combination of free climbing and skyhooking, as only by touch and feel, testing each hold, could I be sure that it was safe to move up. Cracks split off everywhere, but there was little in the way of protection. I eyed each fracture with suspicion – a sign of weakness rather than a place to stuff in a piece of protection. It was a hard choice, but it seemed better to risk a clean fall onto the jagged ledge where Andy lay than to yank the mess of rock down with me. Put simply, there could be no falling. I moved up slowly towards a big roof, the way blocked by a giant flake the size of a car. I assumed that such a feature must be well attached to the wall, otherwise it would have fallen off long ago, so nothing I could do could possibly dislodge it. I began placing cams, one above the other, and moved up, conscious that my rope was running underneath the flake, and if it were to fall, that would be it.

Halfway up I reached high and, retracting the lobes of the cam attached to my daisy chain, I set it in the space between the wall and the flake and began to transfer my weight.

The moment I did, I knew something was wrong. I looked up and saw the cam: its four curved opposing alloy lobes, instead of locking in tight and solid, were instead slowly creeping open. My weight was prising the flake off the wall. Before I could react, there came a low groan that seemed to start deep within El Cap itself and travel out towards me. It sounded ancient, like a two-hundred-year-old oak tree fighting gravity in its final death throes. The flake, which had hung here for perhaps a million years, was about to fall, unlocked from the wall by my cam.

Trembling, I grabbed for the piece below and swung down onto it.

The groaning slowed. Then stopped. The monster fell back under the sleeping spell of time.

I clung to the lower cam, feeling like I was perched on a swaying wooden ladder.

I began shaking uncontrollably, hardly believing I was safe. It was too close. I could have called it a day but instead I shouted for Andy to send up our cheater stick, a long length of tent pole used to navigate past sections of blank rock; and gaining control of myself I reached up with it and bypassed the flake.

A few years later this whole feature broke off, chopping the ropes of the leader to pieces, and smashing inches from the belayer. Incredibly they both survived.

As I climbed up to the roof and clipped an old and rusty set of bolts, my clothes drenched with both the sweat of the climb and the sweat of absolute fear, I wondered what I had let myself in for, and if I were ready to climb in the premier league.

All I knew was that this was a dream that couldn't be dashed by fear. I had to reach deep and find the strength that my heroes had obviously found before.

The route had been named Iron Hawk for two big roofs that split the wall higher up, set like the spread wings of a hawk, and for several days we inched up it. I felt that not dying the previous day had been a big success, and maybe finding Andy ill with heatstroke made me see him as just as human as me, so we began climbing more as equals. There was no division of labour based on competence, the pitches alternated one after the other. It felt great to be back on El Cap, and in many ways I was more comfortable than Andy. Of course he'd almost died there, something apparent by the way he eyed every cloud that passed.

The worst thing about Andy to my eyes was his bowel control. He would have to have a crap once a day, whereas I would go once a week. He seemed to have the knack of being able to drop his trousers and evacuate his bowels at a moment's notice, something he put down to his years of practice with 'Delhi Belly'. He told me a story about getting food poisoning on Changabang, and that his explosive diarrhoea had projected thirty feet down the face, which I assumed was some kind of record. The worst thing about Andy's toiletry habits was he would go the moment he'd finished his food, and the moment I'd start mine. For breakfast we had a big tin of fruit to share, and every day he would eat his half, then in the same motion as he passed the tin to me, pull out a paper bag, pull down his pants, and have a dump. It's not surprising that more often than not I would lose my appetite, the sight, smell and sound unconducive to keeping a mouth full of pineapple and grapes. 'Not eating, youth?' Andy would usually say, taking the tin back off me as, in one motion, he stuffed the paper bag into the now full shit-tube.

On the last evening, we reached the route's only platform and, putting up our portaledge, we sat looking at the sunset. We were both content with what we had done, climbing a hard route with little fuss and no epics or falls, well, that is apart from the death flake. Andy had been good company, and I thought it amazing that I was there with him and, what was more, that I felt his equal on the route. How far I had travelled from the day at a trade show where I was too intimidated even to talk to him. Andy was a great climber, but I wondered how different he was from me.

We got back down to Camp 4 the following night, and met up with a friend of Andy's called Ian Parnell, a relative newcomer to big walling, but already well known as a hard climber. It was a relief to be safe, sat around the picnic table, bullshitting, all the time keeping one eye and one nostril out for the survivalist . . . 'What do you fancy doing next, youth?' asked Andy.

'Why don't we team up and do another wall? I replied. 'Only this time let's try something much much harder.'

The flake groaned like an old man.

I froze as I had the last four times I'd tried to weight it. I stepped back down quickly on a birdbeak, the dirt that had spilled out from behind it clogging up my sweaty eyes, sticking to me in the dark, and to my trembling hands. I felt like a prisoner of war trying to dig his way out of a collapsing prison-camp tunnel. If the flake, the size of a door, broke off, I was dead. I couldn't believe I was wrestling with yet another expanding flake.

'The flake's expanding,' I shouted down into the night, my words travelling along the rope to my two partners thirty metres below with no interruption from solid gear, only tiny pegs and heads. 'I think I might have to free-climb around it,' I shouted again, the words 'OK' coming back up. I knew they didn't really care. They just wanted me to get a move on so they could find a place to sleep.

I began to unclip myself from my aiders and gear, one at a time, methodically, psyching myself up, preparing to launch myself onto the rock with only my hands and feet to hold me there. I wished I had my sticky climbing boots on, not my trainers. I began sorting out my rack, clipping what I wouldn't need to my last piece of gear, reducing my weight, and so the strain on my arms. Finally I rubbed the dirt off my headtorch, then my hands, the grime smearing onto my grubby shorts.

'OK, watch me here,' I shouted, again knowing that they didn't care, imagining them both sitting below on the portaledge, chatting and wondering what the fuss was all about.

I placed my toe out on a small dish-shaped hold to the left of the flake, and grasping its thick edge, I pulled up, my fear increasing the moment my right foot left the security of the sling I had stood in for nearly half an hour, trying to avoid the very thing I was now doing.

I moved my left foot up a few inches, then shuffled my hands one at a time, laying away on the flake like a man climbing a drainpipe. I knew at any moment I could pop off, one foot slip, one greasy hand sliding from the rounded granite flake. But there was no way I could, and so I wouldn't. If I fell, that was it. The idea was unthinkable.

Up I moved, groaning, panting, glad of the dark that hid the drop. Above me, one or two feet higher I could see a slot between the flake and the wall, a place to jam in a cam and rest, out of the danger zone where the flake could break off.

Hanging one-handed, my forearm burning, I fumbled with my tangled cams, searching for the one with the blue sling, but in the yellow light of my headtorch they all looked the same. Almost spent, I just grabbed the one that looked good enough, stuffed it into the crack and, close to puking, clipped in and sagged down onto it.

I wondered why I hadn't just backed off and let someone else try this.

Then the flake broke and we both fell into the dark.

I fell and fell and fell. Everything was black. Black and heavy, the flake pressing on me as we dropped down the wall. I felt no tug from my protection as we dropped, the rope probably cut as the flake sheared.

My brain was numb, totally accepting my fate.

Then the rope began to pull, elastic, still there, my lifeline, pulling hard. I began to slow. The flake slipped away and we parted in space, and I sensed it fall five hundred metres until a delayed boom let me know it was dead and I was still alive.

I was still alive.

Andy began shouting. 'Are you all right, youth?'

I checked that my fingers were still intact, then my limbs, then my face, the only wound a hole in my shoulder. 'Yes,' I shouted back, slowly spinning in space.

'Check your rope isn't cut,' he shouted.

I scanned up, but knew that if it had been, it would have snapped.

'I'm going to jumar back up the rope,' I said, unclipping all the karabiners which had slid down the rope from the gear that had been ripped out. 'I'm going to try and finish the pitch,' I said, suddenly feeling invulnerable, adrenaline shooting through me.

Up I went to my high point, a single rusty rivet. It seemed incredible it had held. There was no gear after it. My life had been saved by an old bolt, probably one found on the floor of a garage.

I began hammering the gear back in, moving up, repeating what I had done, until I reached the scar where the flake had been. Instead of granite, there was now a dirty patch, into which I hammered tiny birdbeaks, forcing them straight into the spongy rock. One, two, three, four beaks saw me to the top of the fracture. I hung from a skyhook and suddenly felt very tired. I felt as if I were melting. I clipped the rope into the hook, even though I knew it would topple off as soon as I stepped off it, and placed a peg above, the steel blade sliding in a few inches until it stopped. I tied it off short, and clipping my rope to it, then attaching my haul line, abseiled down to the portaledge. The rest could wait for tomorrow.

I woke in the morning, and my first thought was of having to go back up and finish the pitch I'd fallen from. My night-time adrenalin was over, and all I could think about as I ate my bagel for breakfast was jumaring back up the rope that hung in space. Perhaps, if I'd been braver, I would just have asked someone else to do it, after all I had nearly died up there. But putting on my gear, it seemed easier just to get on with it, after all if someone asked me to swap I probably would have said no. This was my lead. The haul line hung way out in space, and it made my stomach lurch as I pulled it in tight and attached my jumars. Andy was quiet. I suddenly wished I'd set a better anchor above, rather than a single tied-off-peg.

The sense of vertigo was instantaneous the moment my bum left the edge of the portaledge, inching out into space as Andy let out the rope, the overhanging wall putting far out of reach the illusory safety of being able to touch the rock. I thought about what would happen if the belay above failed, how each piece would unzip below it, and I'd fall, the shock on my jumars cutting into my single lifeline.

Then the belay ripped out.

I was falling. My stomach did a roller coaster flip.

Then I stopped.

A peg zinged past. My belay.

Every molecule of my being attempted the impossible, to weigh nothing as I tried to work out what had happened.

I hung on the rope trying to work out why I wasn't dead yet.

The rope stretched up out of sight. All I could think of was the rope had been held by one of the birdbeaks I'd placed in the flake scar the previous night.

I worked out my options. If Andy or Ian pulled me back to the portaledge he would put further strain on whatever had held me and it could fail. I could hang here and wait to be rescued, but that would be a long wait. Or I could just climb the rope, the most scary option, but also the most promising one.

'OK Andy,' I said, trying to hide my fear, my voice cracking, 'I'm going to jumar up slowly.'

The choice in the end was easy. I would either make it or fall.

Feeling like a man defusing a bomb, I inched my jumars up the rope, trying to minimise every gram of extra strain on the rope.

As I climbed the wall grew closer and closer, until I could touch it, something that brought a strange comfort considering there was nothing to hold on to. I said a little prayer, and asked almighty El Cap to spare me.

On I went, my boots now scuffing against the rock, scared to look up and see what held me to the world.

I moved over a small roof and saw it. A single small flexing skyhook wrapped over a flake no bigger than a biscuit, the one I'd clipped my rope into for some reason the previous night.

I reached the hook and clipped in, then set about preparing myself to finish this difficult pitch.

As I clipped my karabiners and hardware to my harness I felt a sense of shock at what had just taken place. Where had I found that courage? Would I ever have imagined myself so brave? It was as if I was someone else, someone much stronger than me, someone I'd give anything to be.

I started climbing.

On the final day on the wall I led the crux of the route as the sun came up, a pitch named 'Fly or Die' by the first ascensionists, a bulging barrier to the summit split only by a copperheading seam. As I set off, moving slowly and milking everything I had learnt so far, I thought about my chances. The pitch had gained its name after the leader shouted down that if he fell he would have to 'fly or die', any mistake sending him splashing onto a hanging slab beneath. I thought about how I had come so close to dying at least three times in the last two weeks, half a dozen times this year, maybe twenty times in the last five. All these epics meant so much to me, but I wondered how long it would be until it wasn't me telling the story and I was the story itself.

But as I moved on, the wall and the sun at my heels, I felt no fear at all, only an immense joy at being in such a position, the exhilaration of my life in that moment burning through the fear of a death that could perhaps come to me at any moment.

For Emily

Pitch 5 Reticent Wall

I brought up the second bag slowly, my thighs and waist bruised after a week of hauling, my fingertips ragged and my feet throbbing. I noticed that I was moaning involuntarily each time I squatted. I was knackered, exhausted, wiped out, but happy that another day, another pitch was over.

Only nine more to go.

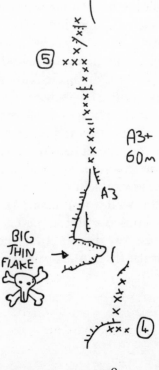

The day had started a little sombrely. I'd woken and my first thought had been to wonder if I'd be alive at the end of it. This had been nothing more than a simple question, like 'I wonder what I should have for breakfast,' or 'Should I have a shower?' I'd noted the night before that on the topo a flake on the next pitch was marked with a skull and crossbones. After the flake on pitch four I had doubted I could handle anything worse. In the end, however, it had gone by with little fuss. I wondered if I were becoming braver, or maybe one can only have so much fear and I'd used my ration the day before.

I thought it was strange how I could become so accepting of danger and of dying. It reminded me of a story about Evel Knievel and his attempt to jump thirteen London buses at Wembley Stadium. The moment he arrived on his bike, high on the ramp that shot down towards the pitch where the buses were all lined up, he knew he wouldn't make it. When asked why he did it anyway, his reply was, 'What else could I do?.' Knievel crashed, breaking his pelvis.

One thing was certain: I was no Evel Knievel. I had never been so scared on a climb. This was probably caused partly by the fact that I was alone, with no one else to bolster my darker moods or share the fear of leading, and more importantly that this WAS one of the most scary climbs anyone could choose to do.

How was it that I could continue on against so much fear? The route seemed to be growing harder by the day. Perhaps that was why. Perhaps each pitch overcome made it possible to plough on to the next one. After all, hadn't the first pitch seemed impossible? Hadn't so many moves seemed beyond me, yet each time I had found myself beyond *them*?

This had always been the problem with me and Mandy. She was normal. She wouldn't and couldn't accept the fact that the thing you loved could be the thing that killed you. She knew me better than anyone, and knew that the harder I climbed, the harder I would want to climb, so she feared that one day I wouldn't come back. Every year we would come to the brink of splitting up. I wanted the guilt-free life of having no one else's worry, to be free to climb what I wanted, not to negotiate for time away as if she was my boss. She wanted a normal husband, a teacher, a lawyer, someone who washed their car and looked forward to city mini-breaks and holidays on the beach. She wanted a normal life and what I wanted was abnormal. Yet each time, when it came to it, we stayed together. We had met when we were kids. We didn't know anything else than each other.

But now I was a dad, I had a job I had to do to pay my mortgage, I was soon to be thirty, and another child was on the way. My climbing partners were moving on – months away in the Himalayas; training to be mountain guides in the Alps – while I sold boots and sat on the beach in Scarborough every weekend. This climb scared me, but not as much as knowing I'd made the wrong choices and lost a better life for all of us.

Are you so scared to face up to what you really want that you'd kill yourself up here?

The sun was low in the sky by the time I'd hauled up the last bag, clipping it to the belay, and backing it up with its haul line to a second karabiner. I was mindful of the story of the three climbers who died when their haul bag came unclipped and, falling to the end of the rope, broke their belay, sending them tumbling down the wall for thousands of feet. A friend who had been on El Cap at the time described how he'd heard a loud noise and seen objects falling down the wall, only realising what they were when he saw arms and legs flailing. Then he heard the sound of them and their bags hitting the ground.

Remembering stories like this kept you alive and on your toes.

I reached down under the haul bag and unclipped my portaledge. I was desperate to flake out. Once the ledge was set up, I lay down and just let the fabric take my weight for a minute, my body relaxing. Then I sat up and took off shoes, gloves and knee pads, clipping them to the edge of the ledge for the morning. Next I slipped off the leg loops of my harness, to let some fresh air get to my thighs. This meant I was only attached by the waist belt, which would reduce the amount of time I could hang before blacking out if I were to fall off the ledge, but I knew I was safe enough: this kind of exposure was no worse to me now than sitting on the top deck of a bus.

I pulled on my fleece, and took a wet wipe from my first-aid stuff-sack to clean my hands and face where the grime was thick and black. My skin felt good, the breeze blowing its dampness dry.

My eyes were heavy with fatigue, but I pulled out my food bag and rummaged around for a can of Coke and an apple, then sat with my legs hanging over the edge, my back against El Cap.

The evening is always the best time on a wall. The climbing is over for the day. Wounds can be licked and food shovelled down. Tomorrow is too far away to consider. There is only the relief of making it to the now. Appreciation of the moment is one of the best aspects of climbing, something that I find missing from normal life, with its countless worries. On a wall there are no thoughts of savings, promotions or pensions. Your future only stretches as far as the next two shiny bolts at the belay above.

I knew I should have a crap, as I'd not gone since leaving Lay Lady Ledge, but the thought was too grim. I always found it hard taking a dump on a portaledge. I remember Andy Perkins telling me that you should practise having a crap in a paper bag at home before going on a big wall 'because although you may think you know where your asshole is, you don't till you've crapped into a bag.'

It could wait. Using all my will power, I leaned over the edge of the portaledge and pulled up the bags that contained my evening meals, finding a bagel and some cheese, too tired to eat anything else. Lastly I found my Walkman in its stuff sack and clipped it to the suspension of my portaledge, to listen while I munched away.

I had set off with about twenty tapes, but unfortunately, on the first day, a tube of sun-cream had exploded in the bag and destroyed every tape apart from one: Simon and Garfunkel's 'Bridge over Troubled Water' – not my first choice of album for such a climb. In fact I had no idea where it had come from – but I was glad of it.

Usually, on a wall, upbeat music works best, making you believe for half an hour that it's the soundtrack to your epic, a drummer boy's beat during battle. Nevertheless, Simon and Garfunkel were good company. My only company. As the sun set, I pressed Play.

Music always sounds amazing on the wall. Combined with exhaustion and adrenaline it enhances your senses. I can hear things I have never heard before, notice subtle notes and key changes, back beats and melodies I have never appreciated. Most of all the music is a welcome escape for a little while.

I lay on my ledge in the dark, bats swooping around me, listening to the gentle harmonies. I felt like a character in one of the songs, strung out and heart-broken, the loneliest man on El Cap. I looked up at the stars, now bright, and made out the shape of the rock against them; the odd glint of a head-torch visible on the wall made it look as if the night was spilling onto it.

The next track began: 'For Emily, Whenever I May Find Her', a beautiful and haunting song. Garfunkel's words drifted in my ears and into the night. Always a militant atheist, I could believe as the music began that a god existed.

Garfunkel began to sing his love song, which made me think of home, and Mandy and Ella. I wondered what they would be doing right now, and if they missed me. I missed them. I thought of Ella, who no doubt wondered where I'd gone. For a child a week is a lifetime, and a month is an eternity. I would have given anything to have seen her right then. She was perfect. Wasn't all this empty and pointless when compared to her? How could I possibly imagine that a life spent climbing, guiding, and spending months in the Himalayas would make me happy? In a few months my son would be born. Imagine the fun things we could do. The adventures we could have. Wouldn't their company, their smiles and questions and laughter, be immeasurably more valuable than climbing alone on a worthless lump of soulless stone? I lay back and thought about Scarborough, Filey, Robin Hood's Bay, seaside towns on the east coast, of sitting on the sand and watching my children play. Mandy by my side, smiling . . .

I woke in the dark to the click of the tape finishing.

Our homemade tent struggles against
hurricane winds on Fitzroy

Jim Hall prepares to descend 56 pitches

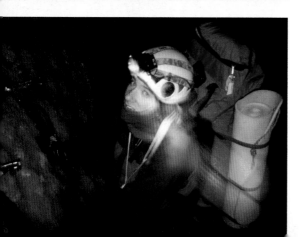

Fourteen hours later
and the strain is showing

Es Tresidder learning the hard way
on the North Face of Les Droites

A long way up, much further down.
Es retreating off the Maria Callas
Memorial route.

(*Inset*) Contemplating a
close-run thing

'You lucky bastard!'
...tt gets the cosy hammock on our
...mpted one-day ascent of Tangerine
...p, one of El Cap's steepest routes.

(*Above right*) My kingdom
for some socks... and gloves.
The water torture begins

So near... Matt reaches the ledge
almost hypothermic

The altar of the gods – Rich breaking trail towards another disappointment. Patagonia 2000.

(*Left*) Most Alpinists just do it for the food and the se

(*Below*) By day five we had run out of food

oing home empty-handed
the walk of shame

The best remedy for an overhang is plenty of water – twenty days' water ready for the Reticent Wall.

From the roof to this point. The biggest fall of my life.

Like going to the gym or pulling a train, hauling on El Cap is best savoured when it's over

Looking down from the last pitch of the Reticent Wall, a climb I'd begun twenty-nine years ago

Dizzy on the summit

An open door. El Capitan as beautiful as the first day I set eyes on her

Hell freezes over

Patagonia. June 1999

Midnight. The four of us stood in a circle and prepared our equipment. I glanced around at Paul, Jim and Nick, watching their eyes dart nervously from behind the narrow slits in their fleece face masks as they attached hardware to their harness, uncoiled ropes, clipped on crampons. No one spoke. I felt a deep sense of unease, almost panic.

A four-man team is designed more for comfort than speed, and there under Mount Fitzroy's 5,000-foot Super Couloir, a fearsome route on its vast North-West Face, with the temperature way beyond cold, comfort was what we needed. Why was I standing with these men? Paul Ramsden, Nick Lewis and Jim Hall were a tight team who'd put up lots of hard first ascents in places like Alaska, Antarctica and the Himalaya. They were gnarly. Hard men. I hardly knew them. I certainly didn't want to climb this route. What were we about to do? It was suicidal, but I knew I wasn't strong enough to speak my mind. They'd asked me to come, had seen something in me they'd liked or needed, and I couldn't back out now, even if I wanted to. As ever, I didn't realise that each of us thought the same about the others.

It was June in Patagonia, at the tip of Argentina, midwinter in the southern hemisphere. This was my first proper expedition – and what an initiation. You could count the number of teams who'd tried to climb here in winter on one hand, unsurprising when you consider the fearsome reputation Patagonia has even in summer: hurricane winds and storms that last for weeks.

Super Couloir
Fitzroy

I was here, gearing up for the longest, coldest, most dangerous climb of my life. It was beyond my wildest dreams, yet now I knew I didn't want to go. I had thought I lived for moments like this, but something was different. I knew I was going to feel different, too.

Soon we began to chill, reminding us it was time to go. We couldn't put it off any longer.

Picking up my ice tools I followed the others and began climbing into the black void under the wide starlit sky.

All I could think about was her.

Mandy had always been determined to have babies. In one of the first conversations we had had, she told me she just wanted to have loads of babies.

I managed to avoid the whole baby-making part for nearly ten years, arguing that it was never the right time. I didn't realise that there is no such thing.

I suppose I knew the game was up when she told me how, when she saw mothers with their children, she wanted to cry. We agreed that we'd give it a go.

Ploughing upwards through knee-deep powder, we were soon swallowed by the narrow boilerplate-sided couloir, which cleaved its way up the dizzying wall. All around us, in the weak beams of our headtorches, we glimpsed the relics of other attempts. Bleached strips of disassembled rope hung frozen and stiff from flakes like old battle flags. Pegs, cams and wires sprouted from the walls, a gallery of lost climbs. I thought about the story of a climber finding a body sticking out of a crack, here, on this wall, its hair blowing like the ends of a tattered old rope as they moved past. I kept my head down and climbed.

Midnight. The contractions began. Mandy woke me up and asked me to start timing them, but by the time the next one arrived I'd fallen asleep. Frustrated by my lack of interest, she pushed me out of bed and told me to ring the hospital – and to put on *The Sound of Music* to take her mind off what was happening.

With phone in my hand, I sat naked on the stairs and

shivered, waiting for someone to answer. I felt unmoved by the coming birth. I wondered if something was wrong with me.

It was too cold for the snow to melt and then transform into ice, so we moved together up snow-covered slabs for the first thousand feet.

My fear and doubt were quickly replaced by the strain of heavy rucksacks, worries about cold feet, and, surprisingly enough, the simple pleasures of climbing, of moving quickly through such a place.

The alpine horror stories which surround it began to recede as we came to grips not with the myth but with the reality of the route. As my hands and feet grew numb, and my eyelids stuck to each other when I blinked, I reminded myself how much I love the cold. Bits of my face stung around the edges of my balaclava.

The light from the moon, silvery and dead, shone down on the blank walls all around us, illuminating the toothy towers and ice cap beyond. It felt unreal, reminding me of an airbrushed sci-fi poster, so harsh and alien. Another world.

I've always found that I had to be pushed into everything: getting married, buying a house, learning to drive. Perhaps having kids was no different? I hoped that as with all those other things, I'd eventually shrug my shoulders and think, 'Well, it's not as bad as I thought.' Mandy once asked me what I wanted most in life, and without thinking I answered, 'For you to be happy.' She wanted a baby more than me and I suppose I knew it was inevitable. It was that simple and I knew it.

Each pitch was harder than the last, with snow giving way to old, fragile ice. The couloir became narrower; the ice running down it was no more than a delicate vein of possibility. With one foot on ice, the other balanced on a vertical band of loose diorite, we cautiously tapped our picks into the thicker smears and hoped for the best, never sure we'd reach a solid belay before the rope ran out.

Anchored to a poor ice screw and an old peg, I stood on my side-points, trying not to put any weight on the belay as Paul made slow progress up a 70° corner. With no protection between us save for the belay, I forgot about my cold feet as I watched him scratch at the ice, carefully piecing together a shaky sequence of delicately balanced moves up a foot-wide, inch-thick strip of ice. Jim and Nick eyeballed us from below, both cut and bruised from the ice we were sending down. Neither of them said anything. We knew what would happen if he fell.

All eyes were on Paul's crampons.

Without warning, a foothold broke as he weighted it, knocking me onto the anchors as it whizzed past. They held.

Paul wobbled on one front point, the weight of his ruck-sack trying to tip him. Then with extreme care, stacking his feet one above the other, he moved up, and regained his balance.

'The ice gets thicker up here and I can see a peg!' he shouted down, but his voice was wobbly.

I looked down at Jim and Nick and felt cheered by their smiles of relief.

The whole baby-making thing turned out to be quite fraught. Nothing was happening. All of a sudden it went from a love thing to a chemistry thing. I hated it, hated the way I was suddenly forced to produce a baby.

As time passed I began to worry that maybe I couldn't, and with that came the crushing reality that maybe it wasn't my choice.

Midnight. I fell onto my bruised knees and hacked furiously at a tiny patch of sloping frozen gravel, my home for the night. I was exhausted after twenty-four hours of non-stop climbing.

We knew we were close to the top, but experience told us that we should get a few hours of sleep instead of pushing our bodies any further into the red. We needed to ration our strength. After all, getting to the summit might not turn out to be the easy part.

Moving around, drunk with fatigue, each of us selfishly tried to manufacture some luxury for ourselves in the overpowering cold: a sling to wrap around the knees, a rucksack to stand in. We didn't ask for much.

The ledge was tiny, our feet dangled over the immense black drop.

Exhausted, Paul untied from the rope then snagged a crampon on Jim's sleeping mat and nearly fell over the edge. They screamed at each other, but I was too tired to care. All I wanted was the sanctuary of my sleeping bag and a hot drink.

The temperature had dropped off the scale of our thermometer.

None of us had drunk more than half a litre of water since we'd left the tent the day before, so once in my bag I forced myself to attempt to get a brew on. Tired, strung out and with zero blood sugar, Nick and Jim argued beside me, as I sat with a numb bum and cold feet trying to stay awake long enough to melt a pan of grit-filled snow.

I wondered what she was doing right now, if she was awake or sleeping. I wondered if she was thinking about me.

Jim sat next to me and slurped down some half-cooked noodles, passing comment on their unusual gritty texture. Until this trip I'd never met Jim, or even heard of him for that matter, yet I was told that he could suffer. On the flight from Britain he'd told the story of how he and a friend had made an unsupported alpine-style ascent in Alaska, of Denali via the South Buttress and South East Spur. The ascent and descent, followed by the walk out to the highway, had taken twenty-eight days. I'd asked him how you climb a route with that much food and fuel. 'It basically involved carrying enormous rucksacks and eating next to nothing, which was just as well as the food got soaked in fuel anyway,' he explained.

On the death march out, half-starved and stalked by bears, they'd lost what little food was left, as well as most of their equipment, while crossing the McKinley River. When they reached the Alaskan highway they were more dead than alive.

'How does this compare?' I asked.

'This was nothing compared to that crazy trip,' said Jim as he cast the sandy dregs of his noodles into the darkness and slumped over asleep almost immediately.

Although forced to sleep in the most ridiculously uncomfortable manner possible, my feet standing in my rucksack so I didn't slide off the ledge, my head resting on my knees, I soon joined him.

Pregnancy began as a blue band almost too faint to see, but there was no doubt. Mandy jumped around with glee; her dream was finally coming true. I tried to look happy, and do the things that fathers and husbands are supposed to do. Deep down I felt a growing sense of unease. I was scared. The only thought I had was of escape.

The baby growing inside her was simply that, four letters that meant nothing to me. It was Mandy's, not mine, it was what she wanted, not what I needed. I began to think that I had to leave, we had to split up before it came. A friend told me that kids did signal the end of your life, but also the beginning of a new one. It sounded like a nice idea, but I could only see the negative.

I realised I had a problem with commitment. I found it hard enough being committed to one person, I couldn't handle the responsibility of a baby as well. Why? What held me back? I hated feeling like this. I wasn't a bad person, but my thoughts were so dark. All I could do was keep my head down as Mandy's baby grew.

The sound of the wind forced itself into my dreams like the roar of a jumbo jet. I didn't know it was real until I woke to find there was no moon, no stars, only that unreal sound in the black emptiness of space above us.

'Oh fuck,' I said, waking the others. A storm was approaching. I knew that we should head down; this route was a well-known death trap in bad weather – but we had put in so much effort to reach this point, with over a kilometre of climbing below us. How could we turn back now when we knew we were so close?

The wind was striking the other side of the mountain, so we still had time to escape. There was no doubt that would be the right course of action. Everyone wanted to go down. Yet because we took this for granted no one said so, and so each of us assumed the rest wanted to carry on. Insanely, this is what we did.

With no time for food and water, we stuffed our sleeping

bags away and set off, almost robotic with fear, gambling that the really tough weather might hold off for one more day.

Very quickly we were back into the thick of the climbing, scratching together a line through thin ice-streaked slabs, grooves and dead ends, that led out of the couloir. The face opened up to form a vast amphitheatre. Climbing in such epic terrain was exhilarating, and soon the storm and the fear receded from our minds. We were now high above the surrounding mountains, climbing fast, looking down onto peaks that two days before we had gazed up at in wonder. The trouble was, here we also got our first sight of giant anvil-shaped clouds advancing fast across the ice cap towards us. All I could do was turn away and try to put the image out of my mind. Then we saw it, white with hoar and incredibly close, the summit of Fitzroy. I could hardly believe it was so close.

Moving together, Paul and I scrambled over huge icy blocks that led us out of the couloir and up to a notch on the East Ridge. We held on tight as we pushed our heads into the ferocious winds and looked down on Cerro Torre far below on the other side. Unable to congratulate each other under the white noise of the wind, we sheltered behind a block and waited for Nick and Jim, our faces warmed by big stupid grins.

When we were all together again, Paul took a deep breath and led an exposed pitch on weather-formed nubbins out of the notch, traversing up onto the north side of the ridge and back out of the wind. Gear flapping, his ropes arching out horizontally, he looked like a stunt man climbing out onto the wing of an aeroplane.

Once back in the shelter of the ridge, we tiptoed out above the couloir, traversing towards the final col from where we could scramble up to the summit. It looked as if we could be there in minutes – until we found our traverse had ended and we had to climb up onto the ridge.

Nick went up, but was soon back, unable to breathe in the wind let alone climb. It was 4.30 p.m. and already the sky was growing darker as we huddled together, aware that it would be impossible to reach the summit before nightfall.

I wanted to go down. I'd fulfilled my half of the bargain, but the others wanted to try and sit it out, gambling that in the morning the wind might abate enough to let us make a dash for the summit. I knew that Patagonian storms often lasted for months; the thought of staying here any longer made me feel sick.

Telling people your wife's having a baby is a real rite of passage, like telling them you've just pulled off a big climb. They know that you're a man. Having children means you're different, you've made it, fulfilled your biological duty. The only problem was that I'd see dads at work, looking fat, tired and fed up, complaining how having kids had quashed all their dreams. People would tell me that I'd have to settle down and stop climbing, that once you have kids your priorities change. No more hard routes.

But I still had so many things I wanted to do.

Scrambling down to a patch of ice perched above the 1½-kilo-metre drop to the glacier, we began hacking out a ledge for our tiny three-person bivy tent. Within a few minutes of the four of us squeezing inside, the flimsy fabric strained against its ice-screw moorings as the first titanic gust hit us.

As the wind moved around and began to blast our side of the mountain, we realised we were trapped until the storm blew itself out, or we were blown off the face. The fabric began buckling wildly, as if a million scared seagulls were striking it from the outside. The edge where our feet lay was lifting and falling as fingers of wind found their way beneath us.

The wind grew. It roared louder than I'd ever heard, then roared even louder again.

The tent lifted and we were airborne.

I imagined her face. If this was the end, I wanted it to be the last thing I'd see.

Mandy started bleeding in the morning. She was only eight weeks pregnant. It was a bad sign. We were staying in London, so went down to the local hospital and waited in the Accident and Emergency department. Mandy cried, fearing her baby was dead. I put my arm around her and felt like crying too but stopped myself. I had to be strong. I felt a deep sense of sadness at the thought of her baby dying. I knew how much it meant to her. I wondered if she would fall apart, if *we* would fall apart, if it died.

The tent tumbled as if it was in wild surf. I heard people screaming and realised I was one of them. I held on to Paul at my side, convinced we were now tumbling out into space, about to be smashed to pulp as we rattled down the face.

We crashed back onto the ledge.

The anchors had held us.

The doctor slid back the curtain, smiling, and told us that everything seemed fine, that he'd examined Mandy and that the unborn baby looked very healthy. There was nothing to be worried about. I felt relieved, wanted to shake his hand. Everything was OK. Mandy wiped away the tears. She looked beautiful when she was happy.

Midnight. Time stretched on, long and terrible. The tent was blown in the air every ten minutes, while the inescapable noise of the wind and the flapping fabric drove us crazy. My body's supply of adrenaline soon ran dry. Unable to cope with the stress, my brain began to shut down. All I could think about was my foolishness, about her love, about what this would do to her if I was to die. I wished I didn't care, wished I could just be remorselessly selfish.

Dawn arrived but the wind only intensified. I shouted that we should fight our way down while we still had some energy, but the others out-voted me, saying we should stay where we were. Fear gave way to numb resignation and we began to shout out stories of other epics we'd come through. We all doubted we'd live to tell this story.

After seventeen hours, the conversation slipped from epics to the mundane and inevitably to women. Nick began describing an ill-starred romance, telling a story of how once, on a climbing trip to Poland, he had been propositioned by a beautiful and famous ballet dancer in Warsaw. 'She was gorgeous, but I already had a girlfriend in England and I told her I couldn't be unfaithful.'

'Did you tell your girlfriend about it?' asked Jim.

'Yeah, when I got home and rang her to tell her how faithful I'd been, she told me she'd met someone else and it was over!'

In our heightened state of fear, we started to laugh hysterically, not only at Nick's misfortune but at the thought of four crazy men talking about sex and ballerinas while trapped on Fitzroy in winter. Tears rolled down our cheeks.

It was then that the tent began to rip apart.

Our lodger Jon took us to the hospital.

Mandy lay in bed in pain while I tried to stay awake beside her. The day dragged on with no sign of any birthing. Busy doctors and nurses popped in every now and then to check on her condition. I walked up and down the corridor, looking at other tired dads. None of them seemed too keen on the whole deal. I went down the hall and rang all the people I needed to keep informed, then sat next to Mandy, again. I tried to talk to her, to do what fathers are supposed to do, but I was only a distraction, so I sat and read instead.

One minute we were in our sleeping bags laughing, the next we were screaming as the tent filled with spindrift and then began to disintegrate around us. My sleeping bag turned into an icy windsock. Furiously, I stuffed it into my rucksack and then squeezed out into the raging storm, holding on to a tangle of frozen ropes. It felt as if I was in the rigging of a ship battling around the Horn.

Hoar frost instantly covered everything. I watched as Nick and then the others appeared, each face hidden behind multiple balaclavas and goggles, all of us dressed in our huge belay parkas. The summit was totally irrelevant now. With wind and snow blowing up, we found ourselves at the top working out how to climb downwards. Gravity had seemingly reverted. Holding on to anything we could, we slowly retraced our steps towards the brèche and the couloir. We had no idea where the other descent routes were; we had no choice but to go back down the way we'd come. It was the last place on earth you would want to visit in such a storm; it was a death sentence, but it was our only escape route.

In the hospital I had flicked through an Australian magazine and done a bit of homework, reading about a winter ascent of Fitzroy's Super Couloir, a route I planned to try that summer. I was uneasy about the trip, my first proper expedition.

I wondered how I would get on with Nick, Jim and Paul, guys I'd only met through work. I'd thought about going to Patagonia in winter for a long time, but I'd never found anyone to share my enthusiasm until I mentioned it to Paul one day when he came in to buy some new crampons. His uncle had travelled around Patagonia one winter and he'd said the weather was much more stable, so Jim and I began to organise the trip. Patagonia in winter – it was still a crazy idea. I thought how I'd now be the only dad in the team, wondered if being a father would make any difference, slow me down or make me more cautious?

A nurse came in and said I should go home. I'd been up for twenty-four hours and she doubted Mandy would have the baby until tomorrow. Glad of the chance for some sleep, I slipped away.

Down-climbing and lowering each other, in order to avoid letting go of the ends of the rope, we arrived at the top of the couloir and clung onto the rocks while we set up the first abseil. Tired and hungry, I imagined we were about to descend over the edge of the world, cloud streaming up out of the void beneath us. The wind ripped at our clothes. We knew full well that in the narrow confines of the couloir the force of the storm magnified tenfold, and there was no chance of escape from rock fall or avalanches. I remembered reading how the climber Gino Buscaini had once photographed a tornado in the couloir. I wondered what horrors waited for us below, and whether I was strong enough to face them. We began to descend.

Midnight. The phone rang. I had been in bed for less then fifteen minutes.

'Mr Kirkpatrick, you need to get here as soon as you can, your wife's giving birth.' I put the phone down and laid my head back on the pillow.

The phone rang again.

'Mr Kirkpatrick, are you on your way?' This time I jumped out of bed.

When I reached Mandy's room she was in full labour with a doctor and midwife helping her. The birth had been long and with complications, the baby twisting inside her. I stood next to the bed and tried to hold her hand. I sat passively and watched. It went on and on. I felt detached. I felt nothing.

Watches froze, time stopped for all of us as we slowly descended. Each of us was alone with our fears. There was nothing to say, and very little chance of anyone hearing it anyway. We thought no further than the next rappel and blessed our gods each time the ropes came down. Losing our ropes to the storm, blown off and snagged on unreachable flakes, or chopped by falling rocks, was unthinkable.

Trying to avoid the couloir as much as we could, we risked a faster plumb line down blank walls: quicker, but totally committing. We could only guess where we were. The walls were now uniformly white with feathered hoar, and thick cloud swirled all around us. At one belay, three of us hung from a small wobbly flake and a single peg, our feet dangling in space as Paul looked for another anchor below. We knew there was worse to come, but accepted it for the chance it gave.

The midwife looked worried and began to sweat. The doctor came back in the room. They talked. I stood up and tried to work out what was going on.

'Mrs Kirkpatrick . . . Mandy . . . we think the umbilical cord might be around the baby's neck. We need you to really push.'

I started to cry. I grabbed Mandy's hand tight and squeezed it. I willed the baby out. Her face turned red. I couldn't stop crying. I didn't want our baby to die.

Unwilling to break out the two other ropes and risk them becoming stiff and frozen too soon, we descended slowly together, rejoined the couloir and scratched across the wall to a familiar belay. Once we were all there, we stayed silent until we retrieved the ropes and then relaxed a little. Now we had a familiar route to travel, even if it was a bowling alley of rock and snow, and held many dangers.

I took a photo and Jim smiled. I wanted to believe I'd live to see it.

'I think it should be about thirty rappels from here,' Nick said, as he slowly lowered Paul into the upwards-driven hail.

The wind dropped for a second and we were immediately blasted by express trains of spindrift. Resigned to our misery, the three of us hung limply off the belay as Paul searched below for another anchor. All of us were half buried in the swelling tide of snow. Don't think any further than the next anchor, I thought. It was a good strategy.

Mandy was urged to push harder, and somehow she did. Then the midwife said she could see the baby's head. I looked away, being a coward, because I was terrified about what I might see. Maybe if the baby was dead, and I never saw it, it would remain unreal to me.

Only the arrival of night signalled that time was still passing. The world was now no bigger than the flickering circle of light from our headtorches. We had lost count of the number of rappels we'd made. I was numb, both physically and mentally. I thought about reaching the glacier and our tent, but the thought was torture: the possibility seemed no nearer than when we had begun. I wondered if we had already died and this was how we would spend eternity.

I stood, unable to move, just waiting for the moment to pass, for whatever would happen to happen and resolve itself. If the baby was dead, we'd get over it. There would be time for other babies.

God, what was wrong with me? Why was I so detached? SO scared.

Did my father feel like this when I was born?

Fourteen hours since the hellish descent began, I climbed down alone, too cold to wait my turn on the endless rappels. Barely in control, slipping and arresting, my headtorch almost as dead as my brain, I heard another pulse of wind break against the face. I stopped in my tracks, as I waited for it to pass. The sound was utterly terrifying, bringing back dark memories of being washed into the sea as a child one stormy Christmas.

I leant into the slope to rest my back, pressed my head into the snow for a second and wondered how far I was from the bergschrund. Without warning a spindrift avalanche poured over me, choking and blinding. I panicked, slipped, and disappeared into a soft helter-skelter of snow that swooshed me down into the darkness.

I came to rest just over the bergschrund and crawled away, too exhausted to think myself lucky. I kept trying to stand, but each time the wind kept hitting me, knocking me over; all I could do was crawl away, utterly defeated. Jim caught me up and passed on by, wrapped in his own sense of survival. Then the others.

I got to my feet and staggered along behind them into the night.

The midwife began to say 'Wait', but it was too late, the baby escaped into her hands. I turned to see it – I couldn't help myself. The midwife's head was bent down, stroking this grey dead thing. She was crying.

I thought for the first time about what sort of person this baby might be . . . might have been. I'd never thought about it as a person before. I wondered about who it would have most resembled, the colour of its eyes, its hair, its laugh, its smile, its first word. I thought about who I might have grown to be. I thought about it loving me and me loving it.

I'm hallucinating now. I see Napoleonic soldiers staggering along beside me, rifles dragging in the snow. I am tortured by the thought that I'll never make it home, no matter how hard I try.

Your family. They are waiting for you.

I plunge down through the snow, glad of the tracks left by the others, although they are filling quickly. Every few metres the wind knocks me over, but I know it has lost, it can't kill me any more, I've won.

I've rationed my energy well, I've had to do it many times before, but now I've never felt so empty. I've been purged of emotion; there is no more feeling of self; my insides have shrivelled into knots of muscle. I'm *totally* empty. I'm about to stall, but the wind blows me on now, back towards our base camp. I think of our nylon oasis, of tea and biscuits, of light and laughter. I think about home.

* * *

I blinked, hardly believing this was happening. Then I blinked again as I saw a change, wanting it to be true. The baby was turning white, then pink. It opened its mouth, its hand jerked, its tiny body wriggled in the arms of the midwife, who raised her head and whispered, 'She's a girl.'

My daughter.

Ella.

Midnight. We kneel in a circle in the snow. This was where our tent had been. Now it's rolling out somewhere on the Patagonian ice cap. There is nothing left but some scraps of material that flap wildly like severed limbs. I'm too dehydrated to cry, and I know that frozen eyes would only add to my pain. I think about Ella, too young to know where I am, but old enough to know I'm not there. I want to be with her, not here with these strangers. I think about those phantom soldiers I'd passed, and of lives, new, old and changing.

Wino

Pitches 6 and 7 Reticent Wall

I had been on the wall alone for seven days, alone but not lonely. All my life I'd been a loner, finding my own company was company enough. As a child I would often wander off by myself, even when out with a group, walking on ahead, just

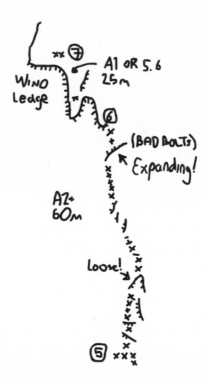

thinking. I would cycle out of the city, or take the train and go camping. I never once felt alone. *I* was always there.

As I grew up, the world seemed to bewilder me: people, emotions, the past and future, destiny and fate, who I was, how I got this way. I often wondered if that was why I became an obsessive; science fiction, drawing, bikes, climbing – I filled up my mind with junk, cramming it so full of clutter that there wasn't any room for any other thoughts, any other emotions.

I remember when my mother was seeing a policeman for a few years, his place in my life slowly turning from my mum's boyfriend to a new dad. His own home and kids were out in the countryside, far removed from our home and the kids we were brought up with. He offered us a chance of a better life. Then one day, out of the blue, my mum told us they were splitting up.

I was probably eleven. I felt a pain inside me, as if a plug had been yanked out and every ounce of happiness was being sucked away, until nothing was left. It hurt. Then I thought about buying a model plane with my pocket money, an Airfix Harrier, and how I'd paint it and set it on an old breadboard that I'd paint to look like an airfield, and how I'd buy some little figures to set around it. In that moment I felt the pain subside. I never ever wanted to feel like that ever again.

You think too much.

While I was climbing there was no time for loneliness or rambling thought. There was no imagining of what it meant to be adrift by myself on this wall. My thoughts could only be focused. There was only 'what next' and the 'what if.'

Focus. Focus. Focus.

There were seemingly endless days of action alternating with exhausted sleep, the transition from one to the other often blurred; I would fall asleep with a mouthful of bagel, and wake with my hands already scraping up the wall.

Then slowly I began to want company up there, another team close by to take my mind off what I was doing, another team that would make this space a little less blank. The nearest team were way over to my right, climbing a route called Pacific Ocean Wall, their actual location hidden from me by the overhanging nature of the route. Only their shouts could be heard in the dark as they joined each other at their last belay and set up camp. I missed the camaraderie of being a team of two or three, sitting together at the end of the day, laughing and joking about life, the pain, hardship and fear shared and so reduced, putting on a front.

On my piece of wall there were now no other teams. Every few days climbers would nibble at the foot of the wall, on routes such as Mescalito or New Dawn, only to bail after a day or so due to a storm, the heat or just bad juju. Now, after a week alone, I woke to see a team climbing up the wall, moving higher than any others had, giving me hope that I might have some company.

I set off to climb the next pitch. This part of the wall was almost featureless, with compact, small, loose flakes and vague seams that took copperheads. It was as hard as all the rest, but with care I made steady progress. Over a week of climbing had fine-tuned my skills, steadied my nerve. I hooked and beaked up the blank wall, taking my time, enjoying the space around me more than I had since I'd begun. Place a piece, test it, get on it. Place another piece, test it, get on it. I felt that I was actually getting somewhere.

You're soloing the fucking Reticent!

After a few hours I reached a point where the route made a rising traverse over an area of granite that looked like layers of onion skin. Each layer allowed a birdbeak to be tapped in, giving me height to reach the next.

I balanced across the wall, bouncing my beaks hard to make sure they wouldn't rip out once I was on them. Each aggressive bounce increased my confidence until, after a few hard yanks, I moved up and looked for the next placement.

With one flake to go until I reached the safety of a bolt, I tapped in the tip of the beak with my hammer, slowly and gently at first, then harder as it began to slip in between the wall and the flake.

CRACK!

The flake fractured, creating a large chunk of loose rock about two feet high. I shot out my hand and held it in place, fearing it would topple away and cut my rope, leaving me hanging from just a single beak. My reaction was instinctual and free of fear.

I took a few seconds to realise I was safe: the wall was so

steep, the flake would miss my ropes and haul bags. I could just let it go.

But what about the team beneath me?

Looking down I knew the people climbing up five hundred metres below would be in the firing line, but there was nowhere else to push the broken chunk of rock. I had to let it fall.

From this height it would kill anyone it hit.

I began to shout 'Rock!' as loud as I could, knowing my words would be lost in the updraught long before reaching them. I shouted again, waving with my free hand. Maybe they were foreign climbers, so I shouted 'Attention!' followed by 'Shit' and a line with every expletive I could think of.

All I could do was remove my hand and allow the flake to topple off the wall, and tumble down into the void. I watched it spin slowly as it gathered speed, until its missile-like shape stabilised it and with a terrible air-ripping hum it shot away, disappearing out of sight under my feet.

I continued to shout, with both hands now cupped around my mouth, knowing that it was too late. It would either hit them and kill them or miss. They were sitting ducks.

It took several seconds for the sound to reach the climbers, the sound of air being ripped apart as the rock came towards them. The moment the sound reached them, they began to move, pushing themselves closer to the wall, ducking behind their haul bags, and trying to get as much of their bodies as possible directly below their helmets.

I wanted to turn away, but I was transfixed, expecting the falling grey shape to strike one of the climbers, a puff of blood exploding from them, smashing and tearing them apart. I would have killed someone.

Then I saw the trees shake. The boom of the flake's impact, far out from the base of the wall, came up to me. It had missed the climbers; the steepness of the wall had saved them.

Now I had their attention.

I sank back in my harness with relief, and shouted 'Sorry'. They weren't taking any chances. Minutes later I watched them begin to retreat back to the ground. I was alone on the wall again.

Several hours after starting the pitch, I climbed up below my first ledge since leaving Lay Lady five days ago. I felt like a man adrift for weeks seeing palm trees on the horizon. An island in the sky. I grabbed the edge of the ledge, threw my leg over and rested there, savouring the special moment. Ledges on El Cap are as rare as islands in the Atlantic, and so, like Lay Lady, this one had its own name – Wino Ledge. It was the size of a double bed, the wall falling away for hundreds of metres on two sides, and was unexpectedly littered with shards of glass.

The ledge had been named by the first man to reach it, a legendary climber named Warren Harding, or 'Batso', famed as much for his doggedness, hard drinking and woman-chasing, as for being the leader of the team that first scaled El Cap.

He had put up the 'Nose' route in 1958, a climb that took forty-five days, spread over several years, to complete. The team chose to besiege the rock, going up and down hundreds of metres of fixed rope, slowly pushing their route as they went, returning to the ground each day. The crowds that gathered to watch this defining moment in American- and world-climbing history grew so large that they began to block the roads, forcing the park service to ban the team from climbing during the summer months. Finally, Harding and his companions left their fixed ropes and made a push for the summit, committing themselves to the longest, steepest climb ever undertaken. Big-wall climbing was being invented by them as they did it. The only people qualified to rescue them if they got into trouble were themselves.

Almost out of water and food, hanging higher than the tallest building in the world, Harding began hand drilling a line of bolts over the final blank overhangs as night descended. On he drilled in the dark, his partners Wayne Merry and George Whitmore hanging below him. It was almost dawn when Harding shouted down, 'Have you got time for one more bolt?'

After eighteen long months of effort, 600 pegs and 125 bolts, Harding, Merry and Whitmore scrambled to the top of El Cap.

The current speed record for the Nose is two hours and forty-five minutes.

After the Nose, Harding went on to make the first ascent of the Dawn Wall in 1970, a climb that the Reticent bisected at this point. On that ascent, Harding and his partner Dean Caldwell were sponsored by a Californian vineyard, which no doubt contributed to the fact that twenty-seven days were spent on the wall, the longest time anyone had taken on a climb without returning to the ground.

Harding, renowned for being tough and hard headed, had climbed the route in the days before portaledges, hanging every night in cramped and claustrophobic hammocks called 'Bat tents' which would fill with water when it rained. So no doubt reaching this ledge had called for a bit of a party. Even here things hadn't gone smoothly, as they were stuck in a storm for four days, surviving on a ration of cheese and 'a fine Christian Brothers cabernet'.

The park service became so worried about the team that they started a rescue at one point, lowering a long string of tied-together ropes down the wall, even though Harding had thrown down messages in tin cans to tell them they were OK. After much hollering and cursing, Harding convinced them he wasn't going to allow himself to be rescued.

The glass on the ledge was no doubt the remains of that fine cabernet.

Harding, short and stocky with raven black hair and crazy eyes, was an icon and hero of mine, the opposite of the athletic norm – 'fitness be damned' as Harding would put it. He was known to be a mess when he climbed, his sheer force of will propelling him on. Once, his climbing partner, a visiting British hotshot, exclaimed that the shambolic Harding couldn't do anything right, to which he replied, 'I know, but I can do it for ever.'

Many climbers would have been dismayed at the apparent mindless vandalism of the broken glass, but I had grown up with glass-covered streets and playgrounds and it didn't bother me, merely adding to the sense of history. It's rare to find yourself sharing the same fears and reliefs as your hero, knowing just how he must have felt, hanging on the wall, then climbing up onto the ledge, feeling solid ground under his feet for the first time in a week. I had one other thing in common with him. I could have done with a stiff drink.

I stood there for a while, feeling the weight being taken by my feet, then noticed a bottle of yellow liquid and a bag of white powder, looking like a litre of piss and a kilo of cocaine.

A present from the Russians. In fact it was a bag of Gatorade drink powder, with a bottle of the stuff already made up, a fine gift to a climber on El Cap, a place where no amount of money can buy you a drink once your bottles go dry. It was a fine gift for anyone but me; my bags were still bursting with water.

After I hauled the bags and set up the portaledge, I took the risk of taking off everything I had on – clothes, shoes, even my harness, attaching the rope to my ankle just in case. I laid out my sleeping bag on the ledge, sat down and felt sun boring into my skin. I looked at my body, changed already, thinner in places, muscles bigger in others. My thighs and hips were a patchwork of bruises, my feet swollen and battered. My shoes were too soft, meaning that the constant standing in aiders had created bone spurs on the outside of my feet, and crushed my toes. Nevertheless it felt so good to be here, to have made it this far.

How would I have been feeling now, if I'd wimped out earlier?

I'd come further than I ever thought possible. I had done amazingly well to overcome my doubts and fears, to overcome myself.

I still had the hardest to come, however. Tomorrow I would have to climb the second most dangerous pitch on the route.

Tomorrow I might die on this very spot, my blood mixed with old dried-up wine and broken glass.

Truths and lies

Yosemite. October 1999

It seemed that no matter how hard I climbed, the thing that was pushing me on could not be satisfied. On the summit I would feel free of it, but in the days that followed it would creep back. Some people have described it as a rat that gnaws away inside you and must be fed. For me it was something else, it was a rat that denied ever being fed. No matter how hard I climbed, I seemed to have the inability to just be happy with what I'd done. I was always undermining my own achievements.

After my two trips to Yosemite with Paul and then Andy, on paper at least, it looked like I had pulled off some pretty hard routes, but soon the initial joy and satisfaction faded and old doubts crept in. Had I pulled my weight? Was it Andy who'd climbed the hardest pitches? Was I just a bullshitter?

There was really only one way to tell, and that was to have a whole climb to myself. To solo a big wall.

The moment I had the idea, standing at the climbing counter at work, I began to giggle. It was so stupidly crazy. It was also just about possible. I giggled some more. It was as if I had been given a million pounds and all of a sudden I could do anything I wanted, only it was a million pounds worth of potential that excited me, the realisation that no one but myself could stop me. There were of course so many reasons why not to try, just to dismiss the idea as ludicrous. But at the heart of it there were those two important words; 'why not'.

I began as I usually did, by thinking about this plan. I needed a wall, and I needed to learn how to solo it. Soloing the Droites and big alpine routes was simple, just grab your axes and go. Soloing a big wall was something more akin to learning to sail, requiring a whole gamut of complex techniques. I began reading all I could, which wasn't that much, the art of big-wall soloing being as exotic and niche as cave diving. I knew of only four other Brits who had soloed significant big walls and two of them had come close to dying, one breaking his leg, the other getting rescued after having almost died of exposure.

On my days off I began going to a local quarry, trying out different techniques, learning how to safeguard myself as I progressed, learning by thinking, doing and then re-evaluating. I didn't have the time or money to do some easy big walls, so I had to learn all I could now.

My first real solo had been that summer, taking place in the dark in the old slate mines above Llanberis in North Wales. It was scary, being alone in the dark, only the hum of the power-station buried deep in the heart of the mountain for company. But I knew that the most important technique I could learn, above that of knots and karabiners and pulleys, was the ability to control my fear. Fear kills all great ideas.

It had taken an age to sort out my belay and stack my ropes that night, and longer still to get my rack in order. Worried that I might leave a vital piece of gear on the ground, I cast the beam of my headtorch around to check for anything crucial. I tried to imagine what it would be like to be on my own for days, perhaps weeks, and wondered if I could be focused enough for that long, if my clumsiness wouldn't finally be the death of me. Eventually I was ready, and began climbing, still running through all the little details I had to get right: placing good gear, the correct sequence of moving up my aiders, making sure my haul line was running correctly. I was about fifteen feet off the ground when I realized a major error in my system: I'd forgotten to clip into the rope, which sat piled neatly on the ground.

Kicking myself, I carefully descended and started again, only this time with the rope. Twenty feet higher I looked up and everything went dark. The battery for my headtorch had fallen off the back of my helmet. Down I went again.

Later that night, walking away from the quarry after having completed the route, I tried to focus on what had gone right, and how to eliminate what had gone wrong. It was clear there was much to learn, and many unexpected problems that would have to be overcome in order to succeed. But I wasn't naive. I knew it would be hard. I wanted it to be hard.

I giggled again, knowing that it could be done.

I told no one of my plan.

As usual I began to focus on a do-able wall, the Verdon Gorge in France, but then moved on swiftly to harder walls, the Dru, the Grand Capucin. Finally I set my sights on the fearsome Troll Wall in Norway, the highest – and most dangerous – wall in Europe. I knew Mandy would be terrified if she knew what I was planning, and so made up an imaginary climbing partner called 'Matt' whom I was meeting out there.

A month later I stood in the rain below the most scary and intimidating piece of rock I had ever seen, black, looming like a bad dream out of the clouds. I knew I wasn't ready, but knew no one ever would be for such a challenge, and so I began anyway, ferrying my gear up to the base of the wall.

Whereas El Cap is silent and majestic, the Troll Wall is always moving, rocks tumbling down, crashing and booming, sparks leaping in the dark. It was a wall straight out of a horror film. The wicked witch's castle, the gateway to Mordor, the entrance to hell. I hid beneath my haul bag, sweaty and wet, and knew it was beyond me.

I hadn't imagined how lonely soloing could be.

Unable to commit to the wall until better weather appeared I rang Mandy to put her mind at ease, her voice making me regret my decision to come. 'How's Matt finding it?' she asked. 'Fine,' I said, wishing I had the strength of my imaginary partner as I stood by myself next to some remote phone box.

The climb proved to be equally illusory. It rained for ten days solid, and each time I ferried my gear up to the base of the wall, my fear grew. The more the rain hammered on my tent, the more my resolve to climb the wall crumbled, the realisation I just couldn't do it.

I lay in my tent and listened to 'The River' by Bruce Springsteen.

Eventually the other climbers who had hung around to climb the wall drifted away to drier climates, leaving me and one other, a Finn who had also come to solo the wall.

I didn't even know his name, but we teamed up and tried to climb it together, perhaps believing our pooled resolve might be enough. But at the first belay, as I watched him smoke a cigarette, fingers shaking, trying to shield it from the mist, psyching himself up, I wondered if he was as out of his depth as I was. Then, ready, he took the stub and pushed it into a crack. In that moment I knew I didn't want to climb with him.

You just don't fuck about with mountains like that. They don't like it, a fact proved an hour later when he fell off the first pitch, ripped out all his gear and landed in a heap at my feet. He was shaken but OK, but our climb was over.

I dug out his stub with my fingers and went home.

A few months later I hung in my portaledge below El Cap and thought about the Troll Wall, and about going home without that climb, about the crushing disappointment. For a while I was broken-hearted, my dream dashed, glad I hadn't told anyone. But slowly I began to rebuild my plan. I would go and solo El Cap instead, where the weather wouldn't play a part. I had no time for doing an easy route, and so chose to try my hardest route so far, Aurora, that terrifying climb I'd heard Adam Wainwright talk about a few years before at the Troll training weekend.

I felt that familiar giggle rising inside me, the excitement that I would begin tomorrow, jumar up the ropes that stretched up for five pitches, fixed high on the route. Could I do it? A haul bag crashed down from the top of Zodiac, the route a hundred metres to my right, cast off by climbers wanting an easy descent. It made a horrible ripping sound, ending in a large echoing thump. It sounded like a body hitting the ground.

I couldn't sleep.

I tried not to think about why I was there. I tried my well tested technique of imagining myself soloing on Stanage, the long gritstone escarpment that hemmed in the west edge of Sheffield's moors. I could smell the heather, feel the brush of the ferns on my legs, the cotton of my laces, squeaking as I pulled my climbing boots tight. I began climbing my usual routes, alone, just me and the crag, a bluebird sky save for the smoke from the cement works. I rebuilt the holds within my thoughts, each one as memorable to me as a lover's body. I could feel my hands cupping rounded edges, or carefully placed and locked in, my shoulders tensing, elbows down, pulling, pushing, stepping, but never too hard. The best climbs are seduced. I could feel myself high above the ground, only my body to save me, from the earth and from my thought. I marvel at the freedom of the soloist, to move without fear, to be free from the thing that pulls like gravity: doubt.

The following morning I started climbing.

Aurora was everything I had hoped and feared it would be. It demanded more than I could give, but somehow what was missing was found. It was almost impossible, only the tiniest chink of possibility for me to find my way, and so day after day I got higher and higher.

As usual my main problems came from the small details, not the large.

Committed to the route I found to my horror that all the belay hangers were missing, which required me to fit my own on the stubs that projected an inch from the wall at the end of every pitch; three steel fingers signalling an end to the trauma and fear of hooks and copperheads. The problem was, although I had brought hangers and nuts, my nuts were metric and the stubs were imperial. Nothing fitted. Hanging there on pitch six, knowing I had somehow to haul my bags up on these studs, I felt the blood drain out of me. Without the ability to retreat all I could do was place the hangers on, then wrap gaffer tape around the studs and hope the weight of my bags would hold them in place.

As I climbed I learned the art of big-wall soloing, and wondered why school wasn't more like this, and how great it would be to have a Master's in big walling.

On the fifth night I sat on my ledge and cut the gloves from my infected and bloated fingers, a reminder that next time I should take more care of them and bring a first aid kit. Over on the Dawn Wall I watched as Leo Houlding had a party up on Lay Lady Ledge. A fellow Brit, but younger and good looking, Leo was the star of UK climbing, bringing a rock-and-roll edge to a pretty conservative sport. For him life always looked so effortless, one long party of fun and climbing. He was one of the few climbers I knew who was fully sponsored, and so could do what he wanted. I wondered why my life wasn't like that, what I could achieve if I wasn't forced to climb in fits and starts. Then I looked at myself, sat there on my own with sausage fingers, eating cold beans, while he drank Tequila with climbing babes across the wall. Deep down I knew the reason was that he was single, with no house, or job, or any ties. This was his life. This was my holiday. I lay in my bed and wondered that if I felt normal here, if things made sense, then why should I go home?

Then I remembered once making a commitment to Mandy, that if she gave me her heart, I wouldn't break it.

The following day I woke up to find a surprise, a three-person speed team climbing up below me. They had started the night before, and had climbed through the dark. They were still many pitches below, so I climbed a pitch and waited for them, shouting down that they had to be careful as my belay was primarily constructed with gaffer tape. I guess they thought it was a joke.

Their imminent arrival created a dilemma as I'd been dying for a piss all day, but didn't think it was fair to go. After all, pissing on someone on a big wall is bad form, especially if they then catch you up. I ended up holding it in all day until tea time. I had a tin of cold stew to take my mind off it, the team only a pitch below me by now, but this only compounded my urgency, the stew putting further pressure on my poor bladder. I was desperate, and so decided I would have to go in the empty stew tin, quickly filling the tin to the brim, lumps of fat and potato floating on the top.

Now I had the dilemma of what to do with the tin. I wasn't keen on the lead climber reaching me and asking why I was holding a tin of piss, so I hit on the plan of pouring it out one drop at a time, hoping it would dissipate before it hit the leader or anyone else below. I lay on my belly, peering over the edge of the ledge, and began pouring. The plan was working, but was far too slow. There was no response from below and my confidence got the better of me, so I poured faster. Suddenly there was a commotion, and the leader began screaming at me to stop pissing on his head. Now I was in big trouble, because when he reached my portaledge he would realise that not only had I pissed on him, but had been pouring it out of a tin can!

For the second time on the route I reached for the gaffer tape, and wrapped the can in tape before hiding it in my haul bag lid.

Eric, Andrew and some guy who'd never climbed a wall before reached me by sundown. Strangely, I found myself washing my face and hands in order to look presentable, feeling a bit like a castaway, cutting off his beard and long hair when he sees the approach of his rescuers. They all looked totally fucked, having been awake for two days already.

No one mentioned the piss incident.

They'd forgotten to bring any belay seats, wooden planks that took the strain off your harness leg loops, and so they shared my portaledge as Andrew geared up for the crux expanding flake directly above the belay. We were all pretty nervous, as this 'Gong flake' pitch was notorious, a grand piano that hung above the belay. If it ripped we'd all be scraped off the wall. We all watched him in the dark, as he carefully taped his way up to the flake, listening to the hollow sound, like a cracked bell, as he used all his skill to place pegs that would hold his weight, but not force the flake off the wall.

BUM BUM – BUM BUM – BUM BUM – BUM BUM.

All of a sudden a loud pulsating beat filled the air all around us. We all looked at each other baffled at the sound until Eric said 'Shit man, you must be scared up there, we can hear your heart beating.'

Then we realised the sound was coming from Leo Houlding's supercharged stereo banging out some Euro Techno. He was having another party on Lay Lady Ledge.

Andrew continued.

A scream ripped through the air, followed by a jangling rattle of gear as Andrew plummeted down, plucking out all his gear as he went. The sound was horrible and for a second we all shrank, expecting the flake to come scraping down the wall with him.

All I could think about was the tin of piss in my haul bag.

Andrew groaned, and we looked up, all still alive. He started up again.

The night drew on, the climbers beginning to hallucinate with lack of sleep. Andrew fell once more, this time when a bat had pushed his cam out of the crack.

It was way past midnight by the time they left, slowly jumaring up, shouting 'Thanks for your hospitality' as they went.

I tried to get back to sleep, only to be woken again when I heard a scream from above. I opened my eyes just in time to see a light fly past my ledge; spiralling down until it disappeared into the rocks at the base of the wall. I felt sick, knowing one of the climbers must have fallen to his death. I had never seen anyone die before.

Then I heard laughter from above, and cursing. It had been nothing more than a dropped helmet with the headtorch attached.

I was glad to be alone again.

Three days later Aurora linked up with the last four pitches of the route Tangerine Trip, and I climbed up to the summit.

You would imagine that the greatest moments of your life would end with a little fanfare. But this one ended with a simple 'Thank fuck that's over' as I dragged my almost empty haul bag to the top.

I took my clothes off and lay amongst all my scattered gear and thought about the climb. I no longer felt the giggles, only pride that this dream had been made real. There was also a slight sadness at its passing.

I was happy. I had kept my faith. I had not given up. I wasn't a failure. It would have been so easy not to have climbed this route. But so many times in the last few days and months and years I had found strength of body and spirit that I would have imagined to be utterly beyond me.

I thought about the Frendo Spur, the Shield, soloing the Droites, and now this, and how each climb had changed me, made me who I am. But why had I wanted more so soon? Wasn't it that I just wanted to recapture that feeling, the same feeling that I had experienced there on the summit of El Cap?

These moments were hard fought and dangerous to find, and some would probably question my sanity, but making a dream reality would always be hard. But in that moment, on the summit, I would have paid any price to feel as I did. To feel proud of who I was. To have believed, and reached beyond my grasp yet still snatched that dream.

I looked over at the Dawn Wall and thought about the Reticent.

Fearometer

Pitch 8 Reticent Wall

I stood naked in a cold white room, a hospital maybe. The room was empty apart from a large black door. My stomach was in knots. I knew that something terrible was beyond it, but I was compelled to go through, even though every instinct I had told me to run away. But where to? There was only one door.

I noticed glass littering the floor.

I touched the door. It was rock hard, cold and stony. I pushed and it slowly swung open. There was only blackness. I was terrified of what I would find in the dark, but I walked on.

I stood in a white room, identical to the last, empty save for another black door. I pushed it open and saw only darkness . . .

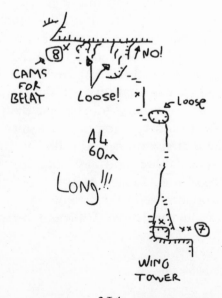

I woke in the dark.

Where am I?

I sat up in my sleeping bag. The metal corners of the portaledge scraped on the wall, the sound bringing me back to the present. I was bursting for a piss.

My muscles were sore, my tendons were stiff, as I stood naked like an old man and pissed off the edge, the heat of me falling for hundreds and hundreds of metres. I shivered, feeling the smooth granite under my feet, cold now after the warmth of yesterday had radiated away.

I noticed I wasn't attached to the rope any more. I wasn't scared. I knew I wouldn't fall.

I lay back down and zipped up my sleeping bag. The dark outline of the rim of El Cap was becoming defined in the predawn. I thought about the dream.

Too much cheese.

I looked at the next corner. It didn't look any easier. Although I was worried about the climbing above, I was also excited; the climbing below had given me confidence in my abilities. Just one placement at a time. I thought about Royal Robbins, and his solo ascent of El Cap. I had met him a few years before at a slideshow, an old man now, but still charismatic, the magic of El Cap still in his eyes. I wonder if, when you're old, all those crazy things you did make more sense. Do the people who doubted your sanity, and questioned your reasons, now question themselves for not having done the same? I like to imagine being a very old man, and looking in my trophy cabinet of life, remembering all those climbs and adventures and thinking it had all been worth it. Probably the thing that bothered me most, especially the older I got, was not the fear of dying, but the fear of getting old and realising I'd let doubt and fear stop me from living the life I'd really wanted to live. And yet I knew that my dilemma lay in the fact that part of me wanted the normal life that Mandy wanted for me – being a normal husband and father. The problem was I was living two lives, in two completely separate worlds. I felt that I had to choose between them. I felt as if I was being pulled apart.

You could die today and none of that would matter.

I've made it this far.

This is the hardest pitch you've ever climbed.

I know I can do it.

Even if you do, you still have the crux.

I got up and stood with bare feet on the cold granite of Wino Ledge and began sorting out my rack for the next pitch, too anxious to wait for the sun. It was so quiet.

What will it feel like if you fall, knowing in that instant that you could not stop?

I thought about my responsibilities, to both Mandy and Ella and also to my mum and dad, brother and sister. So many lives could be changed, even ruined for this. For this. What was this? It wasn't just a climb. I was fighting for my life day by day. There was no fun, only relief; no laughter, only sighs; no smiles, only grimaces. This was torture – mental and physical. I could take the pain in my body, but the agony of anxiety was almost too much to bear.

But you can bear it, every day it gets less and less. This is what you've always wanted. This is what that life feels like. A life of only climbing. Alone. Scared. Just as uncertain as you would be sitting at home.

I prepared my gear as I had done every morning, methodically and with care, making sure nothing was left behind. I reset the belay, triple checking every knot and karabiner. I checked my now tatty topo, even though the way ahead was obvious.

A pillar sprouted up an open-book corner for several metres above the ledge, seemingly devoid of good placements, until it petered out and the corner carried on, blank and smooth. At some point there I would have to move left, out onto the face. One of the second ascensionists had described this pitch as unjustifiable. Any fall would send the leader down onto this very ledge. The lack of any visible protection worried me. Perhaps this pitch was too hard, too scary.

You can only try.

The sun began to lighten the sky.

I felt too sick to eat breakfast, thinking with melancholy that if I were to die I wouldn't mind doing it on an empty stomach, and if I lived and climbed the pitch, I wouldn't really care.

I slipped on my clothes, shoes and harness, feeling my bruises complain as I cinched down the leg loops and waist belt.

I attached my lead rope to my heaviest haul bag rather than directly to the bolts, so that the bag would act as a counter weight. If I fell, the weight of my body would lift it off the ledge, thus reducing my impact force.

I had nothing left to do. I started climbing.

I broke the climb down into the main parts I could see from my position – pillar, corner, traverse – then broke each down into its individual moves. I began with skyhooks and crept up, fingering each edge for the optimum placement. An image came into my mind – of a story a friend had told of seeing a climber fall onto a ledge, smashing his feet, both ankles at right angles, bones sticking out of his shins, blood everywhere.

Don't think about that you idiot! Focus or you will fall.

I took my time and soon reached the top of the pillar where, to my surprise, I found a small flared crack into which I slotted an equally small brass nut, clipping it with relief. It was my first real protection. I felt as if I was getting one over on the pitch and El Cap. Maybe it wouldn't be so bad after all.

On a hard lead I often visualise my very own 'fearometer', a device in my head used to judge just how hard the climbing is. Each marginal piece of protection inches the needle round the dial, pushing it towards the red, until a bomber piece is found, at which point the needle slowly goes back to zero. The more climbing you do, the greater the range and sensitivity of the fearometer, with moves that would once have pushed you instantly into the red, such as hanging from a skyhook, not even producing a flutter.

The problem with the fearometer, however, is that it doesn't measure anything but self-delusion, as simply being on a big wall would push most people into the red. In reality, this wire would be viewed anywhere else as marginal, yet here even marginal protection becomes bombproof, and bad protection becomes good enough.

I clipped my aiders in and moved up.

The pitch went on like this, with each metre surrendering more tiny finds, places to sneak micronuts, birdbeaks and copperheads. I moved slowly, as I knew that the pitch was graded A4+, translated as 'If you fall, you die for sure.'

The terrain began to change as I traversed a long way on just skyhooks. The ledge disappeared out of sight and mind, only to be replaced by big exposure. The ground above a shallow seam sprouted the odd fixed copperhead.

One piece at a time.

I moved very gingerly, again and again, first on hooks, carefully placed, then on heads.

Take your time.

The sun beat down. I drank some water. Time passed.

Think no further than this.

Tiredness began to take hold of me, making me sloppy; low blood sugar increased my anxiety. Each placement seemed worse than the last. My fearometer crept up. I reached a fixed piece of gear, a copperhead made from a lead fishing weight, the softer lead allowing it to be smeared better against the rock. The downside was its lower than normal strength. The wire that had once passed through the head was missing, probably ripped out while being cleaned. I thought about hooking the top of it, but I feared I might prise it out.

You can't afford to fall.

I thought about cleaning it out of the placement, but I wasn't sure I could place it any better. The next possible placement was a long way above, and I would have had to step very high on this one to reach it. *Be creative.* I pulled out a birdbeak and hammered it straight into the lead, the tip sinking in as if it were cheese. Each tap of the hammer, each millimetre further it slid in, the further my fearometer began to slip back. I gave it one last tap.

The head split in half, toppled out of the crack, and fell into space.

The needle shot back round, nearly to the red.

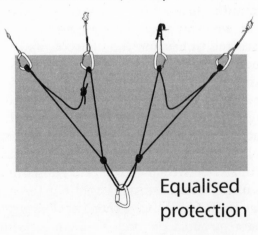

Equalised
protection

Hours passed.

I began tying two or three placements together – a skyhook and two copperheads – hoping that bunched on the same sling they might hold a fall. I clipped as many pieces as I could with shock-absorbing ripper slings, long slings sewn together with zig-zag stitching and designed to rip apart and so reduce the impact force. I knew it was all junk, but it was all I could do to keep the needle out of the red.

Three hours into the lead, I was hanging from a tiny copper-head. I thought I was about to snap, the pressure of keeping a lid on my fear too much to bear. I felt shell-shocked and unable to push myself any further. The needle was in the red.

Calm down.

I hung from the piece, knowing there was no escape, no rescue, but unable to move.

Keep going.

I pressed my head against the rock, feeling that I was about to fall at any second, already hearing the sound, feeling the sick weightlessness, seeing the blur of the wall passing before me as I dropped into space.

Move!

I can't.

One more move.

I was simply too scared.

An hour later I still hung in the same position. I still hadn't fallen. The needle of the fearometer was slipping slowly back, just out of the red. The moment had passed. I stepped up high and placed another head.

You'll be at the belay in an hour or two.

The hammer felt slippery with sweat and heavy in my hand. I had to concentrate on each blow to make it perfect, pasting the head into every crystal of granite.

Get to the belay and you can just go back to Wino Ledge and spend the night there. You don't have to clean and haul today.

I unclipped my rack to place a second head next to the first but, as I looked for the correct size, I fumbled the karabiner. The rack dropped between my feet and spun down the wall, taking most of my heads with it.

FUCK. FUCK. FUCK. FUCK. FUCK. FUCK. FUCK. FUCK.

You're screwed.

I pressed my head against the wall again, then looked up at the last stretch. I had maybe ten more metres to go. My few remaining heads were in my haul bag below. They might as well have been in my cupboard at home.

Maybe you can still put it all together. Keep going.

The pitch stretched on and on, without copperheads, each placement requiring more thought. Luckily there were still the remains of old copperheads left in place, 'deadheads', the wire ripped out of them, either through a fall or while attempting to clean them. I had a few birdbeaks left and tapped them into the tops of some of the heads, telling myself that if the wires ripped out, then the head would still be solid. I hooked others.

I was trying to find the balance between haste and speed, between blind fear and useful paranoia. Never in my life had I concentrated so hard for so long. Yet the pitch still seemed unending.

Just keep moving up – one piece at a time.

Almost all my karabiners, slings and beaks were used up. The pitch was taking me to the very limit of my sixty metres of rope, but the belay was getting closer and closer, out on the wall to my left. Two beautiful bolts.

You could hang the world off them.

Yet seeing them only made it seem more desperate; the nearer they got, the worse the gear became. The copperheads were smaller and smaller. Many of those that were still intact had rusting and corroded wires.

I would have paid any price for one solid wire or cam.

I looked down and tried to work out how far below the last really good piece of gear had been. I couldn't even remember it.

You're going to fall 400 feet if you fuck up.

I won't fuck up, then.

I crept on. The bolts were getting nearer. I imagined the sound of my karabiner gate clicking shut on one of them, that euphoria of relief, knowing I was safe, and had climbed the most difficult pitch of my life.

I was so close now.

I shook the thought away.

Stay with the moment.

I wasn't there yet.

I reached a small roof, under which I had to traverse. The

bolts were no more than ten feet to my right. I looked for the next placement and spied a minute copperhead, the smallest I'd ever seen, its cable still intact but only the thickness of a guitar string.

I wanted this to be over. I was too tired to be afraid any more, resigned to whatever fate would bring. I knew I should test the copperhead, but it was so small that surely it would pull out – and what then?

I had nothing to replace it.

I reached up and just clipped it. My karabiner looked heavy enough to pull it out.

Just be quick.

Breaking the number-one rule I'd set myself from the start, I chose not to test it.

Heart in my mouth, I transferred my weight from the poor piece below, to this worse piece above.

Quickly!

My whole world hung from a small length of steel cable swagged to a lump of alloy, a one-dollar copperhead.

It held.

I looked at it and marvelled at how such a device could possibly hold anyone's weight.

The answer came in an instant. With a roller-coaster lurch in my chest the copperhead ripped out.

You're falling.

Time slowed.

For the first twenty feet I felt weightless, my mind shocked, surprised, my brain trying to compute if I really was falling.

The rope, stretching sixty metres – from me, through dozens of karabiners, all the way back to my haul bags – began to be pulled tight, stretching, trying to catch me.

You're falling.

I felt the rope go tight for a second, my body not yet at terminal velocity. It stretched out, trying to spread the force of me, trying to make my load bearable on the top copperhead.

Time slowed some more.

You're still falling.

I felt the rope stretch out. Each millionth of a second it continued to hold me would further increase the chance of it saving me. Was it too much to ask? I knew it was.

The first piece ripped. The second piece ripped. The third piece ripped.

I felt it through the rope, hopeless; the gear felt as strong as Blu-Tack.

The fourth piece ripped. The fifth piece ripped. The sixth piece ripped.

My body gathered speed. Twenty, fifty, a hundred feet of rock sped past.

Time could no longer be held back, and rushed in. I could hear the sounds of my body spinning down, gear jangling, a long-drawn-out moan of exhaled breath from deep within me.

You're falling.

The seventh piece ripped. The eighth piece ripped. The ninth piece ripped.

I fell. I fell on. I fell so far I thought I would never stop. A hundred and twenty, a hundred and forty feet. On and on.

You're not stopping.

You're going to hit the ledge.

You're going to go further than the ledge.

The rope's snapped?

There was no fear. Fear was knowing you *could* fall. Now I was spinning through the air there was only . . . expectation.

You're going to die!

It doesn't matter.

One hundred and fifty feet.

I stopped.

A piece had held. A crappy, rusty and corroded copperhead the size of my little finger had plucked me back into the world.

Everything was spinning.

I hung there for a second, then screamed out loud.

Why are you screaming?

I don't know, I've just fallen a fucking mile!

No one can hear you.

I hung there in space for a long time. It was all I could do. All I could do. The worst had happened and I was OK. I had been lucky. I savoured the feeling of security, knowing I was hanging on a good piece of gear.

You know you have to go back up and do that all again?

Yes. I can do it.

I clipped in my jumars and started back up the rope.

Mad youth

Chamonix, France. February 2000

Esmond Tresidder was eighteen, almost an alpine virgin, when we ran into each other in Chamonix. I was heading back with Rich Cross from a winter attempt on a route on the Grand Capucin, a needle of rock just below Mont Blanc. As usual I'd had big plans for that winter, but Rich had frostbitten his toes before I'd even arrived on the North Face of the Jorasses and couldn't climb ice. The vibrations caused by kicking were too painful for his toes to bear. We'd had to have a rethink.

The Capucin offered us the chance to suffer without the need to kick, and to climb in a wild spot in the Massif, but after two super-cold nights on the face, we retreated due to the slowness of the climbing. It was difficult to climb hard rock moves in thick gloves and clunky plastic boots. We wanted to practise for a planned trip to Patagonia that summer, but only fools practise suffering. As we skied down the Vallée Blanche, the sense of relief at heading back to a warmer world and food was gradually submerged beneath a familiar depression. I had one week of holiday left; I had to climb something hard before another year of work set in.

We bumped into Es in the town centre as we carried our gear home. He looked like a schoolkid who'd slipped away from his teachers, appearing more like a fifteen-year-old with his painfully skinny frame and schoolboy haircut.

I knew Es well, as he'd worked at Outside in the summer before going to Edinburgh University. No doubt he was here due to my raving about alpine winter climbing all summer long.

I'd interviewed him in the spring for the job, and, although

223

he was a typical 18-year-old, socially awkward, shy, the side of the brain that made people spark and zap still undeveloped, you could tell he was super-keen. He was a champion fell runner, would often cycle fifty miles to work, and really wanted to improve his climbing, going out on the rock at any opportunity. I told him that working in a climbing shop was easy, but low-paid, but that as a climber he would blossom, and no doubt do things he would never have dreamed of as he would often be working with much better climbers. I suppose I wanted to say to him the things I had wanted older people to say to me.

Walking back to the flat where we were staying, Rich hobbling along behind us, I talked to Es and started to form a plan, a way to salvage something from this trip. Rich was happy just to go skiing for the rest of his time, training for the guides' exam he planned to do next winter. I, however, wanted to climb something hard, something harder than I could solo, and so I needed a partner.

Climbers interested in spending multiple nights on a face in winter are thin on the ground. They are a rare breed, and most of those who would say yes are also the type of climber I wouldn't want to climb with. Basically, if you want the job, then you can't have it.

The alternative was to find someone who had no idea what he was in for, and was young and innocent enough to sign on, someone you knew had it in him, only he didn't realise it yet. He would be along for the ride, with me leading everything, and he'd be belaying and seconding. A perfect symbiotic relationship: I couldn't climb without him and vice versa.

As we walked up the stairs to the flat, kicking the snow off our boots, I asked Es if he fancied doing a route with me. He was here to do some easy valley ice climbs, two-pitch pure ice routes which you could get to in an hour and be home again for tea. I was going to suggest something a little harder.

The route I had in mind was called The Maria Callas Memorial route, a kilometre-high mixed climb on my old favourite, the North Face of Les Droites. The route had yet to have a second ascent, and had been put up by three German hard men a few years ago. I'm not sure why I wanted to climb it, but it was probably because it looked like one of the hardest routes in the guidebook – and I sort of liked the name.

On paper, or in the mind of any sane climber, taking a novice on such a route was crazy: 700 metres of steep ice capped by a 200-metre vertical wall of tough free and aid climbing, followed by a final 100-metre ice slope. It was madness, but it would be amazing if we could pull it off. I had soloed the first part and knew that it would be OK for a strong novice like Es, and I would lead the top section, with him jumaring up behind me as I went. I doubted he knew how to jumar up a rope, but I guessed if he was doing a degree he must be clever enough to work it out, even if that degree was in environmental science.

The route would take two days, the first spent climbing the ice slope, the second negotiating the rock shield to the summit. We would have to sleep tied to ice screws on seats we had cut out of the ice and maybe we'd sleep on the knife-edge summit. In alpine north face terms it would be a short outing.

I asked him over a beer.

'That sounds great,' said Es immediately. He had no idea what the words really meant, but the mad glint of youth in his eyes was enough for me to know he had what it would take.

Something was wrong. I was sitting bent over, *pushed* over, unsure for a second where I was. Pinned in place, I was finding it hard to breathe. Something was moving over me like sand, building up behind me, trying to shove me off. My feet thrashed around in my sleeping bag, but I could find only smooth ice, nothing to push against . . .

I woke up. There was a roaring all around and snow really was pouring down over me, building up behind my back and prising me off the mountain. It was a full-on storm, and I wondered if the anchors would hold against the strain.

I unzipped an inch of my bivy bag and looked out.

It was our second day on the face, and the storm had found us squatting in a graveyard for unlucky alpinists, 700 metres up the route, perched on two nicks in the ice just big enough to hold us in check against gravity. The storm was intense and unexpected – good weather had been forecast for a few days. The nature of the face meant snow was funnelling down like Niagara Falls, a terrifying, but thrilling spectacle.

I shouted to Es to see if he was awake. He was, but his black sleeping bag was bent over under the hail of snow; his rope, attached to his harness, and fed out through the zipper of the bag, was pulled tight against the anchor, a peg and nut in a shield of rock behind us.

I told him we'd have to see what happened, perhaps give it a few hours. After all, the weather forecast had been good, so maybe this would clear.

But what if it didn't? I peered down at the line we had taken the day before, up the ice face below us. Now it was a river of powder, metres deep in the places where streams joined to form rivers. There was no way we could get back down the way we'd come up. Going up was also out of the question: the spindrift avalanches would knock us off as soon as we began, filling our faces and cooling us down until we froze.

But we couldn't stay here either.

We were trapped.

I thought about the previous night, as we'd sat brewing up in the freezing dark, tired and thirsty after climbing up to our perch. Es had said that he'd been told by one of his friends not to go climbing with me. I asked why, and heard that his friend had been to one of my slideshows, and that in his opinion I was a 'fucking psycho'.

Almost exactly a year before, two British climbers, Jamie Fisher and Jamie Andrew, had become stuck only a hundred metres higher in just such a storm, pinned down for nearly a week. With no chance of a rescue, they had quickly succumbed to the cold. Jamie Fisher had died of exposure, and Jamie Andrew had been minutes away from death when they eventually managed to rescue him. He was terribly frostbitten, and lost both his hands and lower legs.

Their epic seemed very close.

We too were trapped. We too were fucked.

People often ask me what to do when you have no control at all over the situation you're in. The only answer is that how you react to having no control is often the first step in re-establishing control.

'We'll give it three hours,' I shouted to Es, trying to sound as if nothing was wrong, as if I had found myself in such a predicament many times before. Actually, I had, but nothing quite this bad.

He mumbled something back, but his words were lost to the snow.

I sat and thought about the two Jamies. What would happen to us? What would happen to Es? I felt ashamed at my ambition, for bringing Es here. He didn't have a clue. For him this was about fun, a game, just climbing, but it was anything but. What had I been thinking? How could I be so callous and selfish, getting him into such a mess? What if he had been my child?

What if he dies and you survive?

'Let's get the fuck out of here,' I shouted.

Only fifteen minutes had passed.

Es poked his head out of the cowl of his bivy bag and smiled as if nothing was wrong. I smiled back and wondered if we'd see the end of the day.

With the unrelenting snow trying to bully us off our perches, our only option was to attempt a retreat. I knew I would have to use all my experience to make it down. I was glad I'd survived the retreat down Fitzroy. Now I could call on every scrap of skill I had learnt there.

The only problem was that this was worse.

Getting ready was a mess of cold fumbling, juggling gear, everything buried, frozen or just lost. We pulled up our boots from the bottom of our sleeping bags and strained to get them on, all the while trying to remain in our sloping snow-filled bucket seats.

Wearing every item of clothing we had, we pulled ourselves out of our bags and tried to stand against the force of snow and sort out a system for retreat.

Es was small and very skinny, I was not, so I took the enormous rack of hardware and our single giant rucksack, and got ready to set off down first. The plan was that I would abseil from two anchors, one main one and one back-up. Es, being light and unencumbered, would then take out the back-up anchor and descend on just one, with the belief that if the main anchor held me, it should hold Es. With such a long descent, it was the only way we'd have enough gear to make anchors all the way down, while maintaining a good safety margin.

Triple-checking my abseil device, and trying to kick my crampons into the ice, I lifted my head and tried to smile at Es as I set off. All I could see was his hooded head bowed under the pummelling snow.

I unclipped myself from the anchor and began walking down the face, trying to keep my weight on my crampons and off the rope.

The normal line of retreat was a roaring freeway of snow, and to go that way would have meant death by drowning. We had to head down a thousand-foot steep blank rock to its right. This was our only option, but came at a high risk, as, once we started down, there would be no way to climb back up. We would have to find a crack or spike every sixty metres to make the next anchor. Without this we would be stuck, probably succumbing to hypothermia quickly, left to hang in our harnesses. There was no time for 'ifs' and 'buts' though. It was the only way. It had to work.

Down I went, head bowed under the battering snow, my mind thinking of nothing but the next anchor, holding off my search until I could see the two ends of my ropes sixty metres down.

Locking off the rope, I swung from side to side, looking for a crack or spike under the white-coated rock, my fingertips wiping the powder away, until with relief it offered up a place for a nut, then a small cam as a back-up.

'Off belay,' I screamed, snow filling my mouth as the words left.

Es removed the back-up anchor and slid down the rope to me.

Anchors were difficult to find and construct; snow covered everything. Each time, all I could do was get to the end of the rope and begin swinging left and right, my crampons scraping, brushing frantically with one gloved hand until they uncovered a place I could hammer in a wire or peg, or found a spike or flake over which I could drape a length of our rapidly dwindling five millimetre-thick abseil cord.

The position was incredible. We moved down the blank expanse of rock, snow snaking down in torrents all around us towards the glacier which was still hundreds of metres below but obscured by cloud. Soon I slipped into a familiar pattern of systematic and methodical action, making sure that of the hundred things that could kill us, those which were in my power to avoid were avoided, leaving to fate the few that were out of my control: total anchor failure, huge overpowering avalanche, chopped rope.

At one point, strung out at the end of the rope, all I could find for an anchor was a single incipient hairline crack, and spent several long minutes searching for something better until cold made it hard to hold onto the rope, forcing me to make do with what I had. The only anchor that fitted was our shortest, thinnest knifeblade peg. I slid its tip into the crack, and hammered it in, hoping brute force would achieve a deep and secure fit. It bottomed out after only an inch. Both our lives would have to hang from a peg only a few millimetres thick. It was all there was.

Luckily a thin ledge led across the wall a few feet below the anchor, so I didn't have to hang from it. I could stand with my feet stacked sideways, my body only just in balance, as I shouted for Es to follow.

He came down and I showed him the anchor. His head was bowed under the snow, and I knew he wasn't really taking it all in. The peg was already half hidden under the snow.

'You don't have to clip into the peg if you don't want to,' I shouted, aware that if it ripped as I started down the next pitch, Es would be pulled off with me. 'You can either clip in or just cling to the wall and hope no big avalanches come down.'

It was a hard choice, either die with me if the peg ripped as I went down, or stand on the spot until an avalanche or hypothermia pushed you off.

Es unclipped.

I had no fear as I pulled the rope down, and fed it through the peg. It was obvious that this was all there was. I had no option.

Feeding the rope into my abseil device, Es shouted to me, asking how much further. We'd been moving for about five hours, and still had a long way to go. Neither of us had been able to eat or drink anything, and as Es spoke the air filled with a foul smell that made me feel like vomiting. It was Es's body, much thinner and leaner than mine, probably beginning to digest its own muscle. It was almost comical to be standing there, about to make the most committing abseil of my life, yet I was gagging at my partner's bad breath. I was almost glad to be going.

I stepped down and weighted the peg, watching it bend slightly as my full weight went through it for the first time, then began walking down the wall, trying to think the lightest thoughts possible.

Down I slid for another sixty metres, a timeless span of hope and expectation, imagining the sudden and final drop if the peg ripped.

Nothing pulled, and at the end of the rope I found the best anchor so far, hammering an alloy nut so hard into a crack that it will probably still be there in a thousand years.

My thoughts turned to Es.

'OFF BELAY!'

Es moved around above, clipping into the ropes, then slowly slid down to me and clipped in. After that I thought maybe we could make it.

With a smile of relief I pulled on one rope to drag the other through the anchor. It wouldn't budge. It was stuck. I tried pulling the other one, thinking maybe I had made a mistake, knowing I was right the first time. I was. It was jammed.

I clipped on my jumars and tried to use my body weight to pull it through, trying to imagine what the problem could possibly be. The rope remained stuck. We had no choice but to turn to the unthinkable. Someone would have to jumar back up, trusting the single peg once more, in order to free the rope.

Unclipping the jumars of my harness I passed them to Es. 'Sorry, you have to go back up and sort it out. You're lighter than me.'

Es took them without a word, jugged back up into the storm, and did.

Fourteen hours later we rattled over the bergschrund in the dark, the storm unabated, and swam as fast as we could away from the face, snow up to our armpits, our ropes dragging down behind us. The whole area was awash with avalanche debris, and we knew another could come down and wipe us out just like that, making our slow pace as we lurched through the snow even more traumatic.

At last the ground changed. Horizontal. The snow grew less thick. Safe. We were down. We had made it.

I fell onto my knees and began dry-heaving with exhaustion and relief. Es looked on, swaying in the wind, his eyes wide and bloodshot. I tried to stand up but I had absolutely no energy left.

He pulled me up by my shoulder and smiled, saying he'd get us back to the hut. He was stronger than me now. I knew he would get me back.

He put on the rucksack, strapping one rope to the side and, tying us together with the other in case of crevasses, he got ready to lead off. I tried to steady myself and find the energy for the last leg, tried to show I was OK by joking that the meaning of adventure was being unsure of the outcome.

Es just looked at me, his young face old in the yellow light of my dying headtorch. The sparkle of youth had gone.

Music lessons

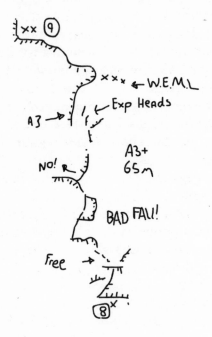

Pitch 9 Reticent Wall

My karabiner closed around the belay bolts at the top of pitch nine. There was none of the usual euphoria. I was just glad the pitch was over. Another pitch closer to this being finished. I was feeling glum.

The belay was special. It featured a tiny sentry-box-type ledge set into the wall, onto which I shuffled my bum and sat on my throne. It was only just big enough for my hips, but I sat there resting my head on my knees, looking down the wall. I'd never felt so drained. I had nothing left to give.

The last two days had been intense. Yet again I doubted I had it in me to carry on.

You're just tired.

I had no idea how I was going to find the energy to abseil down and begin cleaning and hauling the pitch.

You will.

The pitch, like all the rest, had stretched on and on, culminating in a wide crack full of batshit and the bones of small animals. The dust had covered me and choked me until I had reached this tiny perch.

My eyes felt heavy; I just wanted to sleep.

I sat there a long time, my head and arms resting on my knees, and I felt my whole being fall apart. There didn't seem to be one bit of me that wasn't throbbing, bleeding, bruised or close to breaking. I was done in, and just couldn't imagine how I would have the energy to complete the five pitches to come.

You still have the crux to climb, but at this speed you could be there in two or three days. You're faster than Humar.

I don't care.

I hugged my legs and wanted them to hug me back. I felt destitute and alone.

What did you think it would be like? Fun?

I wished I had a phone so I could ring home and tell Mandy how much I was suffering, but I knew she was unimpressible. Climbing was a disease. Climbing was a curse. Climbing was making both our lives hell.

It's not about your climbing.

I thought about talking to Ella, imagined her voice, what she would say.

She would ask when I was coming home.

I often wondered about writing her a letter, to tell her who I was, why I climbed, and why I left her, even though she was the greatest gift I had ever been given. But every time I started, my words sounded like the excuses they were. The only thing I had to give were the photos I had taken of her, boxes full. Through them you could see my love for her. And her love for me.

One day, I would write a book and hope she would then understand that fathers are only children too.

You need to abseil down. It'll soon be dark.

I looked over the wall. To my left I could see a climber leading, heading up to the twenty-fifth belay on the Pacific Ocean Wall, shouting to his partner that he was almost there.

I wished I had a partner to shout to, to clean the pitch, and help me haul the bags.

I looked around, and tried to tell myself how lucky I was, – more people have sat on the summit of Everest than have sat here. I didn't care.

Then I saw something close by, the edge of a piece of card sticking out of a thin crack just above my head. Teasing it out with my fingers I found it was a tatty old business card advertising the services of a 'Lance Millo Eagle – Rock and roll, blues and jazz for all occasions. Banjo and guitar lessons given'. I looked at it and blinked. Inside my head a pilot light came on, and my brain turned over and restarted as it took in how surreal it was to find such a thing here.

Had it been blown up here from the valley, or perhaps it had been left behind by Lance himself, moonlighting as a big-wall climber, maybe the world's greatest banjo-playing big-wall climber? It didn't matter, the card had pulled me back from my self-indulgent funk. The pity party was over and the laughter inside my head reminded me that I was still here.

You're the luckiest man alive.

I stood up on my stiff legs and rigged up to abseil back down to the start, remembering what the taxi driver had said about hard work killing horses.

Give yourself a little slack.

When you're soloing, it's important not to imagine yourself as cold and hard like the stone you climb. You must find some softness within, and see it not as weakness but as compassion and support. You must learn to think about yourself as you would about a friend, a lover, a mother, a daughter. In all the anxiety and fear, you have to make time to love yourself. If you are alone, there are no kind words save your own. This was a lesson I had forgotten. I sat awhile, just admired the view and took a moment to understand what I'd already achieved on this climb.

I clipped in my belay device and double-checked it. Then I slipped once more back down my haul lines. The top now seemed so near.

Safe

Yosemite. April 2000

Airlie moved slowly, so slowly she might well have been climbing down. She tapped at a peg ineffectually, like a sullen teenager hoovering her bedroom.

'How's it going?' I shouted up to her body dangling only six feet above my head. This was the type of comment that would be translated by any leader as 'what the fuck are you doing up there?'

Airlie had been at the sharp end for over an hour.

It was day two of our ascent of Zenyatta Mondatta.

Myself and Esmond sat on wooden belay seats amongst our large and bulging haul bags and shivered; it was only April and a winter chill was still blowing through the Yosemite valley.

'I'm not sure what to do,' shouted Airlie, continuing to tap, a slight wobble in her words. 'I think I might need a mouse beak or something.'

'You mean birdbeak?' I corrected.

Airlie had never climbed a big wall before. Neither had Esmond, and at this rate neither of them ever would.

The idea of climbing El Cap with a novice was pretty outrageous. Two novices doubly so. But here we were, trying to climb one of El Cap's harder routes, graded A5 in the guide book, and the hardest big wall in the world when it was climbed back in 1981. Since then the route had been downgraded with traffic, but was still considered loose and dangerous. A climber died on it few years before, his rope cut in a fall.

'Keep going,' said Esmond, digging his face out of the neck of his duvet, 'you're doing well.' Es had only just recovered from our trip down the North Face of the Droites. On his return to Edinburgh University he'd become withdrawn. But being young and keen, he'd made a swift recovery just in time to sign on for another crazy trip.

'Do you ever get bored on belays?' asked Es, shuffling his bum on the hard wooden belay seat, a plank of wood with rope attached to it. 'Not really, I think you're just glad you're not the one leading,' I said, not mentioning I'd been sitting for four hours already today while he led his first proper aid pitch. It had been graded A4 in the guide book, and had been a baptism of fire, with me shouting up instructions on copperheading and hooking. A novice at the start, by the end of that pitch he'd learnt everything he'd ever need to know.

'How do you know if this mouse beak's any good?' shouted Airlie as she tap-tapped on the tiny peg.

'Just hit it really hard until it won't come out,' I shouted back unhelpfully.

I wondered why I'd chosen to come here with these two. They were friends, and I'd guessed they had the right stuff. Esmond was a young champion athlete and Airlie Anderson was one the best female rock climbers in the UK. I'd realised that I'd become, and perhaps had always been, a die-hard optimist, and this optimism had spread to the abilities of others. Perhaps just as people had taken me under their wing: Dick Turnbull, Paul Tattersall and Andy Perkins. Now it was my time to do the same.

'I can't do it,' said Airlie, as what sounded to me like crying drifted down.

'What's the problem?' I asked, trying to remain patient.

'I'm too slow.'

'Well stop fucking crying and get a move on then.'

That night it rained hard, the storm continuing into a dull and claggy morning, our portaledges and sleeping bags soaking up the rain. Things weren't going to plan and, still close enough to the ground to tie our ropes together and escape, we found the draw of dry beds and showers too hard to resist. We abseiled off, leaving our bags and portaledges in place ready for better weather. I wasn't sure if all of us would return to finish the route, the reality of which far outstripped the crazy dream we'd had in Sheffield.

Staggering down through the dripping woods we found Airlie's boyfriend Matt Dickinson, equally bedraggled, wandering up to meet us, having seen us retreating from the road. Matt was one of those immensely physical people you meet, seemingly pure muscle with nothing to spare. I thought he looked like Frankenstein's climbing monster. He was well known for being a little bit extra. He once attempted to solo the North Face of the Eiger, only to break his leg near the start. Having no insurance, he dragged himself back to the train station and got all the way back to Leeds before seeing a doctor. He had also soloed the Bonatti Pillar above Chamonix, a route that had achieved a mystical quality, higher than even the Eiger, an ascent that singled Matt out as a pretty extraordinary and ballsy climber. I expect he would have done well in the SAS, but in fact he was a supply teacher in between climbing trips.

He'd come to the valley intent on soloing the Nose of El Cap, but to me at least his technique seemed to be lacking a little, his only rope a length of 7-mm cord probably best employed as a clothes line. The difference between me and Matt was that I knew he could probably pull it off through sheer brute force and ignorance of a better way. When I'd asked him how he'd jumared up his rope when soloing the Bonatti Pillar, he just said, 'I used my hands.' He had an awesome self-confidence that he could simply hang on – a confidence I lacked, and so burdened myself with ropes and haul bags. Although I had begun as a rock climber, things seemed to have changed for me and it was no longer about the joy of climbing, as it was with Matt, but simply the struggle of it. In my heart I wasn't a climber anymore, and people like Matt intimidated me a little, because I felt he could see through me. Perhaps that was why I was climbing with Es and Airlie?

We walked down the track, Matt telling us that the storm would clear tomorrow and after one good day a second bigger front would pass through the valley. Matt had to leave for a guiding job in the Himalaya in a week, and it looked as if his hopes for climbing El Cap were as over as ours were if the weather didn't improve.

Standing beside the car, I felt the pressure to grasp something from the trip. The idea of coming all this way for nothing was unthinkable, and so in the time it took me to take off my rucksack I had formed a plan.

'Why don't we both go and climb El Cap in a day?' I suggested to Matt. 'We could set off at midnight tonight, and be at the top before the big storm hits?'

'What route?' asked Matt, helping Airlie with her haul bag.

'Why don't we try and climb Tangerine Trip?' I said 'It's only had one one-day ascent – it's super-steep and I've done the first four pitches and the last three when I soloed Aurora. It would go in a push.'

'Yeah, that sounds good,' said Matt, obviously not having a clue what a stupid idea this was, having no real knowledge of El Cap beyond the Nose.

Airlie turned around and raised her eyebrows then let out a loud laugh as if to prove that we were crazy, and perhaps even relief that for the time being she was off the hook.

Very often in my climbing life I've really questioned if I'm not mentally ill, something that seemed clearly obvious thirty-five hours later, as I clung to a greasy hold with my left hand, my left knee balanced on a smooth sloping shelf, searching for another hold in the dark, my only protection, a sky hook clipped at my feet. That conversation in the car park suddenly seemed ten thousand years ago.

When we'd got back to Camp 4 the previous day, the inhabitants hiding under a carnival of tarps from the rain, I'd begun packing straight away. The Tangerine Trip is one of the steepest routes on El Cap, nineteen pitches long, with no ledges big enough to stand on from pitch two to pitch eighteen. A portaledge is vital, but having one would have slowed us down, and so I left it behind, thinking that without it, and with no chance of sleep, we'd have a big incentive to get to the top. Instead I threw in our wooden belay seat, a plank of wood with swing-like ropes attached to its corners, and a string hammock I'd bought from a garden centre. Our emergency gear was a single Gore-Tex bivy bag and a sleeping bag, which I guessed we could drape over us if we got to the summit in the dark. Matt supplied a bag of food, and I sorted out the rack, taking only the bare minimum. The space that was left in the haul bag was filled with warm clothes. I asked Matt what storm gear he had and he said he didn't need any, just the red fleece he had on, telling me he had 'excellent circulation'. This seemed typical of Matt, who it appeared went out of his way not to conform to the normal manner of doing anything, depending instead on bull-headed stubbornness and grit; wearing jeans when climbing rather than stretchy fast-drying trousers, a heavy duty sailing jacket rather than a lightweight waterproof, a cotton sweatshirt rather than a fleece.

'Matt, if we get in a storm up there it's the most serious place on the planet, there's no abseiling off, no rescue, you'll fucking die if you've only got a fleece on.' Matt didn't agree, and seeing as he was still alive after countless epics I wondered if it was I who was being over-cautious. But being cautious had also kept me alive so far, so I just stuffed in some extra clothes for him instead. While packing, I had found that I had left behind my warm gloves, socks and trousers, plus some vital gear, like our long tent pole used as a cheater stick, in our bags on Zenyatta Mondatta. It was decided that Matt would jumar up our fixed ropes and get the gear, while I soloed the first pitches of The Trip.

The rain stopped and I lay down in my tent and tried to get some sleep. Most speed ascents were made by local climbers who were well rested, and knowledgeable, having done several walls already that season. I on the other hand was just getting back into it, and was feeling neither fit nor fully confident. I thought about Matt, and how he really had no experience for this climb, having almost no knowledge of hauling or jumaring. A speed team needs to be just that, a team, whereas we were really just strangers. I had big doubts about this, but my burning ambition outweighed them, and something inside me was exhilarated by the stupidity of trying. It was as if I wanted to get into trouble.

With midnight approaching I got up, having not slept, and rechecked all our gear. I asked to see Matt's headtorch. Mine was super-bright, with a halogen bulb and plenty of juice in the batteries. Matt's looked like he'd won it in a cracker, or got it free with a litre of petrol. 'Have you got any spare batteries?' I asked, to which Matt produced from his pocket some grubby-looking batteries that looked as though he'd found them down the side of a settee.

It was too late to make a fuss.

Walking back to the base had seemed odd, the woods and wall now silent. We talked a little, but really our thoughts were only of the climb. The best things were the light haul bag on my back, one day's food and water, two ropes and a minimum of gear. I could see the appeal of trying to climb big walls in a day.

Now, nearly twenty-four hours later, I could think of nothing worse or more stupid than pitting myself against a route such as this with so little gear, sleep or talent, stuck on one knee, barely holding on, knowing Matt was sat below, probably asleep, and we weren't even half way up the wall.

I reached up again and tried to find the right hold, any hold, but there was nothing. I had to be off-route. I searched around with my right foot for the aider I had stepped off, the one attached to the skyhook, feeling my knee sliding, the water-proof trousers offering almost zero friction on the glassy granite. I searched harder, trying not to knock the hook off in the process, knowing the next gear was about ten feet below, just an old bent rivet. I tried to control my breathing, and focus, but it was no good, I knew I was about to fall. The worst kind of fall there is.

'Watch me, Matt,' I shouted. 'Watch m . . .'

And I fell off.

It had been a disaster from the start.

I had soloed the first pitch while Matt went off to jumar the ropes, but on reaching the first belay there was still no sign of him, and so, using what rope I had left, I began up the next pitch. I ran out of rope and hung there waiting, worrying that he might have fallen off in the dark. I thought about the reality of him dying; finding his body, telling Airlie and his parents he was dead. Had I asked him if he could jumar?

Then I heard a commotion in the trees below.

'Matt is that you?' I shouted down.

'Yes,' he said, sounding a bit flustered.

'What are you doing?'

'My headtorch stopped working, so I couldn't find any of

your gear,' he shouted back, 'I'm looking for something to use as a cheater stick.'

'Well, unless you can find a folding collapsible stick that's twenty feet long, don't bother,' I said coldly.

I felt mad with Matt, knowing that a stick wouldn't do, and having only shorts, no socks, gloves or trousers, it would be foolish to carry on. It was already nearly 2 a.m., and our time was running out. It was obvious that we should call it off and go down to our beds.

'What do you want to do?' Matt shouted up, climbing language for, 'I don't want to do it anymore.'

This could well be my last chance to climb a route for many months. I'd spent most of my money on the trip and I knew once down, I'd regret not at least trying. The only problem was this was a Yoda kind of route, where there could be no 'try', only 'do'.

'Just jumar up,' I shouted. 'We need to get a move on.'

And so after a full day's climbing, going as fast as we could, but not fast enough, I had climbed into a dead end and was now falling.

I probably would have screamed, but before I could, I came to a jarring halt a metre below. The skyhook, no bigger than the tip of a pencil, had held me.

I tried to be sick.

I knew I had given all I could today, and so, climbing back down to the last rivet, I abseiled down to Matt, who sat slumped in the belay seat, his head resting on the wall, uninterested in me or in life in general.

'I need some sleep,' I said, clipping myself to the belay, suddenly feeling the exhaustion, and the chance of rest, robbing me of the last of my energy. With no portaledge we tossed a coin to see who would get the hammock, but the coin slipped from my hand and fell into the night, so it went to Matt.

I had barely seen Matt since we started climbing. Employing a technique called short-roping, on reaching the belay I would immediately start up the next pitch on what was left of the rope, with Matt jumaring up behind as fast as he could.

Usually climbing a wall is a great way to get to know someone, but this wasn't. We just tried to make ourselves as comfortable as possible.

I got the sleeping bag and pulled it around my shoulders as I shuffled on the belay seat, wrapping a sling around my back to stop me falling off in the night, my helmet my only pillow. It was the equivalent of sleeping sitting on a swing.

I hadn't eaten anything since leaving Camp 4, and with my stomach churning, and feeling nauseous with hunger, I asked Matt to pass me the food sack I'd seen him stash in the haul bag, the only thing I'd asked him to bring. Taking it from the hammock, I opened it to find it didn't contain the cheese and bagels I'd been expecting, only a single glass jar of salsa.

'I brought some chocolate as well,' said Matt sheepishly, his menu obviously designed for a very short ascent.

'Where is it?' I asked, thinking that it would at least raise my zero blood sugar level.

'I ate it when I was belaying.'

We woke feeling like tramps, groaning and rubbing ourselves in the first grey light of morning. I looked up at Matt, looking like a shipwrecked pirate in his hammock, washed up on El Cap. 'Don't worry Matt,' I said, as I began clipping the rack back on, breakfast nothing more than cold air, 'we just need to get to the last couple of pitches in the light and the rest will be easy, in fact I can climb it with my hands in my pockets.' Matt looked down at me, his helmet askew, no doubt wondering where my confidence came from – not knowing that all I had was words, as clouds rolled down the valley.

The day progressed faster than we did.

Half way up a pitch I shouted, 'Send up the rest of the pegs,' to Matt, who hung below me from two bolts, hauling up the bag.

'What pegs?' he replied.

It turned out that Matt hadn't realised that I had been placing pegs, and so had neglected to remove them as he followed. Added to this, although I'd shown him the correct way to remove a cam when jumaring, he had chosen just to pull on them as hard as he could, which had broken a couple. I began to think he was an idiot, forgetting that learning to climb big walls had taken me many years, and I was expecting Matt to pick it up in a day. It was I who was the idiot.

All day the storm grew, rain turning to snow. Luckily the

steepness that trapped us also offered protection, the snow falling metres away. It felt as if we were climbing under glass.

I convinced myself we could make it to the top, but darkness came again with the summit still out of reach, and with it came paranoia. Every placement became a time bomb, every crack expanding, every flake loose. I hadn't slept properly for three days, and my mind was crumbling. I could hear whispers, and my body was acting strangely, sharp pains in my stomach, flashes of light when my eyes moved quickly, and hands that closed involuntarily when I stretched out my arms to place gear.

Feeling beyond wasted at midnight, I knew we had to do the unthinkable and bivy once more, our speed ascent crashing into a third day. Matt jumared up silently, while I hauled apathetically, feeling guilty for suggesting such a stupid idea. Matt never said a word.

This time there were no tossed coins, and Matt got the hammock, which he had to sit in above me, as both anchors were too close together for him to string it out to sleep. He wrapped himself up in the bivy sack, wearing most of the clothes I'd stuffed into the haul bag, a new item going on for each pitch climbed.

My arse was sore from the night before, but exhaustion is a fine painkiller, beating even my hunger for attention, as wrapped in slings, my feet balanced on the haul bag, I dropped into a pool of sleep in an instant, thinking that nothing could ever beat this night for its discomfort, but waking a little while later to find I had been wrong. Matt's string hammock had stretched until his whole weight was pressing down on me, forcing my head against El Cap.

'Matt,' I shouted, 'You're sitting on my head.' All I heard were snores in reply. I felt like sobbing, but it would have required too much energy, and so, too tired to do anything else, I closed my eyes and went into a long period of waking and sleeping, pain on top of pain.

We woke in a cloud, thick mist everywhere, a light wind whistling snow flakes around us. My head throbbed and I felt sick as Matt got his weight off my head and began gearing up to leave. I wondered why no one had called out the mountain rescue, seeing as we were two days late.

Airlie and Es had in fact been to the Yosemite search and rescue and had been told we'd be OK and would just have to sit it out in our portaledge. They didn't tell them we didn't have one. They had come down to the meadow, where people had gathered to check on loved ones sitting out the storm, and found we were the star attraction, binoculars and spotting scopes trained on us through gaps in the clouds. 'Look at those crazy Russians climbing through the storm,' someone had said.

It was late afternoon when we got to the vertical section of the wall. The overhanging world below, with its dry cold drop, was replaced within a few moves by waterfalls and snow. Matt belayed me as I set off up the third-to-last pitch, water draining directly onto him, and pushing him close to hypothermia. Although we were bound together it was every man for himself now when it came to staying alive, and as I moved away up a rivet ladder I saw him doing sit-ups on the belay seat, singing 'One man went to mow,' over and over again. I also got soaking wet, water rushing down my sleeves each time I lifted my arms up, my shoes filling with icy water, my legs burning with the cold wind, with only my waterproof trousers to keep them warm.

I looked down as I climbed. The wall barrelled away into the clouds, the snow whizzing past, mixed with torrents of water drifting from the summit. Perhaps it was malnutrition, but I stopped to take a photo, thinking, for the first time since I'd started, how amazing this was.

With relief I got to the second-to-last pitch, and waited shivering while Matt came up, sleet piling up on my shoulders, my fingers wrapped around my neck for warmth. I could feel my body temperature dropping by the second, every gram of clothing soaked through, forcing me to draw on everything I had learnt in order to stave off the debilitating cold. I began tensing my muscles as hard as I could until they cramped. If either of us succumbed we would die up here in a matter of hours. We wouldn't be the first.

Matt appeared looking grey with the cold. 'Don't worry,' I said as I grabbed the gear off him, 'this next pitch is easy, and the last one is piss.' I was glad I was with Matt, because I just knew he was too stubborn to give in and die.

I set off up, first on easy aid, then switching to free climbing, moving slowly and deliberately on tiny flakes. Snow covered all the edges, forcing me to brush it off with my bare fingers as I climbed, water continuously running down my sleeves as I did so. I thought about my dad's taking us climbing in the rain, and how all those miserable climbs had been perfect practice for this, because although it was desperate, I was making progress. It was a terrible position to be in, yet for some reason I felt exhilarated. Perhaps it was because I could see the end in sight, perhaps it was because I was amazed that I could still climb in such bad conditions, without gloves or socks, or perhaps it was the pure focus of survival that liberated me from the worries of the wall below. We had to get to the top.

I stood in snow up to my ankles and danced and jumped and screamed, waiting for Matt to get to the first ledge on the route, the top just a short crack and an easy slab away, no more than twenty metres.

Matt wasn't coming.

I shouted *safe* again and cursed him for being so slow when we were so near, just some easy climbing, then the descent to warm clothes, food and glorious flat ground.

Matt still hadn't appeared.

I looked down the wall, now almost uniformly white as the temperature began to fall further. I could see that within an hour the upper section would have been ice, and we would have been trapped.

I felt the rope. It was under tension. Matt was coming. Then I saw him, coming out of the storm slowly. Unbeknownst to me his jumars had become choked with ice and suddenly stopped gripping the rope, sending him on a terrifying ride back down the rope and only catching again once they cleared of ice.

Matt pulled himself onto the ledge.

'I need your clothes,' he said.

'What?' I asked

'I – I – I'm dying of hypothermia. I need your clothes,' he went on, stepping into the thick snow, his lips blue and teeth chattering.

'I'm dying as well,' I replied, 'we've just got to keep going.'

I passed him the gear and told him to lead the last pitch, thinking this might warm him up.

Matt was a fantastic climber, climbing grades harder than I could. But as he started up, I could tell he was hurting. He looked stiff and wooden. He climbed the crack and got to the slab above. It was smooth, and shaped like the back of a whale. Instead of climbing shoes, Matt had chosen to wear skate shoes, whose smooth rubber soles offered no grip at all on the snowy rock. They forced him backwards and forwards, trying to find a way up. In the dry a climber could step up it with no hands, now it had been transformed into something impossible, totally friction-less under the snow.

'I can't do it,' shouted Matt.

'Come down then, I'll do it,' I shouted back, irrationally cross with him.

Swapping, with Matt holding my ropes, which were now thick with ice, I climbed up to the slab. It would soon be dark and I had to think quick. I grabbed a skyhook and began scraping it down the rock until it snagged on some unseen edge beneath the snow. I clipped in a sling and carefully stepped up, knowing that if it ripped I could tumble back down to the ledge and probably break my legs.

From the hook I could feel a slight moon-shaped dish or depression under the snow and, wiping it away, I managed to step into it, pressing my body against the rock to gain the most friction possible. I tried not to move a muscle. I had gained about six feet. I looked up and could see a tiny sprouting tree, maybe twelve inches high, on a ledge above. If I could get there it would all be over.

I gathered up the haul line and started tossing it upwards, trying to snag the tree. Again and again I tried, but the weight of the wet rope was too much and each time it slipped back down the slab. I gathered up the rope again, and this time clipped a bunch of nuts and cams to it, then swung the whole lot and cast the rope upwards. It sailed past the tree and disappeared onto the ledge.

I began to pull, slowly, until the rope stopped coming. It was stuck. I stood there, both terrified and immensely exhilarated. I had only one choice and I began pulling up on the rope, my knees braced against the rock, trying to limit the load on the unseen anchor above, expecting it to pull at any moment.

But it didn't.

I reached the ledge and saw the rope was snagged on a block of granite no bigger than a telephone directory, but I had no time to think about this and instead scrambled to a crack, stuffed in some cams and clipped in.

My world suddenly went flat and white. Darkness was no more than a few minutes away and the long descent was still ahead of us. It had almost been beyond me. But I had made it.

I sat down in the snow and began taking in the rope, which had turned as stiff as wire in the cold. An hour slower and we might never have got out of there.

'*Safe*,' I shouted into the storm.

Two days later Airlie, Es and I climbed Zenyatta Mondatta.

Masters of stone

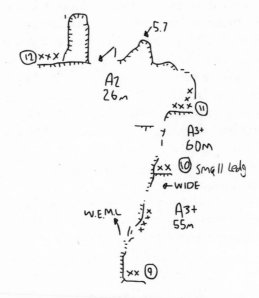

Pitches 10, 11 and 12 Reticent Wall

The morning began with pegs. Lots of pegs.

I moved slowly up a steep corner, my back arched out as I hammered, tapping in short stubby pitons nicknamed Lost Arrows.

The tone of each peg would rise as I struck it, starting low and then singing as it bit down tight into the placement. Nailing pitons is tough, but as with any hard labour it was rewarding to look down at all your work. A line of pegs led back to my haul bags, each peg extended with a red sling so that the rope ran smoothly.

You're getting somewhere.

My shoulder and hand were giving me problems today, no doubt due to the pounding of so many pegs over so many days. In the mornings I'd been waking to find my hands and forearms were completely paralysed, as if I'd slept on them all night. Only after shaking them for several minutes did the feeling, and the pain, return. My shoulder felt as if a hot ember were burning away inside it. I could only strike with the hammer a few times until I'd have to stop and grit my teeth, waiting for the pain to subside. I told myself that the pain was good, that it acted like a speed limit, stopping me from pushing myself too far, but each time I closed my eyes I wished I'd brought some painkillers.

My only first-aid kit was a tiny bottle of tea-tree oil.

My feet were also troubling me, the pain in my arches and toes getting worse by the day, forcing me to dance around in my aiders looking for the sweet spot where they didn't hurt – a pointless exercise; they always hurt. The slightest pressure on the sides of my feet sent spasms shooting through me. I was causing real damage to my tendons, but I knew that in a few days it would be over.

In a strange way my body felt expendable, like all the items of gear I accidentally dropped each day.

All you have to do is keep it together until you reach the top.

The corner was cool, hiding me from the sun for a little while, its texture cold, hard and chalky. Sometimes I would see insects in the cracks, or see long-legged spiders clinging to the wall.

The belay was just above me, a small ledge that I had to reach up to at full stretch so that I could clamber on. I set myself up below, clipping off all my heavy and redundant gear in order to make it as easy as possible. On any climb mantling up is often scary and fraught with challenges, but on this bit I was wearing my trainers instead of rock boots.

Ready, I stepped up as high as I could in my aiders, my fingers inching up until they gripped the edge of the ledge. The surface was shiny and polished, almost like glass, and I could tell it was about a foot deep and maybe three feet long. I swapped hands and dabbed chalk on them to gain more grip, then took my feet out of the aiders, committed, and pulled up.

My arms felt strong after so much work, and I did a pull-up and threw one elbow and one knee over the ledge.

They began slipping off. Something was wrong. It took a moment to work it out. The glassy surface was covered in muesli, which meant I couldn't get a grip.

It could only be the Russians. They must have left me a bag of muesli as a present and the birds had pecked it open.

The situation would have been humorous, if it hadn't been on the Reticent Wall. Holding on with one hand, I tried to wipe the cereal away, only to grab on again with my other hand as my leg slipped off completely leaving me hanging by my arms, feet pedalling, toes fruitlessly trying to find their way back into the aiders.

I pulled up once more, and tried to blow away as much muesli as possible, before committing to a full body lunge onto the ledge, hoping that maximum contact would keep me there.

It worked, and very carefully I reached out and clipped the bolts. What a start to the day!

The next pitch carried on up the corner, then up a solitary hairline crack. I pounded in knifeblades every few feet. The wall was barrel shaped, the exposure exhilarating, and I realised this was the pitch I'd seen Steve Gerberding climbing years before in a *Masters of Stone* video at work.

Who'd have thought one day you'd be climbing this pitch?

The crack turned onto a set of small corners that required copperheads, their tenuous nature increasing my sense of exposure.

Don't blow it now.

I knew I was close to the final pitches.

The crux is only a pitch away.

I hauled my bags up to the top of pitch eleven, lighter now that half the water was gone. I'd climbed and cleaned the last two pitches faster than I'd expected. I still had an hour left before dark. I only had one more pitch to go until I was at the crux. Three more until I reached the top. I knew I was climbing faster than on any other day, but was unsure if it was the climbing that was easier, or if I was getting better. One pitch higher I knew there was a large ledge, and was eager to get there and find a little oasis from the steepness of the wall.

Maybe you just want to see the crux after so long thinking about it?

The pitch began with an easy crack that led to a hanging slab, the climbing changing from aid to free. The clumsy paraphernalia of the climbing below had been left behind, swapped for sticky rock shoes and fingers. The sense of freedom was fantastic. The rock was highly featured, with little nubbins to stand on, a flake to use as a handrail, and easy enough to be fun.

After twelve days of excruciatingly slow progress this pitch seemed to go by at lightning speed. I moved leftwards, fingers curled over the flake, trusting my hands and feet, careful with each movement, tiptoeing, exhilarated by the knowledge that I hung above such a drop. So much space. I was actually enjoying myself.

This could be your last night on this wall.

A few more moves leftward and I stepped onto a wide ledge, the largest flattest ground I'd seen for nearly two weeks. Above me stood the crux.

This could be your last night full stop!

I clipped two bolts, kicked off my shoes and lay down. The rock was knobbly and the ledge poked into my back, but it didn't sag, rattle, or bend. It was hard bliss.

I stared up at the overhangs that bore the summit, only two pitches away. It seemed like so long ago that I'd started, that person and his fucked-up world almost forgotten.

If you climb the crux, you'll be on the top tomorrow.

I scanned the crux: a crack, expanding; a seam, blind and flared; a flake, loose and hanging. Any mistake tomorrow and I would be lying here again on this ledge, only in very different circumstances. I thought about that for a while. How would it feel to smash into this ledge? How much pain would there be?

Can you do it?

Tomorrow I would climb the crux of the Reticent Wall: one of the hardest aid pitches in the world.

Could I do it? I thought I could.

Tomorrow would be my thirteenth day on the wall, the route's thirteenth pitch, but I was beyond worrying about numbers. I thought instead about reaching the summit, lying in the soft soil. I imagined the peace.

I thought about Mandy.

I thought about Ella.

I thought about my unborn son.

I thought about pizza.

I knew it would be OK.

Cold war

Patagonia. July 2000

'*Usted no sabe sobre mama del la?*' asked the woman behind the ticket counter, her face creased with concern.

'We don't understand,' I said, speaking for both me and my partner.

'*La mama, la mama,*' the woman repeated, pointing out of the window at the snow piled high outside. We shrugged. All we wanted were two bus tickets. I thought maybe she had to wait to get permission from her mother to sell us the tickets, but she looked a bit too old for that.

'*La mama,*' she said one last time, now miming snow falling from the sky with her fingers.

Standing in Rio Gallegos airport, in Argentina, on our way to Patagonia, Rich Cross and I shook our heads. Whatever it was, it didn't sound good.

Exasperated by our poor Spanish, the woman left us and grabbed another woman from across the hallway to translate.

It turned out La Mama was a weather system, a nasty relation of El Niño, which had super-cooled the already wintry bottom half of South America. In some parts it had brought snow for the first time in forty years.

She spoke quickly, almost scoldingly at our ignorance, telling us that the Brazilian coffee crop had been damaged by frost, that power was out in many parts of the country, that most of the roads were impassable, blocked by metres of snow. Running her fingers across a map on the wall, she explained that many of the roads had been closed for weeks and that she doubted we could even reach the village of

Chaltén, let alone the mountains. We should go back to Buenos Aires.

We stood at the counter and looked at each other, our bulging rucksacks piled high beside us, and talked over our options. The conversation was short. We'd sunk all our money into this trip, which meant we had no way of changing our objectives. We were already broke and we hadn't even begun. I thought about how I'd left my life in a mess back home, I'd run away from Mandy and Ella, bills and work, gambling that a hard winter ascent would make it all OK. I couldn't even begin to imagine failing here. I'd staked everything. This was my big chance: the perfect objective, the perfect partner, the perfect season. If we pulled this off, I knew I'd finally be satisfied. For me there would be nothing harder. We had to try.

So we bought our tickets.

The bus rumbled through the night, hot and airless, a Hollywood war movie dubbed into Spanish playing at full volume on the TV set above my head. Outside the damp window I caught glimpses of what was to come: snow bull-dozed high, and beyond it nothing. I felt something familiar stirring inside me, something that made me uncomfortable, a deep sense of loss and sadness. I'd been feeling it for as long as I could remember, but I still didn't know why. I tried to block it out. I thought instead about Ella, her face, her hair, her eyes, of holding her hand, squeezing it and feeling her squeezing mine back. We arrived at Calafe, the last town before Chaltén, after midnight. If we couldn't find a ride to Chaltén our expedition would end here. We lay down on the icy tarmac and waited for the morning.

We woke to find a man lashing bags onto the roof rack of a truck. We jumped out of our sleeping bags to ask, in pidgin Spanish, if he was going to Chaltén. He nodded. Mistaking good timing for good luck, we hitched a lift.

The road to Chaltén was a long and rough one, cold, bumpy, the landscape flat and featureless, a desert of rocky brush. It was hard to believe we were heading towards the mountains. The truck bounced and skidded through snow drifts and over icy pools, the deep ruts tossing us around in the back.

The landscape was a vivid introduction for Rich to what was in store. As we peered through frosted windows out at the endless frozen pampas, we could see the road was littered with llamas, starved and frozen to death by the freak weather. We could never have imagined it would be so grim.

Rich was as uncomplicated as usual, unfazed and positive, telling me we could ski to the mountains if the roads were blocked; a round trip of a mere 250 kilometres. My age, no wife, no kids, free to climb and work where he wanted: I envied him. For him climbing seemed to be fun and empty of any other meaning. Why couldn't I be like that? Where had I lost my way? Why was I going back to this wilderness with a sinking heart? It made no sense. Patagonia terrified me. Before this trip I'd wake up and feel gripped with anticipated horrors, thoughts of the cold, the wind, the endless abseils.

I suppose I was returning because I simply didn't know what else to do. Climbing was the only thing that seemed right, the only thing that made sense.

The road stretched on through the pampas for eight hours until, in the distance, we saw Fitzroy, a snow plume perhaps a kilometre long stretching from its summit. I thought back to that horrendous storm, being trapped up there the previous year, how on our return to the village an old man told us that when the stone houses creaked in the village, they knew we would be dead. It appeared slowly, so huge it was hard to believe such a mountain existed. Most people would call it beautiful; to me it looked like a stone thug.

Sliding and skidding into Chaltén through six-foot walls of bulldozed snow, we looked at a town that appeared to have just survived an attack. Roofs strained under the weight of snow, people moved around trying to make repairs, eyes stared at these out-of-season strangers. We knocked on the door of a friend, Ruban Vasquez, who owned the only open hostel in town. When he saw us, he looked shocked that we had made it. We dragged our stuff in and began straightaway to pack for the next day.

Unfastening my skis' safety straps in case the ice broke under me, I shuffled out onto the frozen lake. Rich stood watching from the bank, rucksack off, ready to throw me a lifeline in case I went through. We didn't know that the ice was a metre thick.

We'd been on the move since 4 a.m., slipping out of Chaltén to the moonlight serenade of barking dogs and the muffled crush of our skis forcing down deep powder. At first light we saw our objective: Cerro Torre, a mile-high needle of rock that lies at the head of the glacier. If you were to ask a child to draw a mountain they would produce something like Everest, 45-degree slopes with a pointed summit; Cerro Torre looks like something a teenager would draw: nightmarish sweeps of vertical rock, tortured ridges, and a ghastly mushroom of ice that hangs from its summit. Cerro Torre is one of the hardest mountains a climber could wish for, and no other mountain on earth holds such daunting terrain. A summer ascent was big news. More people had stood on the moon than had stood on its summit in winter. It was obvious why.

I told Rich that the ice was thick enough to hold us, and when he was confident I was right, he followed me out onto the lake.

Our rucksacks were insanely heavy, our hands chilled because the crushing pressure of strained shoulder straps cut off the blood supply to our arms. People often called this style of climbing lightweight: just taking what you could carry, no porters or huge teams of climbers to break down the challenge. Unfortunately to us this style of climbing felt anything but light.

We didn't need a thermometer to tell us the temperature was below minus 30 degrees Celsius, the air burning any exposed skin. I shuffled along, the atmosphere seemingly a vacuum, as if every atom had grown heavy with frost and dropped out of it. When I removed my thick hood and balaclava, it felt as if I'd immersed my head in the waters of an Arctic ocean, the skin tightening in the cold, giving me an ice-cream headache.

How could we climb in this?

After our three-day nightmare on Fitzroy the year before, each of us went home deeply affected by our experiences; you could say we all suffered from a little post-traumatic stress. Everyone looked at life and their future through new eyes, dealing with it in different ways: confrontation, commitment, love. The outcome brought a year of weddings, babies, and separations.

I had gone home feeling like a soldier, thin and tired. It was hard to re-adjust, but I was relieved to be back with my Mandy and Ella. Driving to the seaside one day, I said then that I didn't want to do this any more, and like any addict I had meant it. But words come easily. A month later I had left them again.

It would not end.

I consider myself a simple person, but I was gradually becoming aware that something was wrong, something inside me seemed to be broken, or perhaps unmended. I hated the restlessness in me that drew me to the mountains. It had gone beyond climbing; I was now looking for something but I didn't know what. I was also scared about what I might find. There seemed to be only one cure, one thing that would give me peace. An endgame.

We skied around the edge of the lake, heading for the mouth of the glacier, our eyes fixed on the golden glow of the Torres high above, the moisture in my eyelashes sticky with the cold.

I thought about the route ahead, and tried to imagine that perhaps the sun might warm us on Cerro Torre, yet knew it wouldn't. Then I stared at my feet and tried to think about other things such as the thickness of the ice; then my mind turned to abstract thoughts: whether light rays could freeze, suspending what I could see now, such as this lake, until spring.

Rich scraped up snow into a pan and placed it carefully on the stove, then zipped himself back into his sleeping bag with a theatrical shiver. We had reached the bottom of the mountain by nightfall, finding shelter by digging ourselves in beneath a house-sized boulder. This wasn't a place for camping. The cold, the weight of our packs, and the deep snow had pushed us close to exhaustion on the twenty-hour slog here. In summer you could make this trip in a couple of hours, dressed in a pair of shorts and a T-shirt. I pulled out a picture of Mandy and Ella, taken in the park. The grass on it was the only green I could see anywhere.

'Am I missing you already?' I wondered. It was strange to have such feelings so early. When I was with them I could think of nothing but being in these frozen mountains.

How could that be right; what could I possibly find here?

I thought about Mandy shouting at me in the kitchen the day I left, how she used to worry when I was away – now she just hated me for putting her through it. I knew that my life was unbalanced. There were no fond farewells when I left, only a cold kiss, because that's what you do when someone leaves and you don't understand why.

What if I were to die tomorrow?

Would this make anything better? On the mountain there would be no fun or laughter, no beautiful views, no poems forming in the head. Only fear and cold and anxiety. But I had to believe this route would be worth it.

We made dinner, eating some of the weight we would otherwise have carried up to the base camp tomorrow. Then we lay unable to sleep, listening and talking about nothing, just words, their breath turning to frost that coated the rock above our heads.

In the coldest hour of the predawn morning, we crawl out from beneath our boulder and start climbing up towards the black space in the stars where the Torre stands.

The route is a nightmarish spine that spirals up the tower, bounded on its right by a mind-blowing wall of granite. To reach this ridge we first have to climb 1,000 feet of snow, ice and rock – a route in itself – piecing a line together that will allow us to reach a small col at the beginning of the ridge.

We climb up onto the face, moving together in stops and starts, our hands growing colder as we climb, which means we have to co-ordinate warming them. Like an archaeologist, I scrape about and come across old soft-iron pegs, rattly and loose with cold, and bleached ropes, pulled tight and disembowelled by the moving ice. I wonder who hammered and tied these artefacts here, and what tales they could tell.

Dawn arrives beautifully, but with a price, its vibrant golds and reds heralding a coming storm. I want to go down, but I stop myself from saying it. Rich has yet to experience a winter Patagonian storm, so I keep my fears to myself and carry on climbing, eyeing the wispy clouds that arrive soon after the dead sun.

The first thousand feet are a slog through deep powder,

interspersed with hard pulls into loose, spiky corners. The higher we get, the deeper my anxiety. All the strength I thought I had leaves me. The snow and easy climbing come to an end just below the Col of Patience, forcing Rich to work hard in order to reach the slope above. I had always thought that when this day came, I would find it hard to believe I was actually here on Cerro Torre, and in winter. Now I'm far too aware of where I am and what I'm doing. I'm shit-scared, fighting to stay warm, my mind a jumble of dark thoughts; this is too much, the experience, the dose, far too intense. Shaking, I pray that Rich will back off so we can go down, before I crack. Having persuaded him to come here, I can't bring myself to pull him back. I also don't want him to see I've lost my nerve. The only thing worse would be for me to see *him* crack.

The weather quickly turns moody, then vicious, lashing out at us and sending the wind chill off the scale. Every time a blast comes you feel death brushing past. In the calm moments I hear the musical tinkle of ice particles falling a thousand metres from the summit mushroom, rattling down onto the glacier. Rich shouts that we can dig a snow hole on the Col and wait out the weather. We only have four days' food and I instinctively feel the creaking of a door about to shut. I tell myself he wants to go down as much as I do, but doesn't want to be the first to say so. I stand shivering, looking up at him – a few feet to go and then it would mean that the easiest option would be for us to try and ride out the storm. I don't want to do that.

'Fuck it,' I yell. 'I don't like it . . . let's get out of here.'

Rich looks up, then down at me. He doesn't argue and lowers off. We retreat to the glacier.

'Don't forget how you feel now,' I tell myself as I stagger down. 'Don't come back here.'

The storm lasts six days.

It took us two days to get down to Chaltén. We arrived in time for home-made pizza. Ruban was glad to see us safely back. We used the last of our energy to stamp the snow off our boots and then collapsed at his table, leaving our hated sacks outside in the snow. In his kitchen, I felt warmed with relief, glad to be back. I could see the snow falling thick through the porch light, and felt like never climbing again.

One week later, I scream at myself for being so slow and useless as I try to wrestle my way up a wide overhanging crack, unbalanced by my rucksack, and hindered by my crampons. I'm wasting time and I know it. I scream again knowing it won't make anything better.

In a moment of bravado I once told Rich that I'd never failed to climb anything in my life. Now I stupidly grind and scratch without success halfway up the East Face of Mermoz, a 600-metre face below Fitzroy.

The more I shout, the more impotent I feel in my struggle, hating the world and blaming everything in it, except myself.

I finally reach the top of the pitch, and with feet loosely planted in uncertain snow, I take Rich's weight as he ascends the rope, not wanting him to see how bad the anchor I'm tied to really is.

'That looked hard,' he says, being charitable, while I curse his jumars for robbing me of the chance of letting him find out how hard it really was. He snatches some gear and launches off up the next pitch, an overhanging corner of jumbled rocks, as the flat, cloudy day comes to a close.

My two hours of standing in the dark, dangerously cold, too scared to let go of Rich's rope in order to pull on my down jacket, see Rich through the crux of the pitch but unable to carry on in the darkness. We argue where is best to spend the night, each wanting the solution that entails the least effort on his part. Should I go up to him or he come down to me? Gravity is in my favour so Rich rappels down, leaving his ropes fixed for tomorrow. We chop out two bucket seats in the snow, one above the other. As usual we both strike rock well before achieving comfort, but we're too tired to start again.

I watch Rich wriggle into his sleeping bag below me as I carefully get out the stove and balance it on my knees. Cooking under the shelter of my bivy-bag cowl, I mix cheap dried potato with raw onion and bad cheese, not a meal that's conducive to high morale. Our diet has been abysmal on this trip: not enough calories, not enough food; it affects my psyche. I wonder if perhaps all my doubts can be put down solely to the malnutrition. After only a few mouthfuls, I pass Rich the pan and he scoops food down, hiding in his bivy bag from the torrents of spindrift that pour down the wall. 'You finish it,' he says passing the pan back. It's now peppered with snow. Nearly vomiting, I shovel it down, then, wrapping a sling around my waist and knees, try to find a little comfort.

It really starts snowing around midnight, pummelling us as we sit there, halfway up the wall. Every few minutes I push the snow off the cowl of my bivy bag, the cold clammy weight too heavy to ignore. I turn on my side, my knees hanging in space, and try to fall back into a claustrophobic half sleep.

The snow builds up between me and the wall. My mind tries to form warm memories, of lying in bed, my daughter still unborn, Mandy's bulging abdomen pressed against my back, feeling their warmth and her kicks. Eventually I fall asleep only to dream about cold dead babies . . . Then I hear Ella, two years old, hissing, 'Horsy, horsy,' in my ear. She climbs up onto my face, she starts to suffocate me . . .

I wake up feeling as if someone has placed a plastic bag on my head, and claw at the fabric of the bivy bag, sending the piled snow down onto Rich. I breathe in the snow and cough. Too scared to go back to sleep, I feel inside my jacket for my laminated photo of Ella. I can't see it; only feel the hard bent plastic. I do this to give me some strength, but it makes me feel weaker, reminding me of what a foolish gamble this is. I wonder what kind of father I am. I think about my father. I try not to think about him. I feel I'm falling apart.

I start to cry.

At 3 a.m. we know it's over. Unable to stand it any longer, battered by the heavy spindrift, we get ready to leave. Rich jugs up to our high point to retrieve the ropes while I stand there under the showers of snow. I know I must not forget how I feel right now. I've never felt so alone.

The retreat, a part of climbing I seem to have become expert in, goes quickly, landing us back at our skis muggy and bad-tempered as dawn arrives in the continuing storm. Our old tracks are buried under the thick snow, leaving us with nothing to follow back.

Clipping on the skis, I feel anxious, knowing that even if we find our way to the pass, the slopes back to Chaltén will be loaded with fresh snow. I don't want to die. I decide I'll make sure Rich goes first. He has no kids. To find our way, with no choice, map or compass, all we can do is probe for our old tracks with our ski poles and keep moving.

The driver spoke no English and we spoke no Spanish, but I knew he thought we were crazy as he dropped us off at the trail head and drove off back to Chaltén, back to bed. We were going into the mountains.

We had spent a week waiting for the weather to clear and as it did so, so did my mood. An improved diet of steak, chips, and eggs boiled, fried, or poached, had helped, restoring our energy and morale. I felt fitter and more confident. I'd had time to digest my thoughts and feelings and felt more in tune with the mountains and less negative towards them and myself. We had a week and a half left, and we both felt ready to get to grips with the mountains one last time.

Two days later, as darkness falls, we take turns making a small snow hole high on a remote glacier, the only shelter that will stand up to the pounding of the wind. The weather is nasty, and we shout at each other as we desperately try to dig. Above us lies the North West Face of Fitzroy, but at the moment the biggest challenge is staying alive.

Once we are inside the hole, sealed in by the snow, everything feels back under control. We are in a good position to attempt a route on Cerro Pellone, a Tolkienesque spire on the edge of the ice cap, having hauled seven days' food and fuel over the high Paso del Cuadrado. It occurs to me that our objectives are gradually becoming smaller, as in desperation we try to salvage something from the trip. We know we could do the route in a day. All we need is that day. I place an ice screw above my head as Rich primes the stove for a cup of tea. I hang my barometer watch on the screw, lie back and wait.

'Want another cup of tea?' asks Rich, gaunt-faced as he lights up the stove. He picks a bleached tea bag out of our over-flowing garbage sack and drops it in the pan. The storm is still raging. Six days have passed. All thoughts of climbing have been replaced with thoughts of food, oxygen, and escape. Our supplies are down to almost nothing. We have grown weak, lying bedridden, bodies slowly digesting themselves. On the third day, Rich dug outside for a crap and almost froze to death squatting in the maelstrom. Luckily my bowels have remained still.

The interior of our hole is total squalor. At first, it was only like being in hospital: confined to bed, three poor meals a day, cold white walls. Now the walls are black with soot from the stove, dripping down on us every time we fire it up. Constant tea drinking, our only entertainment, has produced several gallons of urine, which now make up about 50 per cent of our floor. On the fourth day, dizzy and careless about carbon monoxide poisoning, I let my sleeping mat get too close to the stove and it burst into flames. Twisting and scrabbling like astronauts trapped in their capsule, we managed to get it under control, then spent the rest of the day with toxic headaches.

At least our brains are occupied. I do most of the talking. It's hard to be entertaining though. After all, I've heard it all before. Finally, with all words and food used up, we know, as we listen to the wind, that tomorrow we will have to fight our hardest battle yet and get back to Chaltén.

Leaning into the wind, we bolt for the col, carrying our skis, trying to breathe. I try to cover every inch of my face but my skin and eyes still feel as if they're being dragged through gravel. I visualise myself storming ashore on D-Day, my heavy skis some kind of cumbersome weapon to be carried through the thundering enemy fire. I can feel the soles of my feet beginning to go hard, beginning to freeze. I know I'm close to getting frostbite, but I'm beyond worrying about such trivia. Our old footprints stand out proud from the wind-scoured slope, a trail of crumbs to follow through the screaming wind, as we both drop down onto our skis and take cover, exhausted.

'Not far,' I shout at Rich as we cling to each other, feeling naked and exposed even in our thick layers, waiting for the eye of the storm to blink and let us pass over the col.

It seems cruel to have come so far, to have suffered so much, and all for nothing. It's easy to say that I'm not cursed, that I am blessed: lucky in just having the chance to come and fail, to steal a moment in such a high places, to survive, victorious or not.

But that's not true. It's all bullshit.

I came to win, came as I always do, in order to justify who I am and what I have become; now I don't even know what that is. The rot inside me, the cancer of desire, feels unbearable, now it knows it won't be sated. There's a malignant discontent in there, and without a climb there will be no peace. When – if – I pass over to normal life I know I will drag this feeling with me.

What do I want, why can't I be happy with what I have? I want to escape.

I want to climb something so difficult that I'll never feel like this again.

As the wind draws its breath, the two of us spring up and run for our lives.

Psycho

Pitches 13 and 14 Reticent Wall

I woke at dawn. I lay there for a while and waited for the sun to arrive at the ledge. Almost at the top of the wall the sun came early.

There was no rush.

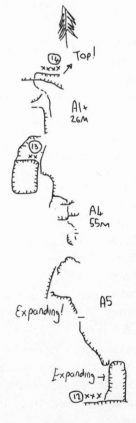

It was colder here than down below. Now I could see snow out on the Sierras. I was glad of my warm sleeping bag. I snuggled down into it.

It's not every day that you attempt to climb the hardest, most dangerous pitch of your life.

I thought about what it had taken to get here – not just the hundreds of metres of rock directly below, but the hundreds of pitches, kilometres of rock, ice and snow that I'd climbed in the past to get myself to this point in my life.

It's just climbing, don't be so melodramatic.

The sun lit up the wall. I sat up and went and dangled my feet over the side of the ledge, enjoying the drop, and ate my last bagel, watching the light spreading down the wall below me.

How long would it take for a crumb to fall?

I thought about the pitch, what I'd been told, what I could see.

The first part was yet another expanding crack.

If you mess that up you might get away with just a broken leg.

The next section was a leftwards-trending seam, probably requiring tiny copperheads and birdbeaks.

Got to be careful there.

I considered the consequences of a fall. Maybe I would survive, but I would probably hit the ledge on my side. Maybe it would be better to die straight away.

You don't want to lie smashed and semi-conscious, feeling sorry for yourself.

At least close to the top I had some chance of a rescue.

Only if someone sees you fall.

The crux itself involved hooking a fragile flake. With no gear to hold a fall, any mistake would be terminal: a two-hundred-foot fall onto the ledge.

These are only facts.

It was strange and unexpected, but I felt no anxiety, no fear, no emotion. A river of clear water flowed through me. Everything I had ever done had led to this point and I was ready.

I began by emptying all the water that remained in my bottles, and, along with those I had already used, placed them in my haul bags, to turn them into makeshift crash mats. The trick was to half unscrew their lids, so the air would escape neither fast nor slow. That way they would neither crumple too quickly nor cause me to bounce over the edge.

I positioned the portaledge below the first part of the pitch. If nothing else, this took my mind off the rock beneath, and might even turn a break into a sprain.

Lastly I emptied out the water from the bladder I carried on my back like a rucksack, inflating it instead. I knew I'd be too busy to drink. It would save a little more weight, and being inflated meant it might protect my spine.

It's all an illusion.

Next I laid out all my equipment: cams, nuts, pegs and hooks, checking each one for damage before I clipped and racked them on my harness. We had many things in common: tired, beaten up, scarred with a thousand wounds, a thousand placements. We were older. My hands were still swollen but now the pain felt good. They felt like the hands of someone who could feel.

Either way, you'll soon get a long rest.

I clipped my hammer to my harness, its once square head now rounded with abuse, its hickory handle stained with sweat. I thought back to the day it had arrived in the post all those years before, new, shiny, a blank page. Now every scrape, scratch and impression told a story. We had travelled a long way together and I was glad we'd made it this far.

I stacked my ropes, once a hated task, now one I savoured, a therapy of hands and Perlon, first the lead line then the haul line. I felt for damage as they passed through my fingers.

I put on my helmet. New when I began, it was now scratched and beaten, sponsors' stickers flapping like old skin, unimportant now. Lastly I slipped my sore naked feet into my shoes, left then right, always the same. I tied my laces, thinking back to how difficult I'd found this simple knot as a child, just as I found it difficult to tell the time, to read, to write. I wished I could go back in time and hug my then self, take away the feeling of inadequacy, and whisper that one day all these things wouldn't matter, that one day I would be more amazing than I could imagine.

It was 9 a.m. A beautiful cool morning. The snow stretched clean out across the Sierras on the horizon. It was quiet. There had never been a more perfect moment.

I began.

*   *   *

A Lost Arrow.

A Skyhook.

A small cam.

The climbing is automatic. There is no emotion, no fear, no doubt. There is only the correct option.

A knifeblade.

A cam hook.

A knifeblade.

The hours pass more slowly than the metres, but this is immaterial. I can only climb as well as I can.

A birdbeak.

A birdbeak.

A copperhead.

I finger peg scars in the rock to judge what once fitted best and fill them again. I bounce as hard as I dare on the gear to test its strength. I don't look down at my landing. I won't fall.

A copperhead.

A copperhead.

A birdbeak.

I hook up to a huge crumbling flake, a rock celebrity. It's unstable, it's weak, it threatens to kill, that's what I've been told. I have to ride it, as if it's a wild animal. I put my hand on it and stroke it calm. It's misunderstood. I hook it and step up slowly. It lets me.

A hook.

A hook.

A smaller hook.

The flake ends.

Thank you.

I hang there for a moment and wait for my fearometer's flickering needle to settle again, breathing slowly, conscious I mustn't rush.

Savour this moment.

I feel so at peace, conscious that this is not what I had expected. Something has changed in me. I feel calm.

I'm enjoying this!

I look down and marvel at my position, immune now to the exposure. I try to take in everything around me. I won't be here again. I notice two people standing on the rim of El Cap a few hundred metres away. It seems strange to be watched after so long alone. Then one of them begins shouting: 'Psycho, psycho, psycho!', the words drifting over the huge void between us. It makes me feel that people are thinking about me. I wave back.

I can see a crack up to my left. I know when I reach it I will be safe forever. That will be it. I will survive. Between me and salvation lies a blank stretch of rock, its surface covered by a mosaic of small round pancake-sized exfoliating flakes. It seems you could peel them off with your fingernail. Like me, they barely cling to the wall. I look hard at the flakes. I must hook one, the one that is attached just enough to hold me. Make the wrong choice and that's it. Pick the right one and that's it. There is no hesitation, only thought. I imagine what others must have thought. I choose the one which looks the most secure and hook it, stepping, swapping my weight over to it.

It holds me.

It defies reason to do so.

This flake is a time-bomb, but I already have the next piece in my hand, ready to fire into the crack.

I step up higher, my hand outstretched, the cam retracted waiting to spring.

Once 8,000 kilometres stood between me and tomorrow. Then only 900 metres. Now it is measured in centimetres . . . and now millimetres.

I hold the cam's trigger back, knowing that when I let it go, the cam will expand and lock within the crack. That will be it. But instead of letting go, my fingers hold tight. I am no longer connected to the world.

I enjoy the sensation of the void all around me, of choices, so many made to reach this moment: everything I ever did, the good and the bad, all I wanted, every experience coming to just this moment.

This very moment.

I let the trigger slip from my fingers.

I lay in the dirt with my shoes off. It was almost dark. A cool breeze carried away my smell and replaced it with that of the manzanita bushes all around me. Alone for so long I'd wanted to find someone, to tell them where I had been, what I had done, not for ego or glory, but so I could believe it myself. But there was no one there to listen. I realised then that I had not spent so long alone since I'd been in my mother's womb.

I wondered if I should have a cry. It seemed the appropriate thing to do.

Don't be so melodramatic.

Happiness can make you cry.

I looked at the pile of hardware and ropes beside me, my helmet, shoes and harness, spotted my dad's wire, and wondered what he'd say. What would anyone say?

I felt sorry for all my pegs and hooks and cams; life savers for so long, they meant nothing to me now, simply heavy things I had to carry back down. It seemed appropriate to thank them, and my ropes, and my haul bags, and my body, so I did, then said it again to no one in particular.

I pulled out Ella's toy train and held it up against the sky. Then I kissed it.

The crux had taken less then four hours. A blur. Clipping the belay had meant nothing, I already knew I was safe. Once it was over, I raced to climb the final easy pitch, a crack that led to a roof. I should have known that it wouldn't let me just walk away. It surprised me, harried me, played tricks and scared me. I became frustrated, annoyed it was making life tough; hadn't I suffered enough? Didn't it know who I was, what I'd done to get there? I was too tired to realise that this was all part of the wall's grand plan.

It had one final lesson to teach me.

I reached the roof, the path across it a line of old pegs, placed by my heroes, Royal Robbins, Warren Harding and Charlie Porter, and many others. Clipping from one to the other I became aware of how they must have felt as they passed this way, with many routes converging on this last section. I looked down at the tiny trees, nearly a kilometre below, and felt a tingle of vertigo, a shiver of fear. Some would think of me as a hero for soloing a route like this, but climbing a wall only makes you feel mortal.

I had just soloed one of the hardest big walls in the world, but, probably like my heroes, I felt only humbled and transformed. I had my answer.

I pulled over the roof and arrived at a small ledge, the wall leaning back now, the top very close. The smells began to change, from an austere stink of toil and fear, to the simple aromas of earth and trees and life.

I kissed the rock one last time and scrambled on to the summit.

Now I lay on the soil. I closed my eyes and listened. The world sounded more beautiful than I could ever have imagined. There was only silence, both without and within me. Like a junkie, his arm full of heroin, I no longer thought about my next fix. I had overcome myself.

I lay there for a long time, relishing the new-found space, along with the lack of clawing gravity.

I can't fall off the world any more.

Finally, I knew it was time to go, so I packed one haul bag, leaving the other for later collection, and began walking down from the summit, along the rim, heading for the series of abseils that would take me back to the base of the wall.

My legs felt weak under the load; my body was much thinner than when I'd begun nearly two weeks before. My headtorch picked out the right path down steep slabs, yet all of a sudden I felt exhausted. I sat down again and tried to compose myself. Then I noticed something, something so beautiful it's impossible to describe. Voices.

I followed the sound, scared for a moment that I'd imagined it. It had happened many times before. Then I heard it again. Then laughter. Now I felt like crying. I stumbled down and came across two men sitting in sleeping bags behind a rock. We were strangers, but we were also fellow travellers. They smiled at me. I smiled back. We were the same.

'Hello, do you mind if I sleep here with you guys?'

It had been a long time since I'd talked to anyone but myself.

'Sure thing – pull up a rock,' they said, switching on a battered CD player. New music spilled out.

They were silent as one rolled a fat joint, which he offered to me first. 'No thanks,' I said.

'Why?'

'Smoking's not good for you,' I said. We all laughed.

'Where have you come from?' asked one of the climbers as he dug out their remaining can of beer, wrapping it in their last few wet wipes to cool it down.

'The Reticent.'

No one said a word.

'How was it?' asked the climber with the can, pulling the tab.

'Not too bad,' I said. After all, it couldn't have been, I'd climbed it.

Down

We woke together and talked. We didn't want to rush from the place we'd worked so hard to reach. We had a lot in common. We talked about music, we talked about drugs, we talked about women. We didn't talk about climbing.

Finally, we knew we had to leave. The descent was long and pretty tough, especially with our huge haul bags, and if we were to make it down before dark we knew we had to go.

I'd descended this way after every previous ascent, so I thought about all those other times, touching familiar trees, scraping down the same old rocks. The abseils were as scary as ever, sliding down the ropes with the haul bag pulling at my harness. Eventually all that was left was the long dusty trail back to the parking lot.

As we staggered through the trees, talking to take our minds off our aching knees, trying to keep our distance from each other's smells, it occurred to me how normal I felt. Everything seemed the same. I hadn't done anything. I hadn't changed up there – or if I had, I had quickly reverted to who I had been. I began to think about the route, how it hadn't been so hard, how two years and several other ascents might well have reduced the difficulty. I felt a tinge of disappointment. I wondered what was harder. What could be next?

Finally we broke out of the trees and stepped onto the parking lot. Dumping our bags, we collapsed on top of them and tried to stretch our sore backs, our clothes soaked with sweat. Never again.

I looked up and saw something familiar through the trees. I stood and walked forward until it spread out across the sky above me. It was the Dawn Wall of El Cap. Even though I'd

seen it so many times, its beauty and size remained un-
diminished. I traced the line of the Reticent with my eyes.

How did you climb that?

The others joined me and we stood together and marvelled.

Glossary

ABSEIL. To descend a rope using a *descender.*

AID CLIMBING. Climbing using *gear* for resting or making progress.

AIDER. A ladder-like *sling* used to climb up when *aid climbing.*

ANGLE PEG. See *Peg.*

ARÊTE. An outward pointing bit of rock; a ridge or rib.

ASCENDER. A device for climbing a rope when all else fails.

AXE. Climbing ice axe that can be swung into ice or turf. Used in pairs.

BEAK. A tiny peg the thickness of a credit card.

BELAY (noun). A place where you attach yourself to the rock.

BELAY DEVICE. A piece of equipment which you use to control the rope when *belaying.*

BELAYING. Fixing a rope round a rock, pin, or other object, to secure it.

BERGSCHRUND. Crevasse that forms between a mountain face and the moving glacier at its base.

BETA. Knowledge of trick moves or *protection* or just about anything about a route available before you start.

BIRDBEAK. See *Beak.*

BIVY BAG. Gore-Tex sleeping-bag cover.

BOLT. An expansion bolt fixed permanently into the rock face to *protect* a climb or form a *belay.*

BREAK. A horizontal crack.

BULGE. A small rounded overhang.

CAM. A complex expanding *nut* with three or four opposing camming lobes, used in cracks of all sizes.

CHALK. Magnesium carbonate used to dry the hands when climbing.

CHICKENHEAD. American term for a small lump of intrusive rock which sticks out of a slab.

CHIMNEY. A crack wide enough to fit your whole body into.

CHOCKSTONE. A piece of rock which is jammed immovably in a crack.

CHOSS. Soil, dirt, rubble, stones, vegetation, in fact anything other than good clean stable rock.

CLEANING. The act of removing *protection* placed by the *leader*, performed by the *second* as he/she follows.

COPPERHEAD. Alloy or copper *nut* that can be hammered to fit in *seams* and flared cracks allowing progress but not *protection*.

CRUX. The hardest move on a *pitch* or the hardest pitch on a climb.

DAISY CHAIN. Long *sling* with multiple places to clip into, and used in conjunction with *aiders*.

DEADHEAD. Fixed *copperhead* with broken clip cable.

DESCENDER. A friction device used when *abseiling*, such as a *figure of eight* or a *belay* plate.

ÉTRIER. See *Aider*.

EXPANDING FLAKE. A *flake* that moves when pulled on, or which looks as if it might move or even detach completely if pulled hard enough.

FIGURE OF EIGHT. The most commonly used knot to attach a climber to the rope.

FIXED. See *In situ*.

FLAKE. A partially detached section of rock which will often yield good holds along its detached edge.

FREE CLIMBING. Progressing up a route by using your body rather than the gear.

HAMMER. Wooden-shafted hammer used to place *pegs*.

HAUL BAG. Large heavy-duty rucksack (150+ litres) used to hold all your big-wall gear on the climb.

HAULING. The process of dragging up your *haul bags* after each *pitch*.

HEAD. Short for *copperhead*.

HEX. A large alloy *nut*. Sizes range from finger to fist.

HOOK. See *Skyhook*.

IN SITU. Latin for 'in place'. Used for *protection* that is found on the climb, placed by a previous climbers including *pegs* and bolts.

JAMMING. The technique of inserting part (or all) of the body into a crack to make progress.

JUG. An excellent hand hold.

JUMARING. The technique of climbing a rope using jumar clamps.

KARABINER. An oval metal hoop with a springloaded 'gate'. Rope and *protection* are attached to karabiners. Also known as a 'krab'. Karabiners come in many forms, and arguments about which is best occupy many hours in gear shops.

KNIFEBLADE PEG. See *Peg*.

LEADER. The person going up the route first; the one who solves the conundrum of 'how do you get the rope up there then?' Hence 'lead a route' and 'leading a route'. Is followed by the *second*.

MANTLE. Short for *mantleshelf*.

MANTLESHELF. Technique used to establish yourself on a ledge below a blank piece of rock.

MICRO WIRE. The tiniest of climbing *nuts*, being the size of a large pinhead, with an equal amount of strength.

NUT. The simplest form of *protection*. A metal wedge threaded on steel wires, intended to go into cracks and stay there. The name comes from the practice of 1950s climbers, who used motorcycle nuts.

OFFWIDTH. The most awkward width of crack: too wide for fist jamming, but too narrow to *chimney*.

PEG A simple length of steel, either U-shaped (angle peg) or flat (knifeblade) with an eye in one end for clipping the rope to. Hammered in place.

PENDULUM. Swinging on a length of rope in order to obtain a distant hold.

PITCH A section of a climb, usually close to a rope length (45 metres).

PITON. A *peg* or spike hammered into a crack to support a climber on a rope.

PLACEMENT. The place in the rock face where *protection* is actually positioned.

PORTALEDGE. Folding bed made from alloy tubing and nylon and used on a big wall.

PRO. Abbreviation of *protection*.

PROTECTION. Also known as gear. The devices that climbers use to prevent themselves from decking out.

PULLEY. Metal wheel used to increase the mechanical advantage when *hauling*.

QUICKDRAW. Two snap-gate *karabiners* linked by a short *sling* equal one quickdraw.

RACK. A collection of *gear*, usually attached to loops on a harness.

RAPPEL. Another word for *Abseil*.

RIVET. A 5 mm x 50 mm machine *bolt* hammered into a drilled hole on blank sections of rock.

SCREAMER SLING. A shock-absorbing *sling*.

SCREWGATE. A locking *karabiner*.

SEAM. A very thin crack, one too small for any *protection* wider than a *knifeblade piton*.

SECOND. The person who *belays* the *leader*, and gets the fun of taking out their *protection* on the way up. Being the second is generally less dangerous than leading, because you have a rope above you – except on traverses, when it can open you up to big swings if you fall off and the leader has not put in enough protection.

SHIT-TUBE. Plastic tube used to store bodily waste when climbing on El Cap.

SKYHOOK. Small steel hook that will hold a climber's weight when placed on a small *flake* or flat edge.

SLING. Loop of rope or tape, useful for racking *gear* or looping around *chockstones* for *protection*.

SOLO. To climb without ropes, or to climb alone with ropes.

STATIC ROPE. Compared with a dynamic rope, a static rope does not stretch significantly when loaded.

TORQUE. Technique whereby a climber places the pick of an ice *axe* in a crack and twists it.

WIRE. Short for a *nut* on wire.